$50.00

HD
2745
.B733
2015

'A fascinating and honest account of the opportunities and pitfalls of life as an independent director. Gerry Brown has a unique blend of executive and non-executive experience and his book brims with authority and useful tips. For those of us on boards, *The Independent Director* is a must-read.'

—Hugh Lenon, Chairman, Phoenix Equity Partners

'I thought there was no justification for another business book, least of all on corporate governance. I was wrong. Gerry Brown offers a rare mixture, deep thinking combined with practical experience, tested and conveyed via a rich array of eclectic corporate cultures and against different business cycles. No business problem is unique; a good independent director with the right chemistry operating in an appropriate corporate culture can prevent avoidable mistakes and mitigate others. Whether you are setting out to be an independent director or you are a seasoned traveler, this book is a must-read.'

—Peter Waine, Director, Hanson Green

'This book is a lively and thought-provoking read which rightly acknowledges the increasingly central role of the independent director on company boards. It provides an accessible guide to what independent directors do, how they do it, and why. Drawing on numerous real-life case studies, it demonstrates the variety and complexity of the dilemmas faced by the independent directors. It will be useful both to those who sit on boards and to those who wish to know more about this increasingly important component of modern corporate governance.'

—Dr. Roger Barker, Director of Corporate Governance and
Professional Standards, Institute of Directors

'Gerry Brown is a businessman of great experience and exceptional incite. His understanding of the critical role of the independent director is unusually perceptive. Professors are frequently asked to serve as independent directors by a wide array of large, small, and aggressively growing corporations. With its eleven cases and eight themes, *The Independent Director* will be a great help for anyone needing to understand the pressures of this role and its important responsibilities. I believe this book will be an excellent background resource for case studies in schools of Business, Law and Health Sciences, as well as Public Policy and Management Programs. It will be on the required reading list for my Health Policy course in the School of Public Health next year.'

—Chester W. Douglass, DMD, PhD, Professor Emeritus of
Health Policy and Epidemiology, Harvard University

'A comprehensive and practical review of issues facing independent directors in today's ever-increasingly complex business environment. Eleven varied and detailed case studies from Gerry Brown's personal experience are described to provide the reader with a broad array of business examples that become interwoven with important issues facing boards. The stage is set perfectly for penetrating discussions of difficulties and nuances surrounding decisions independent directors must make. Provocative, educational, opinionated, and entertaining—a must-read!'

—Dennis Gillings, Executive Chairman,
Quintiles Transnational Corporation Inc

'With the ongoing controversy about corporate governance, you would expect there to be an excellent book on the role of non-executive directors. Now, thankfully, there is. In this book, Gerry Brown has laid out with great clarity his own extensive practical experience and wisdom, putting meat to the bones of the academic literature on which he builds. The product is an account of the how, what, and why of being a non-executive director that should be compulsory reading: and not just for non-executives. This book should be on every MBA reading list, and even—given the accessible style—on advanced undergraduate syllabuses. Like every good book, it calls for repeated reading. Each time round brings new insights and provokes new thinking about how boards function currently, and how they should function in the future.'

—Robin Mason, Dean, Exeter Business School

'Gerry Brown has it right. In his introduction to his book *The Independent Director*, he observes that there are a great many books on governance and legal issues for independent directors. However, these books are handbooks that attempt to keep independent directors out of trouble. There is little that has been written for independent directors on the affirmative side. Rather than just playing defense to prevent shareholder lawsuits, minimize liability, or, above all, follow the governance processes, Gerry Brown has something novel to offer: how about a director that moves the company forward? His book offers the details of case studies as a foundation for themes that provide specific tools, in word and chart form, to help directors work with management to develop a strategic focus and move the company forward. The book is a welcome addition to the resources for independent directors and provides boards and directors with the tools and insights they need to contribute to business success.'

—Marianne M. Jennings, Professor Emeritus, Legal and
Ethical Studies in Business, Arizona State University

'This is an important and impressive book. It seems amazing that such a pivotal role has rarely been covered in this way. As Gerry articulates, to look at the role solely as an act of governance is to fundamentally diminish its key function: to ensure that both executive and non-executive directors are focused on creating shareholder value. All too often in the work we do with boards, the remit of the independent director is, at best, undervalued—Gerry is not only educating the reader but creating a debate that can only lead to better-quality board performance, whether that is within the context of a private equity-backed or publicly traded company.'

—Matthew Blagg, CEO, Criticaleye

The Non-Executive Director's Guide to Effective Board Presence

The Independent Director

Gerry Brown

First published 2015 by
PALGRAVE MACMILLAN

Palgrave Macmillan in the UK is an imprint of Macmillan Publishers Limited, registered in England, company number 785998, of Houndsmills, Basingstoke, Hampshire, RG21 6XS

Palgrave Macmillan in the US is a division of St Martin's Press LLC, 175 Fifth Avenue, New York, NY 10010.

Palgrave is the global academic imprint of the above companies and has companies and representatives throughout the world.

Palgrave® and Macmillan® are registered trademarks in the United States, the United Kingdom, Europe and other countries.

ISBN 978–1–137–48053–8

This book is printed on paper suitable for recycling and made from fully managed and sustained forest sources. Logging, pulping and manufacturing processes are expected to conform to the environmental regulations of the country of origin.

A catalogue record for this book is available from the British Library.

A catalog record for this book is available from the Library of Congress.

Typeset by MPS Limited, Chennai, India.

To my wife, Clemencia, children and family, without whose constant support and encouragement throughout my working life I would not have this story to tell.

Contents

List of Figures and Tables

Figures

Tables

Acknowledgments

My thanks go to many people:

To Morgen Witzel, who has done so much to help me to convert my dream of writing this book into reality;

To Marilyn Livingstone for preparing the index;

To Mario, for working the miracle of transforming all of the illustrations into the correct format;

To Cayetana, for preparing the website and marketing plan, and making the videos;

To Francisca, for copyediting and finding quotes;

To my brother Ben and Juliana and Alexander for checking the draft manuscript;

To all of the people who have worked for me directly or indirectly in all of the companies globally, especially to the frontline secretaries, Margaret Moss at BRS, Jane Wiltshire at Exel, and Colleen Hillyer at Quintiles;

To all my work colleagues, including the board members, of all of the companies;

To all my friends with whom I have consulted about the book, whether at dinner or on a golf course; especially Steve Abel, Barry Bateman, Patrick Dunne, Robin Headlam Wells, John Farrant, Martyn Pellew, Stuart James, Peter Weston, Mike Bundy and Geoff Whitehead;

To Farzaad Engineer for the material on Quintiles in India;

To everyone who agreed to be interviewed and quoted in this book: Justin Atkinson, Robbie Burns, Lawrence Christensen, Chris Collins, Jeremy Curnock

Cook, Richard Daw, Steve Edge, David Frankish, Dr Dennis Gillings, Charles Hammond, John Harvey, Mike Innes, Jean-Charles Julien, Alan MacKay, Andrew Marshall, Simon Massey, Ken Merron, Fran Moscow, Francis Peck, David Richardson, Crispin Simon, Sir Peter Thompson, William Underhill, Stuart Vincent, Peter Waine, Chris Welsh, Patrick Wilson, Ron Wooten, and Toshi Yamada. To those who have endorsed the book.

About the Author

Gerry Brown is currently Chairman of NovaQuest Capital Management, a private equity firm focused on life sciences. Prior to this, he was Chairman of NFT Distribution Ltd and Senior Independent Director of Keller plc, the global leader in ground engineering. He was also Chairman of Biocompatibles International plc; the Senior Independent Director at Forth Ports plc; and he represented 3i on the board of Vantec Corporation—a management buy-out from Nissan in Japan—until their very successful exit. Previous other independent directorships include Chairman of U-POL Ltd, and Director of CH Jones Ltd, Michael Gerson Ltd, and Datrontech plc. Gerry has also been an Independent Director of Quintiles, the largest global provider of biopharmaceutical development and commercial outsourcing services.

Prior to his career as a chairman and independent director, he worked for many years as an international senior business executive working in supply chain management, covering a variety of market sectors. He served as Operations Director of Exel plc (now DHL), was a board member of TDG plc, and Chairman of Europe for Tibbett and Britten plc. He is a Fellow of the Chartered Institute of Logistics, a board mentor with Criticaleye, and a member of the Council of the University of Exeter.

chapter 1

Introduction

> Do not hover always on the surface of things, nor take up suddenly with mere appearances; but penetrate into the depth of matters, as far as your time and circumstances allow, especially in those things which relate to your profession.
>
> — Isaac Watts

The independent director (and, by extension, the independent chairman) has one of the most important jobs in business today. Over the past twenty years, a series of government and industry reports in the United Kingdom (UK) and the United States of America (USA) have focused a great deal of attention on the role of the independent director. Those reports, and that attention, have come in response to a series of industry and corporate scandals, the latest being the banking crisis of 2008. Subsequent codes of corporate governance around the world have laid more duties and responsibilities on the shoulders of independent directors, who now bear frontline responsibility for ensuring good corporate governance and accountability.

But that responsibility, important though it is, is only the beginning of the job. Independent directors and chairmen also have a crucial role to play in directly adding shareholder value. They do so through, for example, their involvement in the development of company strategy, especially international strategy, and by enabling more effective management of risks.

An independent director is both a coach and a referee. He or she acts as a guide, mentor, and wise counselor to the firm's executives. Good independent directors bring with them a wealth of knowledge from their own executive careers. They provide examples of best practice they have seen elsewhere; they recommend trustworthy consultants and advisors; they bring experience of working in different sectors and global markets, which the existing team may not have. They help guide and shape strategic thinking, perceptions, and understanding of risk. The one thing they do not do is get involved in day-to-day management; that is the province of the executive, and the boundary between their separate roles must always be respected.

At the same time, the independent director is just that: independent. He or she stands back from the firm and examines it with a critical eye. Through both the main board and various committees, he or she ensures that the company is managed in the best interest of its stakeholders; not just the shareholders (though that is the common perception), but employees, customers, and society at large. He or she oversees the company's compliance with all relevant laws and regulations, and ensures that it is governed in a moral way.

If the independent director detects failings of governance, then it is his or her duty to speak out and warn the board of what is happening, even if the board does not want to hear it. This takes courage, of course, and courage is one of the key attributes of any successful independent director. But the consequences of not speaking out can be dire. "What were the non-executives doing?" asked the *Financial Times* in the aftermath of the banking crashes.[1] It can be argued that the answer in many cases is that they were not doing their jobs effectively. The same applies to companies caught up in scandals, like the rash of corruption and bribery allegations that has run through the pharmaceuticals industry in recent years. Independent directors should be watchful for incidents of malfeasance and use their powers to stop them.

Why This Book?

> I can calculate the motion of heavenly bodies, but not the madness of men.
>
> — Sir Isaac Newton

The job of an independent director has become much more important, and I would argue too that it has also become much more challenging and difficult. But what is the public perception of the role? Here is a summary of opinions:

A task for which no one is qualified.[2]

— *Financial Times*

The list of attributes required of the non-executive director is so long, precise and contradictory that there cannot be a single board member in the world that fully fits the bill. They need to be supportive, intelligent, interesting, well-rounded and funny, entrepreneurial, objective yet passionate, independent, curious, challenging, and fit. They also need to have a financial background and real business experience, a strong moral compass, and be first-class all-rounders with specific industry skills.[3]

— *Financial Times*

Good governance and strong management have never been more important to the health of … capital markets. In this context, non-executive directors have a critical contribution to make to the efficient running of companies, which in turn impacts the performance of the UK economy as a whole.[4]

— Alastair Walmsley, London Stock Exchange

Murray Steele, a former non-executive director and now lecturer at Cranfield School of Management, comments on how ill-prepared most independent directors are. "Few new directors are trained in what it means to be a member of a board," he says. "Many don't even understand the basics."[5] Another observer comments that in times of crisis, many non-executive directors look after their own reputations first and foremost, rather than devoting themselves to helping the management team resolve the problems.

There are thus many different opinions about the role of the independent, or non-executive, director, and much more media attention is now focused on these directors, especially whenever a corporate scandal comes to light. I therefore thought it was important to share some of my own very diverse experience as an independent director in order to shed some light on the problems and challenges faced by independent directors.

The purpose of this book is to explain what independent directors do, how they do it, and why. It begins by showing, through a series of case studies, the variety and complexity of issues faced by independent directors. It goes on to explore key themes that are critical issues for boards. The book is aimed at people who are interested in becoming independent directors themselves one day, or who simply want to know more about the role and what it entails. It is my hope also that some serving independent directors will also find it useful.

Importantly, too, the role of independent director is expanding into the non-profit sector and many institutions now have independent directors, or trustees, or governors; for example, my own most recent appointment was to the Council of the University of Exeter. Directors in these non-profit organizations are often even less well trained and prepared than those in the corporate sector, and I hope that many of them will also find this useful.

My intention in writing this book is to fill what I perceive to be a gap in the market. There are already a number of handbooks in print that describe the function of the independent director, concentrating largely on legal frameworks and responsibilities under law and regulation. These are invaluable, and every serving or prospective independent director should read at least some of these to ensure they understand the regulations and boundaries of compliance.

But none of these books, it seemed to me, describe what it is like to *be* an independent director. The role requires much more than mere compliance. Independent directors are members of a team, the board of directors. They have to learn their roles in that team—and to some extent, create a role that suits them—and learn how to manage complex relationships. Even more vital than learning the rules and regulations, they need to learn the importance of true independence of thought and spirit, and how to maintain that independence in the face of adversity. They need to learn how to create vision, drive change, mentor and support colleagues, assess risks, and monitor and audit performance. Of course, they may have had the experience of doing these things already in their executive roles; but they will find carrying out these tasks in their new role to be very different. The purpose of this book is to convey some of the knowledge and skills involved, and to discuss the issues that lie beneath the frameworks of rules and responsibilities. Ultimately, we will not only discuss what independent directors *do*, but also what they *are*.

The foundation stone of this book is my own experience. I took on my first non-executive directorship in 1996, and over the subsequent two decades I have been an independent director or chairman of eleven different organizations. Some have been small family businesses, while others have been major global companies. Some were publicly owned, others owned by private equity houses or other private owners. Some were domiciled in the UK, some in the USA and one in Japan, but nearly all had an international dimension and my duties as an independent director have taken me to many corners of the world. I have worked across many sectors, too, including logistics, construction, biopharmaceuticals, manufacturing, medical devices, information technology, chilled foods, ports, property, financial services and higher education.

In the course of those two decades, I have been involved in difficult and sometimes unpleasant situations. I have had to deal with underperforming executives and the announcement of trading downgrades to investors. I have reviewed health and safety in the aftermath of workplace fatalities. My very first independent directorship was of a company that had to be wound up—a very trying and difficult time for all concerned. But I have been fortunate in most cases to be a director of very successful companies, and I have seen and participated in many splendid examples of best practice. In the course of this book, I will describe these incidents and practices in more detail and then lay out the lessons to be learned.

I should emphasize, however, that this is *not* an autobiography or a memoir. This is a book about the role of the independent director and, while it is underpinned by my own experience, I also use examples of other companies and directors, and refer to academic and journalistic books and articles for support. Importantly, many other people have contributed to this book. More than thirty of my colleagues and business associates—including independent directors, chairmen, chief executive officers (CEOs), consultants, investment bankers, lawyers, audit partners, coaches, head-hunters, private equity partners—came forward to provide their own views on the role of the independent director. Their contributions have been invaluable, and this book would not have been the same without them.

The Importance of Independence

Throughout the book I have used the term "independent director," only using "non-executive director" where specific UK usage is intended. In the USA, the official title of the role is "independent director"; other jurisdictions have different uses, and, as mentioned earlier, terms such as "trustee" and "governor" are often used in non-profit circles.

I prefer the term "independent director" because, to me, the name reflects the true nature of the role. Independent directors are just that: they are independent. Yes, they work closely with the executives, sometimes mentoring and coaching them, but they are always aware of the line separating them from the executives, and they know that crossing that line would compromise their independence.

Independence is important because it allows a detached, dispassionate view of the company and its actions. Executives are very close to the company; they have to be, it is part of their job. But, as some of the CEOs interviewed for this book are quick to point out, the executives are often *too* close. Consequently, they have difficulty seeing the forest for the trees. They need people around them who are able to step back and see the broader picture.

Executives also need challenge and stretch. They need people who can critically analyze their ideas, point out risks and errors and help them see and understand more clearly. This is why even small private companies and non-profit organizations are appointing independent directors in ever-greater numbers. They realize that having independent, critical minds in the boardroom sharpens their own thinking and gives it more focus. The CEO's job can be lonely, and having an independent chairman or senior independent director to share business problems with can be very helpful.

Independence also means that directors don't go along with everything the executives say. When they see something that they think is wrong, they say so. That is a very important part of their duty. Their loyalty is not to the executive team; it is to the company as a whole. This can result in some very tricky situations. Tact, negotiation skills and a good sense of humor are also part of the armory of any good independent director.

Independent directors are often appointed by shareholders and, especially in private equity-owned companies, they may have quite a close relationship with the owner. This might be seen as a contradiction: how can someone who reports to the owners of the business be truly "independent"? It is true that independent directors are there to represent the interests of owners and shareholders. But it is equally true that it is in the best of interests of the owners and shareholders that the company is run well, efficiently, and in compliance with the law. Failure to do so rebounds on shareholders as well as the company (and, increasingly, on independent directors themselves, who can be prosecuted if the company breaches the law). If shareholders wish to do something that is not in the best interests of the company, then it is again the duty of the independent director to point this out and recommend an alternative course of action.

Structure of the Book

Books of this type often start by discussing key themes and then provide case studies by way of illustration. In this book, I am doing it the other way around.

I start by discussing the importance of executive experience and how my own experience shaped my role as an independent director. I then move directly on to case studies of eleven organizations, listed here alphabetically:

- Biocompatibles plc, a medical technology company
- CH Jones Ltd, a fuel wholesaler
- Datrontech plc, a computer memory distributor
- Forth Ports plc, an operator of seaports in Scotland and England
- Keller plc, the world's largest ground engineering company
- Michael Gerson Ltd, a removals and relocation company
- NFT Ltd, a chilled food distribution company
- Novaquest Capital Management, a private equity fund specializing in life sciences
- Quintiles Transnational Corporation, the leading global biopharmaceuticals research firm
- U-POL Ltd, a manufacturer of automotive repair materials
- Vantec Corporation, a logistics firm and spinoff from Nissan

Each case study is divided roughly into three parts. A profile of the company and its recent history is followed by a discussion of the key boardroom issues in which independent directors were involved. The third section of each case is a description of the "lessons learned": takeaways that can be applied to other organizations.

These eleven cases are my raw material. I use these to construct eight central themes. I start with the role of boards, discuss their purpose and function, what can go wrong and how problems can be solved, stressing the need for teamwork between executives and independents. I go on to discuss ownership and how different ownership types impact on the board, and affect the role of the independent director.

I then move on to strategy, an issue of paramount importance for boards and therefore for independent directors. Not everyone agrees on the extent to which independent directors should get involved in strategy. I believe they should be fully involved, and will explain why in more detail. One of the most important aspects of strategy is globalization, and we shall go into this in detail too, showing how independent directors can help companies that intend to expand internationally.

The fifth theme is risk. In this theme we shall see what independent directors should be doing, how they should get involved in risk management and the approaches to risk that they must take. I then discuss the role of external advisors and consultants and how independent directors are involved in their selection and management.

I come next to the executive team, and here I discuss the critical relationship between independents and executives—and especially, that between chairmen and CEOs—and how independent directors can both support the executives and remain independent; as we said above, acting as both coaches and referees at the same time. The final theme is the role of the independent director itself, summing up learning from the case studies and the other themes to present a comprehensive picture of the role. I look at two important subsets too, the role of chairman and the role of the senior independent director, or SID.

Finally, after summing up the main lessons of the book, I offer a short chapter on building a portfolio. This is intended specifically for those who are interested in becoming independent directors. There are many ways of doing so, but I suggest it is a good idea to have a plan, just as one might plan a career. What kind of independent director do you want to be? What sorts of companies do you want to work with? I offer a few tips based on my own experience and that of others, a list of dos and don'ts, and finally a description of "the good, the bad and the ugly" independent director. It is up to you to choose which kind you want to be!

chapter 2

Executive Experience

The first important point to make about independent directors is that they must be men and women of experience. Their value to the boards on which they sit and the companies they help to govern lies partly in their own intelligence and ability, but also in the wisdom and experience that they have accumulated in their previous careers.

That can include, for example, sector and industry experience, as well as experience of running operations, international markets, making and implementing strategy, building and managing networks, and relationships with other people. Before becoming an independent director, it is a great advantage to have served in senior executive roles, not necessarily as a CEO but certainly as a board-level executive director with a considerable amount of responsibility. Independent directors need to know and understand the responsibilities and tasks of the executives. Without that knowledge, they will find it very difficult to discharge their own duty to advise the CEO and his or her executives from an independent perspective.

Chapter 3 of this book is devoted to understanding what independent directors do and how they do it, and we will come back to this point about experience and discuss it in much more detail. For the moment, before looking at the case studies of my own independent directorships, in this chapter, Chapter 2, I will describe briefly my own executive experience and what I learnt from that period in my career. We will then see how that experience maps onto my work and contributions as an independent director in Chapter 3. As will also be shown in Chapter 3, my experience was not all-embracing: when I became an independent director I found myself in plenty of new situations where I needed to learn, very quickly, if I was to be effective. In every case, though, my previous experience gave me a platform on which to build, and a field in which I could make some sort of contribution.

I took a combined honors degree in economics and economic history at the University of Exeter, followed by a postgraduate qualification in teaching from the University of Reading. Initially I took up a career as a teacher before going into business. I decided on a career in personnel and training, there being a close link between these and education, and I felt that helping people to develop themselves and realize their potential was also a good way of giving something to society. In 1979, I joined the National Freight Corporation (NFC), starting in training and moving soon after to the human resources department.

NFC

NFC was established as a state-owned company in 1948 as a direct result of the Transport Act of that year. It was a sprawling conglomerate engaged in everything from waste disposal and landfill to home removals, as well as conventional road transport. Like many of the state-owned conglomerates created after the Second World War, NFC never lived up to the expectations of its founders. The group was heavily burdened with debt, and although some parts of the group operated efficiently, debt and interest payments swallowed up all its profits and more.

NFC was privatized in 1982, the first high-profile privatization, and held up as an example of a successful privatization. Unlike other large privatizations, such as British Petroleum and British Gas which were sold on the open market, NFC's privatization was a buy-out with a difference: ownership was open to all employees, not just management. One of the driving forces behind this move was group CEO Peter (later Sir Peter) Thompson, who led the negotiation with government and the City in the run-up to the buy-out. More than 10,000 employees and pensioners bought shares, contributing £6.1 million of their own money. [1] (Interestingly, some of the senior managers who led the buy-out had met in 1982 at Aberdovey. The Aberdovey Golf Society still meets more than thirty years later, under the chairmanship of Sir Peter.)

Peter Thompson then drove forward a new strategy for the group, consolidating and focusing on profitable segments. In 1982 turnover was around £400 million and profits for that year were about £20.5 million; by 1993 turnover

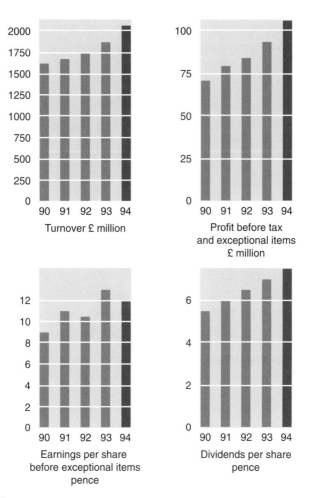

FIG 2.1 Financial highlights

had reached £1.3 billion and group operating profit was £126 million, and by 1995 turnover had climbed to £2.3 billion, with around half that income derived from outside the UK. In 1991 the company was floated on the FTSE 100 index. Figures 2.1–2.3 and Table 2.1 show the steady improvement in the company's financial position during the first five years after the buy-out, and the company's growth and expansion thereafter.

British Road Services

British Road Services (BRS) was in many ways at the heart of NFC. Originally a road haulage business, after privatization it was transformed into a diversified

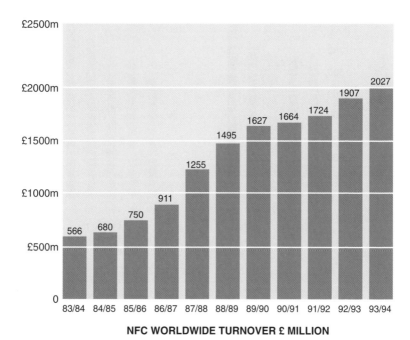

FIG 2.2 / **NFC worldwide turnover**

company involved in activities such as general haulage, contract hire, truck rental, distribution, and warehousing (Table 2.2).

As part of Peter Thompson's shake-up, the company was split into a number of regional business units. These proved to be very successful, empowering local management to grow the business and improve profits. However, the culture of BRS was still heavily rooted in the company's road haulage background, and change and diversification were not always regarded in a positive light.

After a few years at head office, I took a post initially as personnel manager and then director of personnel at one of BRS's regional subsidiaries, Midlands BRS. This was something of a baptism of fire. At the time, the trade unions in Britain were very powerful, and part of my role involved negotiating with the unions' leaders. Some of the trades union leaders were honorable men, but others were not really interested in their members and were instead pursuing personal power. Some of union leaders and shop stewards actively campaigned against the buy-out and the transition to employee share ownership. I had to go directly to the employees and explain the buy-out, including the benefits to them.

MOVING SERVICES			
UK	**EUROPE**	**NORTH AMERICA**	**PACIFIC RIM**

Allied Pickfords
 	
Bullens/
Pickfords
Industrial
 	
Hoults
Removals
 	
Pickfords
 	
Pickfords
Record
Management
 	
Radcliffes
Transport
Services
	Allied Pickfords
	- Bulgaria
	- Czech
	  Republic
	- Hungary
	- Poland
	- Romania
	
	Allied Varekamp
	- Netherlands
	
	Allied Pierre
	- France
	- Luxembourg
	  Netherlands
	
	**Irish Security
	Archives**
		Allied Van Lines
		- USA
		
		**Allied
		International**
		- N. America
		
		Allied Canada
		
		**Pickfords
		Records
		Management**
			Allied Pickfords
			- Australia
			- China
			- Hong Kong
			- Japan
			- Malaysia
			- New Zealand
			- Singapore
			- United Arab
			  Emirates
			
			**Pickfords
			Records
			Management**

INTERNATIONAL LOGISTICS			
UK	**EUROPE**	**NORTH AMERICA**	**PACIFIC RIM**

Exel Logistics
- Grocery
- Industry &
  Consumer
  Services
- Tankclean
 	
BRS
- Car Auctions
- Car
  Processing
- Car Lease
- Taskforce
- Truck Rental
 	
Lynx
	Exel Logistics
	- Belgique
	- Deutschland
	- France
	- Iberica
	- Nederland
		Exel Logistics
		- Canada
		- Mexico
		- N. America
		
		Merchants
		Home
		Delivery
		Services
		
		Merchants in
		Home
		Services
		
		SFD (Service
		Furniture
		Delivery)
			Exel Logistics
			- Hong Kong

FIG 2.3 / NFC worldwide activity

My ambition at that point was to make a career in personnel, but my boss and mentor, Steve Abel, pointed out that I would be a far better personnel director if I had line management experience as well. So I took up a post as area general manager of Midlands BRS working for Allan McPherson. I later moved

TABLE 2.1   NFC worldwide resources

Employees	35,376
Commercial Vehicle Fleet	15,410
Trailer Fleet	10,168
Car Lease Fleet	12,889
Owner Drivers	1,513
Ambient and Chill Warehouse Capacity	3.8 m²
Frozen Warehouse Capacity	1.1 m³
Operating Locations	921

TABLE 2.2   The BRS Group

THE BRS GROUP
8 500 transport professionals
8 000 trucks
150 depots
60 heavy vehicle workshops
60 truck rental depots
5 000,000 ft² of warehouse space

to BRS Western to work for Ron Irons. This was an exciting time in BRS, for this was the beginning of the outsourcing boom and companies were eager to outsource their logistics. Frozen food company Bird's Eye, part of the Unilever group, was one of several companies that transferred the management of its cold stores and fleet to us.

After spectacular growth through the early and mid-1980s, NFC was affected by the post-1987 recession. The company was able to offset the worst effects of the downturn thanks to its growing overseas business, particularly in the USA. By 1992, 37 percent of NFC revenue came from outside the UK. Much of this growth was being driven by a new venture created in 1989, Exel Logistics.

Exel

Exel was established under the leadership of Robbie Burns to create a single worldwide brand for NFC's warehousing and distribution operations. We established Exel Logistics (Exel being short for excellence) to create what we believed was the world's first global logistics brand. The senior executive responsible for the brand was Martyn Pellew. I joined Exel as a board

AUTOMOTIVE	ELECTRONICS	UTILITIES
FORD	ICL	NORTH WEST WATER

APPAREL	ELECTRICAL/VARIETY	PACKAGING
BHS	ARGOS	CARNAUD METALBOX

DRINKS & BREWING	PETROLEUM	CHEMICALS
BASS	ASDA	SHELL CHEMICALS

BULK EDIBLES	GROCERY RETAIL	GROCERY MANUFACTURE
MILK MARQUE	J SAINSBURY	BIRDS EYE WALL'S

FIG 2.4 Exel's markets, with examples of clients

member responsible for the temperature control division. Four years later I was appointed chairman of Exel UK, also with responsibility for Spain. I went on to become managing director of the industrial, consumer and services division and, in 1994, operations director of Exel/BRS UK.

Once we had brought together all the different logistics businesses within BRS and elsewhere in NFC under the Exel umbrella, our next step was to establish a strategic direction. We needed to decide which market sectors we would concentrate on, and in which countries. Twenty-nine business sectors have a logistics requirement, and it was not possible to concentrate on all at once. Thus, we had to decide on which areas to focus. Figure 2.4 shows the sectors that Exel entered, although it should be added that the process of entry was very much an evolutionary one.

Much of our growth was organic, but we also aimed to make strategically chosen acquisitions that would give us footholds in particular markets, adding capacity but without becoming over-geared (this was in line with group policy, which stressed that gearing levels should not be too high; the average was about 55 percent).

In North America, the acquisition of several existing firms made Exel Logistics the largest independent provider of warehousing services. As well as food and grocery, it also served clients in sectors as diverse as health and beauty, automotives and commercial banking. By 1990, the North American division contributed 40 percent of Exel's total profits.

In Europe, Exel's revenue and profits also grew rapidly, thanks to the securing of significant contracts in France and Spain, and also the acquisition of the leading Spanish distribution company, Sadema, and the French chilled distribution company, BOS. We also made acquisitions in Germany and the Netherlands.

Growth in the UK was strong too, again thanks to Exel's strong position in the food and grocery sector. The temperature-controlled distribution industry had suffered during the downturn, but as the economy began to revive Exel moved strongly into this area. In particular we worked with Tesco and Sainsbury's to help them establish regional distribution centers, and we also worked with Kwik-Save and Safeway. By 1992, temperature-controlled distribution made a major contribution to Exel's profits. In our non-food business, we also expanded into industrial markets, working with a major supplier of plumbing and heating equipment and a steel company, and built a major presence in print media and book distribution. Overseas, Exel continued to expand in the early 1990s, establishing a presence in Asia-Pacific for the first time and also entering Mexico in partnership with Procter & Gamble.

Employee-Ownership and Performance

There is no doubt in my mind that the employee-ownership program was one of the reasons for NFC's and Exel's success. The employees who bought into the company were committed to the business because they owned it. Their own personal wealth increased, of course, through dividends and when the share price went up, but they also became genuinely interested in the company.

Sir Peter Thompson recalls how several thousand employee-shareholders used to attend shareholder meetings, where they asked articulate and intelligent questions. On one occasion, he says, when the board had decided to dispose of the waste management business, "the board asked the employees if they would wish to accept the offer (and inducements were offered to influence the decision). However, the employees felt that this was an important business and they opposed the decision. We listened to them and respected their views as shareholders and employees, and in the end we changed our decision and did not sell."

"We do not want NFC's employee ownership to be measured solely by profitability, the value of the shares and the number of millionaires it has created," wrote Sir Peter Thompson in 1990, "but by whether a company is emerging that has a culture and values that are respected by its own employees and the wider community in which it does business."[2] That vision was largely realized. The employee-owners cared about NFC and understood its business model, and because they understood they worked harder to create value for customers.

The impact of employee ownership on performance was immediate and dramatic. Within the first year of the buy-out, NFC's profits had increased by 28 percent. New acquisitions in the UK and North America led to an 18 percent rise in overseas profit contributions. Dividends per share rose from 30 pence in the early 1980s to £3.50. And as already noted, the overall turnover rose from a few hundred million to more than two billion in the space of fifteen years. That growth was in large part due to the commitment of our employees.

End of an Era

Sir Peter Thompson stepped down as chairman in 1990. In his final annual report, he said: "My time at NFC has been rewarding, and in many ways we have been trailblazers. I thank employees and shareholders alike for their support as well as their challenges and, at times, bloody-mindedness—but, above all, for making it such fun."

He was succeeded by James Watson, who then stepped down in 1994. Shortly before this Peter Sherlock, the CEO who had recently succeeded the long-term NFC stalwart Jack Mather, also resigned. The board recruited a new chairman, Sir Christopher Bland, who brought in Gerry Murphy as new CEO. Sir Christopher made it very clear that he did not believe in the concept of employee-share ownership, and it was decided that the system would be broken down. The culture and values that had made NFC a great business eroded away. I was not there to see it happen. In the two years following the appointments of Sir Christopher and Gerry Murphy, many of the one hundred most senior managers at NFC left the company. I was one of them.[3]

TDG and Tibbett & Britten

From 1996 to 1998, I was an executive director at TDG (formerly Transport Development Group). I was divisional managing director of the plant and vehicle hire business, and the group director responsible for property and purchasing. This was another logistics company with turnover in excess of £500 million and with subsidiaries in goods transportation, distribution and warehousing, as well as hire. It operated in continental Europe as well as the UK. TDG was a holding company, with many fingers in many pies. The board decided to rationalize and downsize the company, combine some of its subsidiaries to create a divisional structure and sell off some subsidiaries. The plant and vehicle hire business was one of these.

In 1998, I moved to Tibbett & Britten, an international logistics group with a turnover in excess of £1 billion, working in thirty-three countries and in sectors as diverse as retail, clothing and textiles, food, high-tech, and automotives. I was chairman for mainland Europe and worked with John Harvey, the very dynamic group chairman whose creation Tibbett & Britten had been. This post helped me to build on my previous international experience and gained me a great deal more experience of working across national and cultural boundaries. I retired from Tibbett & Britten, my last executive post, in 2000. (Incidentally, in 2004 Tibbett & Britten was acquired by my old firm, Exel.)

Personal Experience

What did I learn from this experience, which lasted for twenty-nine years, from 1971 to 2000? The first thing was experience of senior management. By the time I left Exel, I had held a variety of general management and director posts, and had experience across the board from personnel and industrial relations to operations. I had some specialisms—temperature-controlled distribution, for example, and logistics more generally—but I also had the broad experience of managing large organizations. My job as operations director had involved responsibility for a turnover of £930 million, over 17,500 employees, eight million square feet of warehousing and 20,000 vehicles. Logistics is a service industry, and I was fortunate to have worked across the whole company, giving me exposure to business issues in many different sectors.

I had also acquired much international experience, particularly of continental Europe and the USA. I was later to learn that international experience can be a very important asset for an independent director. Today, international experience is not quite in such short supply as it once was, but even now companies often struggle to find board members who have in-depth, relevant experience of working in other markets.

I learned a great deal about business development, especially at Exel, which, though it brought together existing businesses, had many of the characteristics of a start-up, particularly in terms of branding. I learned how to build relationships with customers and bring in new business, not just in the UK but also in other countries and cultures. I learned how companies grow organically, and had helped BRS and Exel in particular to a high level of organic growth. And I gained much experience of the growing international logistics market, experience that would later prove useful in a wide variety of contexts.

Another very important area of experience was the evaluation of business performance. My general managerial and executive duties taught me about accountability and change management. I led operational and asset reviews. I had learned a considerable amount about property management, a highly important aspect of management for most companies. I learned about operating efficiency and how to increase it through, for example, more creative approaches to procurement and requiring suppliers to add value.

My work also required me to learn the principles of risk management, and I was now familiar with this increasingly important subject. I conducted environmental and health/safety audits and security reviews, and I established business continuity plans to ensure that our business could carry on even if a major disruptive incident were to occur.

I also learned the essentials of strategy, both strategic thinking and execution. I formulated, evaluated and reviewed strategic plans and conducted strategic resource reviews. I oversaw a number of acquisitions and disposals and became familiar with the negotiation processes that are part of every acquisition. I also learned about the emerging field of e-commerce, and management information systems and their potential.

Finally, I had always been interested in people management, but my experience of top management gave me a new set of skills. I had learned, for example, how to mentor and coach others and build their capabilities in order to develop them and make them better fit for top management roles of their own. I had been involved in training, selection, and recruitment at senior levels and knew how the processes worked. And again, thanks to my international experience, I was more aware of the nuances of working in different cultures. I should add too that along the way I had received senior management training at London Business School, Harvard Business School and the NFC Senior Management Programme.

I say all of this, not to show off, but to explain the kinds of skills and experiences that I had to draw upon. This was my raw material, which I used as the basis for a career as an independent director. As I remarked earlier, I would find that I still had a great deal to learn about a great many things. Executive experience was the essential foundation upon which I built my later career. And this point is important. As an independent director, you will be called upon to deal with many, if not all, of the issues I have just mentioned above. Whether you succeed will partly depend on how familiar you are with each and what your previous experience can tell you.

So, as a would-be independent director, what should you do? The answer, in my experience and that of my colleagues, is to try and put yourself into positions where you can learn about all of these issues: people management, international management, risk and strategy, and business development and team-working. The best independent directors are all-rounders, who have specialist knowledge but are not fazed by anything that comes their way. Again, I am not trying to boast about my own experience, or to claim that I was a "superior" independent director. But, though a mixture of chance and design, I had a varied executive career that gave me a broad range of relevant knowledge. My advice is: don't leave this solely to chance. Try to plan a career that will give you that broad knowledge.

Lessons Learned

One of the major issues that affected NFC, causing the breakdown of the employee equity participation scheme and the company's culture as a whole, was the lack of board continuity. Over a very short time, there was a complete change in the board and the senior executive team. There was very little in the way of succession planning. The whole philosophy and culture of employee ownership and involvement died. A second important issue was NFC's strategy of internationalization. The management was learning by discovery, and consequently made many mistakes. The board really needed experienced independent directors to give guidance.

Sandy McLachlan, in his study of the NFC buy-out, makes some interesting observations. "The NFC buy-out," he says, "is an example of the real benefit that can be obtained from the contacts and wealth of experience which older and wiser men [sic] can offer."[4] He goes on to say that in advance of the buy-out NFC directors talked to a wide range of people, often quite unconnected with the company or the buyout, to ask their opinions and advice, and he believes that it was this wide range of ideas and thoughts that contributed to NFC's success.

Looking back, the one overriding lesson to take away from my time at NFC and Exel was the importance of experience itself. Later on in this book I will talk about the need for diversity of experience, the wide range of opinions that McLachlan mentions. But at a deeper level, it is the expertise, the contacts, the networks and the professional and personal experience that independent directors have that makes them valuable. No one is good at everything, and experience levels will always vary. People will also have personal interests in certain subjects, such as my own long-standing interest in developing people. Depth and breadth of individual experience changes from person to person.

A board must assemble a group of people with complementary interests and experience, who can work together and fill in the gaps in each other's knowledge. It is the group, not the individual, that becomes the all-rounder. If a company can put together such a board of directors and advisors, then it has at its disposal a very powerful tool for competitive advantage. But it is rare for an executive team alone to have enough knowledge at its disposal. The board needs independent directors to round out and complement the specialized, and sometimes rather narrow knowledge, within the executive team In conclusion as I transitioned from my executive career to that of an Independent Director I developed with the help of Ron Vaughan some criteria for selecting an NED role.

These are shown in (table 2.3) and played an important part in my deciding to join the boards of the companies that are the subject of the case studies in the next chapter.

TABLE 2.3   **My criteria for selecting an NED role**

| Challenging role |
| Could contribute and add value to the business |
| Respected the other directors, especially the chairman (and the private equity house if a PE partner involved) |
| Good chemistry with the management team |
| Company operates internationally |
| Complementary to other roles in helping me to build a diversified portfolio |
| Interesting and different to what I had done before |
| An opportunity to learn, especially in different sectors |
| An opportunity to invest |

chapter 3

Case Studies

Datrontech plc

Datrontech, founded in 1994 by entrepreneurs Steve King and Ian Boyle, was a computer memory distributor. In the words of Patrick Wilson of Hawkpoint partners, who advised on the flotation of Datrontech the following year, the company "was dominant at what it did, and did it very effectively." The company grew rapidly through acquisition, buying up other memory distributors in America and Europe. Most of this growth was funded by debt.

At its peak Datrontech had, through its eleven subsidiary companies, five offices in the UK and operations in ten countries employing more than 600 people. The company had three strategic focus areas: components, value-added networking (including remote access, mobile computing, connectivity and high-end network storage) and information technology (IT) services, with a focus on training. However, many of those subsidiaries either underperformed or were not fully integrated into the company (or both), with the result that while revenues rose, profits declined. Turnover in 1995 was £130 million with profits of just over £6 million. By 1999, turnover had more than doubled to £265 million, but profits had halved to just over £3 million.[1]

The computer industry was a complex one, with a number of different players. Figure 3.1 shows the role played by distributors, acting as middlemen between original equipment manufacturers (OEMs) and assemblers, and companies such as HP and Toshiba which "made" computers and sold them.

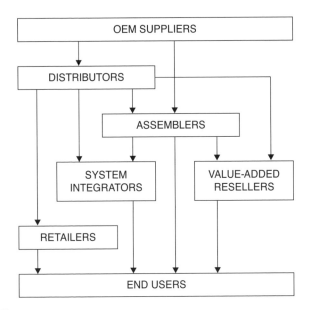

FIG 3.1 / Industry structure

Other important players were value-added resellers, who took basic products and added additional services and support for end users, for example by designing customized configurations, and systems integrators, which design and build entire systems.

This sector was, and is, very volatile and cyclical with periodic lows, sometimes even when the rest of the economy is performing well. In 1996, the market for computer memory was heavily oversupplied, not just in Britain but worldwide, and in 1997 prices fell by as much as 70 percent. Distributors were particularly vulnerable to being squeezed; value-added resellers and systems integrators were less affected. Even without these cyclical pressures, distributors faced severe competition in a market that included a large number of major corporations which had strong market power. Success in this market was dependent on the efficient handling of high-volume, low-margin products. Datrontech's distribution business, unfortunately, was characterized by low volumes and high margins.

Datrontech's response was to try to reduce its dependence on the memory business, diversifying into other areas and trying to move into the value-added market. In 1997, several subsidiaries which distributed memory products in the

USA and Europe were sold and other operations were scaled back. Acquisitions included a software original equipment manufacturer (OEM) and a Dutch-based general distributor, International Computer Products (ICP), which also had an assembly operation. A professional management team was installed, including a chief executive, Mark Mulford, who had a strong industry track record. A new independent chairman, Raymond Way, was appointed in 1998. A strategy for the UK market was put into place: six business units were consolidated into one, and investment was made in supply chain infrastructure to reduce costs and improve operational efficiency.

However, the distribution business continued to suffer, especially in central Europe where revenues failed to meet forecasts. Overall, the company still lacked a central strategic focus. The attempt to move into the value-added market was strategically sound but poorly implemented. Finally, and ultimately fatally, the company was heavily burdened by debt from earlier acquisitions.

A difficult year of consolidation followed in 1999. We restructured part of the debt, and re-organized UK operations as described above. But the company needed a complete restructuring to rationalize its operations. Unfortunately, we never got the chance to carry this out.

In 1999, turnover fell from £265 million to £208 million and the company posted a loss of £4.8 million. Mark Mulford departed in early 2000 and a new CEO, turnaround specialist Ray Peck, was appointed in his place, but by August 2000 it was clear that the company was in trouble. KPMG was called in to advise. The consultants' report suggested a way forward for the company and indicated that the business was viable in the long term. Initially the banks supported the idea of a new business plan. But in November the banker we had been dealing with at Natwest, our main debt holder, moved on from his post. His successor announced a reversal of policy: the bank would no longer support us. When Natwest pulled the plug, we were left with no choice but to call in the receivers. Datrontech was wound up, although some of its subsidiaries did carry on.

One might be forgiven for asking why I joined this company—and even more for asking why I stayed! Initially I was approached by a headhunter, who asked if I would be interested in becoming an independent director for a recently floated company that needed guidance on corporate governance issues. Then I met the banker who had advised on the flotation, Patrick Wilson of NatWest Markets, and discovered to my surprise that he had been one of my pupils when I was a schoolmaster.

Patrick Wilson was very open and honest about the situation at Datrontech. Here were two clever, very independent entrepreneurs who had never run a quoted company. I had experience in international logistics and of managing people, so I could understand their business and advice, and I was also familiar with the rules of corporate governance for quoted companies. Patrick Wilson hoped that I could bring some discipline to the company, particularly in areas such as strategy and reporting. Altogether I served on the board for just over three years, until the company was wound up.

Board Issues: The Search for Focus

Datrontech is a classic example of a company that had some good businesses but was running out of cash. The primary cause of the problem was the debt burden. Steve and Ian had expanded too broadly and too quickly, and now Datrontech was, literally, paying the price.

The move into the value-added market was a sound idea, but here again the expansion was opportunistic rather than planned and the company ended up with a random assortment of unconnected businesses: portable add-ons, data connectivity, retail. In addition the separation between distribution and value-added meant that Datrontech was effectively running two different types of business models under one roof.

The board was confronted with a variety of strategic issues. Firstly, there was the need to divest some of the poorly performing or badly integrated subsidiaries. We managed to dispose of a few of these in 1997 and 1998, but not enough. Secondly, we needed to get control of the overseas subsidiaries, which had been operating under only limited control from UK headquarters. The CEO had left overseas subsidiaries to run their businesses, and there was little in the way of synergy. Financial and operational control over the European subsidiaries, in particular, was inadequate.

Thirdly, there was a pressing need to consolidate the UK operations and reduce costs. Here there was a clear strategy and, by 1999, this had been achieved. Fourthly, there was the need to move out of the distribution of low-margin products, where there was a clear strategic threat, and focus more systematically on new areas such as value-added markets. Fifthly, there was the need to deal with the company's debts. Here again, we had partial success, reducing the debt from £18.1 million down to £12.5 million in 1999. Finally, there were differences of opinion as to how the company should be run by the two founders, Steve and Ian, who remained on the board, and the rest of the board, including the independent members.

The search for focus was illustrated by the departure of Ian Kirkpatrick as chairman soon after I joined the board. His resignation was the culmination of a dispute between himself and the two founders, both of whom continued to be involved in the running of the company. When Ian departed, I served as temporary chairman for six months, with one of my tasks being the recruitment of his permanent successor, Raymond Way.

We worked steadily at the problem and, reflecting later, Patrick Wilson believes the strategy put in place was the right one. "But as ever," he says, "it is all about implementation." We did what we could to try to strengthen the company by encouraging the management team and the board to recruit additional resources to cope with the expansion of the business and the changing market, but the going was slow. Acquisitions continued to be a thorn in our side. New subsidiaries, once purchased, were given a great deal of independence and let go their own way; they were not managed or reviewed effectively from the center. This is, I should add, by no means a unique case. Executives are often very good at acquiring other businesses, but not always well-suited to managing them. Day-to-day responsibility for running subsidiaries is handed to someone else, and the senior executives move on to the next big thing.

That can work, if there is a strong management team in place and a culture of pulling together and working towards a single goal. If these are lacking, then there is a real danger of losing focus. That is particularly the case when a business is being run by its founders. Entrepreneurs are used to running things their own way. But, as Patrick Wilson says: "It is exceptional that these individuals are surrounded by people as good as themselves." They need to step back and let professional managers take over the day-to-day running of the company. Psychologically, that is a very hard step for entrepreneurs to take. Some never take it.

We continued to believe, right up until November 2000, that the company could be turned around, but when the banks stopped supporting us we were left with no choice. Directors, including independent directors, have a legal responsibility to make sure that the company is solvent. Once insolvency is declared, the independent director is there to represent the interests of shareholders; but when directors are also shareholders, conflicts of interest can emerge. What is in the best interest of the executives might not be in the best interest of shareholders; for example, it is not unknown for directors of companies that have gone into liquidation to pick up subsidiaries at a cheap price and thus turn a profit for themselves. The liquidation had to be handled in such a way that all the shareholders, including the external ones, were treated fairly and no conflicts occurred.

Lessons Learned: What Can Go Wrong

Datrontech shows what can go wrong if a company lacks a focused strategy and effective managerial controls. This company had grown very quickly from small beginnings, and it showed. Acquisitions had been made almost randomly, with little thought for how they might support the broader strategic goals (whatever those were). That meant that the more profitable parts of the business ended up supporting, and in effect cross-subsidizing, poorly performing subsidiaries, with consequent impacts on profits and cash flow. The lesson is: create a strategic focus and strategic goals and then concentrate on those, rather than getting side-tracked by tempting opportunities along the way.

That problem might have been solved by stronger managerial control from the center, and as noted we did make some progress in this area (though once again, not enough). Centralization is always a tricky issue for businesses, which diversify across geographies or market segments, or both. Too much centralization and the subsidiaries are straitjacketed, forced to do things "the company way" regardless of whether this is suitable for that particular time and place, and unable to act to take advantage of local opportunities. Too little centralization and companies go their own way; they are managed according to the whims and interests of their own chief executives, without thought for the rest of the company and its needs. Datrontech clearly fell into the second category.

More generally at Datrontech, the quality and strength of the senior management team were insufficient bearing in mind the issues facing the company. There were also too many management changes: two different CEOs and three different CFOs in a few years meant there was little continuity.

And of course, there is a lesson to be learned from the debt issue. It is not so much lack of profitability that kills companies, as lack of cash. Even profitable companies will fail if they cannot manage their cash flow; and of course, by 2000 Datrontech was no longer profitable. Expansion in the early days had plunged the company heavily into debt. More should have been done, early on, to reduce and manage that debt. We could probably have solved the strategic and organizational problems of Datrontech given more time. It was the debt issue that sank us.

Being an independent director in this sort of environment is not easy. When things are happening that you think are wrong, then you have to speak up. But this has to be done carefully and diplomatically. You cannot simply go into the first meeting and start telling people they have got it wrong; you have to get to know the business first. You then have to establish a position as someone whom the rest of the board respects, and whose opinions they respect. Then, as an independent director, it is important to remember why you are there. Your role is to represent the shareholders. Part of your task is to remind the executive of those interests. In the end, though, there are limits to what you can achieve. What you can do is state clearly what you think, and why. How well your views will be received depends in part on the respect that others have for you, and the relationships you have with them.

Nor is necessary to do all of this at open board meetings. As an independent director, you are there to advise the chief executive. I have found that quiet conversations can be very effective. There is nothing secretive about doing this; it is simply that people often respond better in informal situations than in formal ones. Passing on your opinions quietly to the CEO is one way of making yourself heard. And again, whether the CEO listens will depend on whether he respects you and your views.

However it is done, it remains the job of the independent director to challenge the executive, to push and stretch them, so that the company does not end up trapped in the same old ways of doing things. Patrick Wilson puts it very well. "Non-executive directors are not there to be executives or manage the business," he says. "They are there to question, to make the executive think outside the box. The most effective independent directors are those who say, 'Why are we doing this? What kind of business are we, and do we want to be? What do we want to look like in five years', ten years' time? Why do we want to look like that? What do we need to do to get there?' The job is to make the executives think about things they do not normally think about." He thinks the job of an independent director is a tough one, and it can be, if the independent directors and the executive do not agree on fundamental issues.

Why did I stay at Datrontech? I have never resigned from posts in difficult situations; I have always stayed to see things through, and I think that is the right thing to do. At Datrontech, this was not easy; at the end, the company had major problems. I had a responsibility that I could not walk away from.

That could have rebounded on my personal reputation, and I am sorry to say that I have known independent directors who put their own reputations first and resigned from companies when the going got tough. I feel strongly that this is wrong. The independent director has duties to others that should take precedence over self-interest. In fact, having a strong sense of integrity and acting accordingly *is* probably the best way of ensuring that your own reputation *is* protected, no matter how bad things may be around you.

Quintiles Transnational Corporation

Quintiles is the global leader in clinical development and commercial outsourcing services to the biopharmaceuticals industry. The company was founded in the USA by Dr Dennis Gillings, then a professor of biostatistics at the University of North Carolina at Chapel Hill. Born and educated in Britain, Dennis had been working with pharmaceuticals companies since 1974, consulting with them on statistics and data management. He set up Quintiles in 1982.

From small beginnings, Quintiles went from strength to strength. In 2013, the company employed 27,000 people in around 100 countries. Worldwide, revenues in 2012 were $3.7 billion, with a profit of $543 million. By any standards, the company has been a tremendous success story.

Quintiles' services were divided into two areas. Firstly, Quintiles offered a complete clinical development outsourcing service for new pharmaceutical products, including testing, analysis, and evaluation. The company had capacity in every major therapeutic area—with cardiovascular, neurology, diabetes and urology, oncology, anti-inflammatory, infectious diseases and gastroenterology being among the most important—and employed a range of specialist scientists and practitioners across the globe. Thanks to its size and economies of scale, Quintiles could provide product research and development services that were both cost-effective and yielded greater chances of success.

The second area is what Quintiles describes as "integrated healthcare services," or the bringing of new products to market. Pharmaceuticals companies invest huge amounts in development and clinical trials for new products, $1 billion or more for a "blockbuster," and these costs are rising (Figure 3.2). Times to market have increased, with development times now taking an average of eight years, and often longer. Increasing government regulation, the prospect of global healthcare reform, price pressure from other players and the "patent cliff" are all piling further pressure on the industry.

Quintiles provided expertise which helped companies to manage the research and development process. Services at this level included costing of projects, provision of sales reps, process optimization (for example, to speed up commercialization when an early result is required), IT and technology management, negotiation of rights and other contractual/legal issues, advice on regulatory issues, market research, information gathering, and data management.

In the late 1990s, Quintiles also established a controversial third division, corporate venturing. This involved Quintiles investing in some of its clients' products and sharing risk with them, an unusual thing to do at the time.

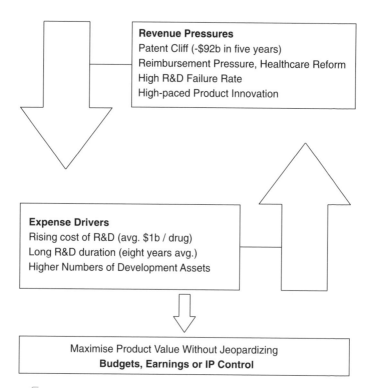

Revenue Pressures
Patent Cliff (-$92b in five years)
Reimbursement Pressure, Healthcare Reform
High R&D Failure Rate
High-paced Product Innovation

Expense Drivers
Rising cost of R&D (avg. $1b / drug)
Long R&D duration (eight years avg.)
Higher Numbers of Development Assets

Maximise Product Value Without Jeopardizing
Budgets, Earnings or IP Control

FIG 3.2 / Industry drivers in pharmaceuticals

In the eight years from 1990–1998, the company grew from $10 million turnover to over $1 billion. The lion's share of this growth came from acquisitions, of which there were more than thirty. These acquisitions gave Quintiles the capacity to offer a wide range of services, which have been crucial to the company's success. Diversification meant a greater range of services could be offered and Quintiles developed full-service offerings for clients. At the same time, size gave economies of scale that helped Quintiles keep its costs down, which in turn gave it a competitive advantage over its rivals and made its services an attractive option for companies considering whether to outsource new product development.

In 1994, Quintiles was listed for the first time on the NASDAQ exchange. This yielded mixed results. Dennis Gillings recalls that the share price fluctuated unpredictably: "Sometimes it was very high, sometimes it was very low." There was a feeling that the market had not properly valued the company, especially the corporate venturing business.

In the late 1990s, the pharma industry entered a period of change. A number of big firms merged and others slowed their development programmers. As a result, the market for Quintiles' services slowed. The industry press noted that some of our acquisitions, such as contract sales and informatics, were not performing as hoped and, in the end, we had to issue a major profits warning. The share price slumped.

Frustrated by these swings and roundabouts and with the market still flat, in 2003 Dennis decided to take the company private. The buy-out was achieved with the support of several private equity (PE) houses, notably Bank One; later, TPG, Bain Capital, 3i and Temasek also got involved. Thanks to the support of these PE houses and strong ongoing partnerships with blue-chip clients in the pharma industry, Quintiles continued to expand. Growth was particularly spectacular in the Europe-Middle East-Africa (EMEA) region. In 2003, EMEA contributed $40 million to Quintiles' global profits; by 2011, this figure had risen to $400 million. In 2013, Quintiles went public once more, this time on the New York Stock Exchange. The share price rose at once, to the pleasure of investors. TPG still regards this as one of its most successful investments ever, with an eventual return of ten times the original sum invested.

I have known Dennis for many years, since we were both students at the University of Exeter, part of a group of friends who still meet regularly. In 1998, he offered me an independent directorship on the board and asked me to take over as chairman of the audit committee. I accepted the post for several reasons. Dennis was a friend, and I have always felt that personal relationships really do matter in business. Secondly, this was a NASDAQ-quoted company, and I thought that being involved with an American-listed company would be an interesting new experience (it was, though not always in a good way). Thirdly, the job of audit committee chairman is very important. And finally, the company was engaged in a field—life sciences—with which I had not had much to do. I felt that this was a great opportunity to learn.

I joined the board in 1998. One of my early challenges was to find a new external auditor after the current one, Arthur Andersen, was caught up in the Enron scandal and collapsed. After the buy-out in 2002, I served as chairman for the EMEA region. In 2011, Quintiles spun off its own corporate venturing fund focused on life science, and I left Quintiles to chair the board of the new company, NovaQuest.

Board Issues: Growth Is Good, but It Is not Always Easy

"I've always had a pretty clear idea of where I want the company to go," says Dennis Gillings. As we saw above, rapid growth by acquisition was a big part of the strategy. Scaling up allowed Quintiles to move with its globalizing clients, understand the issues and risks they faced, and partner them in a variety of projects.

That was the upside. The downside was that acquisitions had often been made quickly, and were not always integrated into the company. Some of the parts of Quintiles didn't fit well with each other and some of the acquisitions needed to be disposed of, but with all the attention focused on acquisitions, no one was thinking much about disposals.

On the board, one of our duties was to oversee the scrutiny of proposals for new acquisitions. As well as due diligence on the companies to be acquired, we also needed to ask whether the acquisition would "fit" with Quintiles. Would this new firm and its facilities and people help to take forward our corporate strategy, or was this just an "impulse buy," a reaction to a perceived opportunity?

So long as acquisitions were closely aligned to the existing business there was no real problem. Issues arose when we began to diversify into areas outside our core competence, such as pre-clinical trials (which involved the controversial subject of animal testing) or medical informatics. Would such diversifications fit, or were they going too far? Our task was to question each proposal and make sure the acquisition was being undertaken for the right reasons.

Sometimes, the board would reject an acquisition that the executive directors had set their hearts on. "As an executive director of a growing firm, you have to be pretty hard-charging," says Dennis. "Sometimes, the independent directors get in the way of this. But I have to say, sometimes it is a good thing that they do so." These disagreements could have turned into "us and them" arguments with one side lined up against the other. Fortunately, at Quintiles both sides saw these disagreements as chances to reflect and discuss the issues. Usually we managed to arrive at a sensible and realistic solution without blood being spilled (metaphorically, of course). Good communications within the board were essential to this.

After the company went private, the private equity firms that now owned a majority of the company imposed their own discipline. Some major disposals were made, particularly the early-stage pre-clinical trials business and the logistics business. There was more of a focus on organic growth rather than growth by acquisition. But the strategic issues of *how* the company should grow, rather than *whether* it should grow, remained of prime importance.

After the private equity firms became involved, too, there was much more focus on capital management. The view of the private equity firms was that Quintiles could be much more heavily leveraged than it was. I think all of us involved recognize that we learned a great deal about capital management and financial discipline from the PE firms.

One of the issues that generated discussion around the boardroom table was what to do with the corporate venturing business. Not every member of the board was happy about venturing. Running clinical trials for clients was one thing, but investing in client projects and sharing risk with them was another. In effect, Quintiles was bearing some of the cost of development, and this was seen by some as being outside our core competence. On one occasion it was proposed that we invest $300 million in a joint venture with Eli Lilly, our largest corporate venture to date. The discussion at board level went on at considerable length with many people feeling—at least at first—very uncomfortable. We did eventually make the investment, and it was very successful, but the question of whether we really should be involved in corporate venturing continued to rear its head.

More significantly, analysts never really understood what we were doing in corporate venturing, seeing only the risks and rarely the upsides. This was a significant factor in the underperformance of the company's share price, which led directly to the buy-out. Six years later the problem was finally solved when the corporate venturing arm was spun off into a separate company.

Another strategic issue that confronted the company was globalization. Once again, it was easy to acquire subsidiaries overseas; it was far harder to make those acquisitions pay off and add value to Quintiles. In 2002, despite having expanded overseas, Quintiles was still a very centralized company. Its culture was very North American, and like many North American companies it had its own particular, very set ways of doing things. Like many North American companies too, its management were not particularly sensitive to the ways that things are done in other parts of the world. There is a tendency to believe that the same rules and same management practices that work in North America will work everywhere. We were very fortunate to have some senior executives who had international business experience, like John Ratcliff, Mike Mortimer and Derek Winstanley. We also had a strong senior management team in EMEA including Hywel Evans, Brian Lowson, Jeff Thomis and Steve Preece.

Notwithstanding this, when I took on responsibility for EMEA, the tensions between global and local were ever-present. Our clients were developing global product lines. Clinical trials needed to be carried out to the same high standard, no matter where in the world they were done; if we did a trial for Roche, for example, there was a particular standard to which we had to deliver, regardless of whether the trial was carried out in America, Belgium or India (indeed, this ability to deliver to the same standard around the world was one of our selling points). Similarly, when dealing with issues such as IT, we needed common IT platforms that were shared around the world.

Table 3.1 shows the challenges we faced at EMEA. We had to grow the business, increasing profitability, margin and cash generation. We had to invest in line with the global strategy of the company, but balance this growth with the needs of the regions. In particular, we had to take cognizance of local conditions in different countries. Thus, if we wanted to set up a facility in Eastern Europe, we had to learn about employment conditions in Eastern Europe and offer terms that would attract the people we needed there. Not all of our business was with global pharma companies; we had plenty of regional customers as well, and their needs had to be catered for.

The manager in charge of business development for EMEA once came into my office in a state of despair. "I'm tearing my hair out," she said. "I'm being told by the US that we have to offer a service to [one of our clients] at a particular

TABLE 3.1   Challenges for the Quintiles EMEA board (2003–2010)

Strategic
Ensure that global strategies for each service line were balanced by the regional dimension
Develop geographic expansion plans, for example, Middle East and Africa
Oversee major investments e.g. new EMEA HQ, new offices and labs, IT systems
Promote the development of commercialisation away from being a commodity business

Financial
Grow the business organically faster than 10% pa
Increase the profitability year on year
Increase the margin year on year
Increase cash generation

Operational
Improve productivity in the clinical business
Achieve operational excellence
Oversee the management development plan
Integrate acquisitions
Achieve cooperation between global business lines
Promote partnering with Global Venture Fund

price. But that pricing structure doesn't make any sense here. How do I make them understand what the local market needs?" The problem, as so often happens in multinationals, was that they often weren't thinking multinationally at all; they were still thinking in North American terms.

As Dennis says, he had a clear idea of the strategic direction that Quintiles needed to follow. But, as has often been remarked, setting strategic direction is comparatively easy; implementing strategy and making it work is the difficult part. Quintiles faced a number of strategic decisions: whether to go private or remain public; whether to expand by acquisition or focus more on organic growth; whether and how to expand internationally; whether to remain a centralized organization or to decentralize and give the regions more autonomy.

Independent directors were involved in all of these issues. Their role was to scrutinize proposals and decisions, offer advice and, where necessary, challenge the received wisdom within the company. On several issues—for example, strategy, acquisitions, auditing, the recruitment of a CEO, incentives for management, governance of quality, disposals and capital management, and the whole process of taking the company private—we made valuable contributions. Dennis Gillings believes that "independent directors bring an objective balance to the company's decision-making and review process," and cites auditing in particular as one area where independent external advice is essential. Executives are busy and tend to make snap decisions, or else have a personal stake in matters. Independents "have no axe to grind. They help move the decision to the right place."

Lessons Learned: Being an Outsider-Insider

That independence that Dennis Gillings talks about is indeed one of the most important benefits that independent directors bring to a company; but as we saw earlier with Datrontech, that is only achievable as long as the independent directors remain independent. That independence again involves a balancing act. Independent directors have to be, at one and the same time, both part of the business and outside it.

It is absolutely necessary to learn what is going on in the business. It is not necessary to understand the technical side of the business in every detail, but you do have to have enough knowledge to understand the underlying business and how it functions. At Quintiles, I began by going around the company, talking to people and learning. When I went into labs and scientists told me what they were working on, I would ask them to show me. Later, when I became chairman of EMEA, I had to do the same thing with our operations throughout the region. I embarked on a steady programmed of site visits, going out to each country and each facility, meeting people and walking around the "shop floor." That, in my view, is the only way to really learn how a company works. In the case of EMEA, too, the knowledge gained from these visits enabled me to go back to the board and challenge the predominantly North American way of doing things, and recommend changes.

I say this to make the point that independent directors cannot simply sit on their hands. They need to become involved in the company, understand its culture and its operations, and be prepared to advise on any aspect of the business if required. (Remember, according to the law in most countries, independent directors can be held legally liable if things go wrong, and ignorance of the law is no excuse.) At the same time, independent directors need to remain detached and preserve their independent point of view. That "objective balance" that Dennis Gillings talks about is one of the things that makes us valuable to the chairman and the executive. If independents start to identify too closely with the company, they are in danger of losing their objectivity.

One of the roles of the independent director is to ask questions of managers and hold them to account. If the independents fail to do so, then what happens? Sometimes, it means managers pursue their own path without the necessary regard for what is good for the company, or its shareholders.

On the other hand, when independents assert their independence, there is a danger that an "us and them" atmosphere can develop. That did not happen at Quintiles, largely because we retained good relationships. The fact that Dennis himself remained open to new ideas and facilitated debate was of paramount importance. Founders of companies—especially highly successful ones like Quintiles—can become rather godlike and unapproachable, but Dennis has always been willing to engage. He knows that it is better to take people with you than to try to enforce your will on them.

A lot thus depends on the personalities on the board, but it is still incumbent on the independent director to make sure that those relationships exists, that the lines of communication are open, and remain open. As a director, you will only make your voice heard if people are willing to listen to you. Being able to communicate and empathize with others, sensitivity to diversity and a general understanding of human relationships are all key skills for an independent director. Otherwise, the insider-outsider will in time cease to be an insider.

The insider-outsider's watching brief over the organization touches on other areas too. As Dennis says, busy executives tend to make decisions quickly. More generally, observers such as the management academic Henry Mintzberg have noted how managers tend to make decisions that will give quick results and gratification; they reach for the levers that are easiest to pull. I mentioned above that Quintiles had undergone a number of reorganizations. In my experience, reorganization is one of those easy-to-pull levers. When managers see a problem in the company, they look for reorganization as a quick fix. When in doubt, reorganize. Others see reorganization as a kind of Holy Grail, the pursuit of which will ultimately lead to the perfect organization (which, of course, does not exist).

Many perceived organizational issues are in fact matters of behavior, which reorganizing will not deal with (and might even make worse). Challenging reorganizations, asking whether they are really necessary, and whether the time and cost expended on them will yield value, is another of those questions that independent directors need to ask. The same applies to the management of people. Some executives like to hire and fire people; these are instant decisions with clearly visible results. But we know that underperformance is sometimes a matter of a good person being in the wrong place, or lacking the skills they need to do their job properly. In my experience, a very small amount of training can often yield impressive results in terms of personal performance improvement. Watching out for these kinds of situations and encouraging executives to think more about building and developing people rather than simply hiring and firing them is another area where the insider-outsider can do something valuable.

Finally, there is the issue of personal learning and development for the independent directors themselves. When Dennis asked me to join Quintiles, he knew I had no experience in life sciences; to him, my useful skills lay in areas such as audit and international business. But he also wanted someone from outside the sector to come in and look at the company with a fresh pair of eyes. This gave me in turn the chance to learn about an entirely new area of business and expand my own horizons. One of the consequences of this was my joining NovaQuest in 2011 (of which more later). The final lesson from this case, then, is this: learn as much as you can, about everything that is going on around you. You never know when it will be useful.

Vantec Corporation

Vantec is a Japanese-based logistics company, founded in 1954 as part of Nissan Motor Company (now Renault-Nissan). It specialized originally in the packing and transportation of automotive components. Like all the big

Japanese conglomerates, Nissan's logistics needs were met by in-house sub-sidiaries, of which Vantec was one. The company remained part of the Nissan group, and its executives were very much "Nissan men."

The Japanese financial crisis of the late 1990s affected the automobile industry particularly badly. Fluctuations in the yen, shortage of capital, and crisis and consolidation in the global automotive industry generally was putting some of Japan's best-known names under pressure. Nissan's financial performance was particularly badly affected, and the company had little choice but to begin looking for assistance from outside. A "strategic alliance" was formed with Renault in 1999, and Renault's Carlos Ghosn became CEO of both companies.

One of Ghosn's strategies was to re-focus the group on its core competencies and get rid of non-essential subsidiaries. Divestment would also raise cash, which the Nissan side of the business badly needed. Vantec was identified early on as a target for a spin-off, and in 2001 it became one of the first major Japanese companies to be sold as a management buy-out (MBO). The major backer was 3i, with PPMV taking a smaller stake. Okuno Shinsuke, who had been managing director of Vantec when it was a subsidiary, now became chairman and CEO of the new, independent firm.

Vantec was a healthy company see the SWOT in table 3.3. At the time of the MBO, it had a turnover of around $780 million and pre-tax earnings of nearly $42 million. There was also strong growth potential. The stagnant economy meant that Japanese firms were forced to change the ways they operated. Logistics was iden-tified as an area where cost savings could be made. Foreign companies including Exel, TNT and Deutsche Post were looking for opportunities to expand in Japan but Vantec, as a home-grown company, had a competitive advantage. Vantec was also one of the first Japanese companies to become an "advanced logistics solution provider" that provided a full logistics package, including management, transpor-tation, warehousing, information and the like down the full length of the supply chain. This model caught on in Japan, and demand was strong.

After a period of settling in following the MBO, Vantec began to expand its operations. It embarked on a series of acquisitions enabling it to diversify into other markets and/or acquire important skills and technology. Among the first acquisitions were another logistics firm, Ikeda, which had also been supplying Nissan, and also two former subsidiaries of Mazda.

By 2003, the company employed nearly 3,000 people, with more than 1,500 at the parent company and the remainder at various subsidiaries. It had sixty-three warehouses with 300,000m² of covered space, and a fleet of 2,700 vehicles. Operations had been divided into nine separate services. Table 3.2 shows the divisions, major clients, sales and number of employees.

As Table 3.2 suggests, Vantec had also successfully moved away from its purely Nissan roots. Nissan and its subsidiaries continued to be major clients, but Vantec also picked up other automotive customers. Mazda was one of the non-Nissan customers, and the company also built long-term relationships with two components suppliers, JATCO and JIDECO. Outside of automotives, Vantec continued its relationship with Ryoshoku, but Coca-Cola also became a major client; by 2003, the soft-drinks giant was Vantec's second-largest client after Nissan. Another food company, UCC Ueshima Coffee, and convenience store operator Family Mart also became important clients. Finally, Vantec began to plan for further international expansion (Autrans Europe and a US subsidiary had already been established in 1990). Today, Vantec Europe is one of the most important subsidiaries of the company.

Throughout this period of growth and expansion there was discussion and debate about the future of the company. I will discuss this in more detail below, as it was a major issue that the board had to confront. That Vantec would be sold was a given. The main question was whether to sell to a foreign company, such as Deutsche Post or Exel, or to a Japanese firm. In the end the faction favoring a domestic sale won out, and in 2004 Vantec was sold to Mizhuo, then Japan's largest bank, for a very attractive exit price.

This again proved to be a good move all around. Mizhuo Capital Partners was the first MBO fund to be established by a Japanese bank, and already had a track record of successful acquisitions and subsequent initial public offerings (IPOs). Itosaka Minoru, president of Mizhuo, was very supportive of the company, and Ohata Yasutoshi, the senior independent director appointed by Mizhuo, was a very able man. Mizhuo helped guide Vantec through a merger with another logistics firm, Tokyu Air Cargo, which added more diversity to the company. Two years later, in 2006, the company was floated on the Nikkei index, again at a very attractive premium for shareholders. The market valued the company at ¥60 billion, four times the value of the original MBO.

I joined the board at the time of the MBO in 2001. The first invitation came directly from 3i, the private equity firm, which had invested in Tibbett & Britten where I had spent two years as chairman of the European division. 3i had asked John Harvey, chairman of Tibbett & Britten, to suggest someone who had experience both of international business and of logistics who could work with a strong Japanese chairman and CEO with a view to a successful exit. John put my name forward.

TABLE 3.2   Vantec divisions and customers

Division	Business description	Major customers	Sales (JPYm)	Employees
Transportation	Transportation of vehicle parts between facilities of automotive OEMs and beverages between bottlers of major beverage companies. Includes handling, storage and delivery	Nissan Nissan Group Cos Coca-Cola Other automotive OEMs	38,050	525
Automotive SCM	Comprehensive SCM and 3PL solutions. Harbour transport, KD and Service parts logistics	Nissan Nissan Group Cos JATCO JIDECO	11,311	100
SCM	Comprehensive SCM solutions including storage and delivery of shops of daily necessaries, alcoholic and soft drinks and foodstuffs; warehouse management, SCM information system services and inventory control	UCC Coffee Ryoshoku Planet	7,890	100
International	Freight forwarding, customs brokerage, operation of bonded warehouses, international air/sea cargo consolidation and insurance agency services	Nissan Nissan Group Cos	6,352	86
Kyushu	Responsible for all operations in the Kyushu region. Operations including general and harbour transportation, export and moving services	Nissan Nissan Group Cos	5,059	154
Hokkaido	SCM services in customer facilities, harbour transportation and air forwarding	Corporate (50%) Individual (50%)	1,791	58
Machinery installation	Disassembly, transportation, re-assembly and installation of heavy machinery	Nissan Nissan Group Cos	1,743	49
Other	Lease of vehicles, iron scrapping, other	n/a	129	n/a
Total			74,477	1,088

TABLE 3.3   The SWOT of Vantec

Strengths	Weaknesses
Experienced management and employees Automotive sector Product offer, logistics expertise in: - Multi-modal - Transport long distance - Local distribution - Ambient warehousing - Picking - Packing components - Export documentation and clearance - Import documentation and clearance - Heavy machinery Assets: - Warehouses, network of 13 major and 27 minor locations in Japan Diversification experience into retail Subcontracting Quality ISO9001 Profitable	Inadequate SCM experience Operational IT systems Dependence on Nissan Loss making business e.g. Home Removals Short term contracts, no volume guarantees Poor margins e.g. packaging Low level of Automation Solutions Sales Marketing Image Procurement Return on Nissan business Quality of warehousing Age of senior team No global standards

Opportunities	Threats
Cost reduction: - Productivity - Subcontracting - Suppliers Improve Nissan contract Grow business in: - Automotive sector - Other car manufacturers - And commercial vehicle manufacturers - Component suppliers - Diversify into other market sectors - Similar requirements to automotive Select highly profitable sectors International Offer wider more profitable product offer e.g. SCM Alliances / partnering Attractive market, growth of outsourcing	Competition New entrants to Japanese market Global automotive industry volume 11% down Customers and margins Amount of change management required Power of Nissan

I went out to Japan and met Okuno Shinsuke, and we got along at once, in part thanks to a shared passion for golf. Okuno-san wanted someone who could help him transform a former in-house subsidiary into a free-standing business and develop a forward-looking strategy. Here again, I had some useful experience thanks to my background at Exel, and I had also visited Japan several times with Quintiles. On the downside, I did not speak Japanese, and this certainly made the job more challenging! I found Japan a very, very different environment in which to work, for reasons I will describe in a moment. I stayed on through the sale to Mizuho and for another two years after, leading operational reviews, hosting customer visits, overseeing account management and contracts. At the invitation of Okuno-san I also ran a number of seminars on management issues, helping to introduce Vantec's managers to Western practices. I departed after the IPO in 2006.

Board Issues: Crossing Cultures, Crossing Boundaries

Several issues confronted the board of Vantec when I joined. First among them was reducing the reliance on Nissan, ideally to the point where Nissan would account for no more than 50 percent of the business; Nissan was cutting costs every year, and would become less significant as a client with the passage of time. We needed to decide how to expand, diversify and grow the company, and we had to decide how and to whom it would eventually be sold.

All of these issues, in fact pretty much everything we did, were complicated by the cultural divide between Japan and the West. I don't mean just the cultural problems encountered by myself and Ken Merron, the 3i advisor who was the other principal non-Japanese board member, but the challenge of re-orienting Vantec itself in a world where international competition was becoming a daily reality.

Vantec, when I joined, still thought of itself as part of Nissan. All the senior managers were long-established executives in the automotive industry; all were in their fifties. In Japan, certainly in those days and still to a great extent today, there was not a lot of job migration between firms. People joined a company at the age of seventeen or eighteen years and stayed there until they retired. They were steeped in knowledge of their own industry, but their experience outside of Japan was limited.

One exception was Okuno Shinsuke, who had worked in America and had a fair command of English. Ken Merron from 3i spoke Japanese fluently, but I and the other Western independents did not. It was agreed, not without reluctance, that board meetings would be held in English to accommodate the key Western shareholders—primarily so that the records of the meetings would be in English—and some of the Japanese executives required translators so that they could follow proceedings. (After the Mizhuo buy-out, board meetings switched back to Japanese and I was the one in need of a translator.) Language issues at times made it difficult for both sides to understand what was really going on.

There were many other cultural problems and ways of doing things that were baffling to the outsider. In governance terms, there was a lack of understanding of the concept of individual responsibility. For example, one of our subsidiaries failed to deliver on a contract to a key client. When we investigated we found that it was almost impossible to get to the bottom of the problem, because everyone protected everyone else. Another issue was charitable donations to organizations outside the firm. When we started looking at these it was very hard to tell whether these organizations were charities or something else because the laws and regulations were, at least to us outsiders, very opaque. There were a great many "shades of grey," which made establishing corporate governance responsibility very difficult.

Vantec was a traditional Japanese company. Workers wore a uniform, and there was a company flag. The culture was one of solidarity, the firm as a kind of family, "we're all in this together." There was a strong belief that Japanese and Western companies had different ways of doing business, and Vantec should stick to the Japanese way. Westernization—indeed, change of any sort—was bound to provoke resistance. The management buy-out itself was a novelty in Japan, and some people at Vantec were clearly trying to pretend that it had not happened and that things would carry on as before.

Others felt that the company had to be "protected" from foreign interference. Okuno Shinsuke, the chairman, in particular felt that 3i and PPMV, the main foreign investors, did not understand Vantec. He insisted that Vantec had to be run as a Japanese company. Needless to say, this did not sit well with 3i and PPMV, who wanted to move Vantec away from its traditional roots make it a more international and modern business. Okuno believed that the private equity companies were only interested in making money—which was true up to a point—and had no interest in the welfare of the business or its employees.

"Ours was a very successful business," Okuno said later, "and this was a high-profile deal. Our partner had to be absolutely right." But he had doubts as to whether 3i was the right partner, and wondered whether the private equity firm really had Vantec's best interests at heart. "As the years rolled along," says

Ken Merron, "it became clear to Okuno, who was a perceptive man, that 3i did not have a long-term commitment to Japan."

Okuno Shinsuke was both part of the problem and part of the solution. He was ambitious for the company and wanted to drive it forward. But he was destined for a career in politics; his father was a member of the Diet, the Japanese parliament, and it was expected that Okuna in time would succeed his father and become a Diet member himself. His desire to make Vantec a success was therefore tempered to a degree by his personal ambitions.

I had a good relationship with Okuno, and he was very generous and hospitable towards me during my time on the board. On some of the issues we faced, such as international expansion and reform of the company pension plan, he was very forward-looking. Also, he got things done. The other executive directors tended to follow his lead; they would do very little until he gave the signal, and if you wanted something done, the fastest way was to get Okuno on side. He was also very willing to hire a CEO with international experience, Yamada Toshi, who played a major role in the subsequent growth of Vantec.

However, on one issue in particular he was adamant. When 3i and PPMV sold their stake in Vantec, the sale must be to a Japanese firm. That was important to him, on both a professional and personal level. 3i, on the other hand, had always favored a sale to Deutsche Post or Exel or one of the other big international logistics firms, a move they felt would help take Vantec into global markets. This was a major source of dispute between 3i and Okuno. "Right from the beginning, the two sides had completely different perceptions of what the deal meant," says Ken Merron. There was a fundamental mismatch of ambitions, which neither side seems to have realized until the MBO was completed. In the end Okuno got his way and Vantec was sold to Mizuho Capital Partners.

Despite the cultural problems and tensions, Vantec was a successful company, and the price paid by Mizuho was a reflection of this. The appointment of the forward-thinking and internationally-minded Yamada Toshi as CEO was a big step forward. He brought fresh thinking into the boardroom and his enthusiasm for the company was infectious. "I always thought Vantec was a company with a great future," Toshi says. "We just needed a sound strategy and a change of business consciousness to take us forward internationally. Once we had that, everything was fairly straightforward."

The main choice facing us was whether to grow the company through geographical or product diversification. In the end we attempted both. We moved away from pure dependence on Nissan, first by associating with Mazda and other automotive companies and then moving into the food, beverage and grocery sectors. In geographical terms, we expanded in the USA and Europe, but the big growth in automotives at the time was in China, where Shanghai was emerging as a center of car production. Renault-Nissan moved into China in a big way, and brought Vantec along as its key distribution partner.

From the outside, Vantec looked like a growing, forward-moving company. Inside, away from the public view, things were rather more fraught. That is not uncommon; successful companies often have their own tensions and internal conflicts. Managing those is another part of the task of the independent director.

Lessons Learned: Give and Take

My role on the board was to represent the shareholders, 3i and PPMV, but I was also part of the link between them and Vantec. That job was not made easier by the disagreements over direction and the cultural barriers between them.

The only way to break down the barriers was to build relationships. I spent much of my time working on my relationship with Okuno, and with some of the other senior directors too. We played golf; I have always loved the game, and now it came in very useful for I could talk to my colleagues on the golf course, away from the business setting, and build a rapport with them. The Japanese were eager to share their old and very rich culture, and I spent much of my time eating meals in Japanese restaurants, visiting temples, watching sumo wrestling and so on. I learned a great deal about *sake*, and I also learned that there is a limit to my appetite for Japanese theatre. But it was through these kinds of interactions that I began, slowly and patiently, to build relationships.

Once these relationships were in place, I could talk with Okuno and the others. Instead of dismissing me as a foreigner who knew nothing about Japan, they would listen. I spent hours talking with Okuno about the relationship with 3i and PPMV, and how he had to work with his shareholders, not simply do things his own way. I talked with him about partnerships with international firms, and made introductions to my old firm Exel. None of this would have been possible if the relationships had not existed in the first place. Of course this issue was more acute in Japan, where often people will not do business with you at all unless there is a pre-existing relationship. But the basic principle holds true in every culture: it is far better to build relationships and take people with you, rather than trying to push them to do what you want.

Another lesson, which we have seen to some extent in the other companies looked at so far but which is very much highlighted here, is the need for companies spinning off from a parent to look at cultural issues, not just financial and structural ones. An MBO of any kind requires a cultural change, a shift in mentalities. Whether an MBO succeeds or fails very often comes down to the issues of whether senior management has been able to make that shift.

At Vantec, there was a need to change from the "in-house company" mentality to that of an independent company. For example, under the old regime if Vantec needed investment it simply went to the Nissan board and, provided it could make a reasonable case, got it. As a free-standing company that was no longer possible. Vantec had to learn to stand on its own.

As an independent director, representing a shareholder with a planned exit in mind, part of one's job is to help speed up that change process. That requires two things. Firstly, it requires working with the chairman and CEO to help change the internal culture. Very often this is done by changing people, bringing in new faces with different experience who will shake the company out of its rooted ways of doing things. That is why the appointment of Yamada Toshi as CEO was so important at Vantec.

Secondly, the independent director needs to encourage the shareholder to be an active investor. People management is critical, a fact which private equity firms sometimes forget. They can sometimes concentrate too much on targets and not enough on the people have to hit those targets. Reminding them of the need to build relationships and helping them to do so is a big part of the job of the independent director. So, although your primary responsibility is to the shareholder, in reality you often end up serving as a middleman or link between the two. Being an independent director sometimes means holding the doors open so that the two sides can be encouraged to talk to one another.

Keller Group plc

The Keller Group is the world's largest ground engineering firm. In 2002 it employed 4,000 people and had a turnover of £360 million; by 2013, employee numbers had risen to 7,000 people and turnover to £1.3 billion. Key market areas are the UK and continental Europe, North America, East Asia and Australia, but Keller has people working across much of the world.

Keller has provided engineering services for more than 150 years. The company has its origins in two firms, the German engineering company Johann Keller, founded in 1860, and the ground engineering division of global engineering giant GKN, established in the 1950s. In 1974, GKN expanded into Europe, acquiring Johann Keller as the first step in that expansion. Other acquisitions followed, the most significant of which was the American ground engineering company Hayward Baker, bought in 1984. In 1990, Dr Mike West led a management buyout from GKN. To distance itself from its former parent, the new company took the name Keller. In 1994, Keller was listed on the London Stock Exchange.

For the most part Keller continued to stick to what it does best—ground engineering—although there has been some diversification (for example, a social housing division, Makers, survived until 2007 when it was disposed of). Ground engineering is the branch of engineering and construction that deals with what lies beneath the ground's surface. In the words of the Institution of Civil Engineers, "The engineering behavior of the ground is fundamental to the way most structures behave. What lies beneath the Earth's surface is often the most uncertain element of a construction project." Ground engineers go into a building site, survey the ground to make certain it is stable, and then provide the foundations to ensure that the subsequent building, once built, stays up. As can be imagined, this is highly specialized work, which requires a great deal of technology and skill, and also has profound health and safety implications not just for the builders but for subsequent users of the buildings.

Keller has worked on some of the most high-profile engineering and construction projects in the world. In the UK, as well as the Olympic Stadium in London, Keller was involved in the Crossrail project, the building of the O2 arena (formerly the Millennium Dome), the revamping of part of the British Museum, the Channel Tunnel Rail Link, West India Quay and Belfast City Airport. In the USA, Keller subsidiaries provided services to building projects at the Capital Building and Supreme Court in Washington DC, the Dallas Cowboys football stadium and the Chicago Trump Tower, as well as projects to build bridges, dams, marinas and power stations. In Dubai, the company was involved in the highly complex work that led to the building of the Palm Islands, two offshore artificial islands with a luxury resort complex, and across Europe and Asia it has worked on a wide range of projects from the Amsterdam Central Station to Changi Airport in Singapore.

Keller's services fall into the following broad categories:

Piling and earth retention. Piling involves the installation of structural elements to transfer foundation loads through weak soils to stronger underlying ground. The piles support the weight of the structure on top and ensure its subsequent stability.

Specialty grouting. Specialty grouting strengthens areas within the ground, and also reduces the permeability of rocks and soil, thus controlling the flow of groundwater, which can de-stabilize structures.

Anchors, nails and minipiles. These are devices, which improve the stability of the ground, and are often used to underpin and stabilize buildings, slopes and embankments.

Ground improvement. This area consists of a range of services that prepare the ground before a construction project begins, and is particularly important in areas of high seismic activity. Common soil stabilization techniques include a combination of vibro-compaction with stone, concrete or lime columns, along with soil mixing and injection systems.

Post-tension concrete. Post-tension concrete cable systems are used to reinforce concrete foundations and structural spans, enhancing their load-bearing capacity by applying a compressive force to the concrete.

A good example of the services Keller offers is the Millennium Dome in London. The largest structure of its type in the world, the Dome is supported by twelve masts. For each of these, Keller designed and built twenty cast in-situ piles (that is, the piles were cast in the ground, rather than being cast elsewhere and hammered into the ground), each 480mm in diameter. Those masts nearest the Greenwich Tunnel and the river Thames received additional support in the form of 750mm piles. A series of 600mm anchor piles and 133mm ground anchors were then constructed to tie down the roof cables that held the Dome's pillow-like roof in place. Finally, a further series of 10,000 350mm piles were driven into the ground to support the exhibition space and core buildings in and around the dome.

All of the mast piles and 7,500 of the exhibition-space piles had to be completed within twelve weeks. At one point, Keller was completing over 1,000 piles per week on the site, using twelve driving rigs and two other rigs to emplace the anchor piles. As the company's own literature says, not without a certain element of feeling, "despite a number of very large obstructions, the work was completed on time."

When I joined the board in 2001, Keller was already a global firm, offering foundation services and specialist services in thirty countries. Following a later strategic review, the company was restructured into four divisions: North America, Europe-Middle East-Africa, Asia and Australia. The divisions were highly independent, and had their own finance, human resources (HR) and other support services. The individual divisions traded independently, sometimes under different brands. In Europe, for example, the company traded under the Keller name, but in North America the company trades through six subsidiaries: Anderson Drilling, Case Foundation, Hayward Baker, H.J. Foundation, McKinney Drilling and Suncoast. Figure 3.3 shows the Keller business model.

As Figure 3.3 shows, Keller had a global reach but its focus was very much local. Every engineering project is unique: different clients have different needs, and different sites pose different ground engineering challenges. Staff on site had to have the freedom to solve problems as they encountered them, rather than being constrained by corporate procedures.

But the company also thought global, and there was a great deal of cross-fertilization and sharing of best practice between the divisions. (This was not always the case. One of the outcomes of the recent strategic review was to bring the divisions closer together and encourage greater sharing of knowledge.) Keller's CEO Justin Atkinson calls it a company with "a British brain, an American engine and a European heart". The American operations were the largest and most profitable, but the intense competition in Europe, coupled with a tradition of technical know-how, meant that many innovations in service came from there, and were then diffused around the rest of the firm.

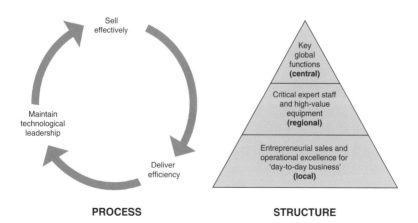

FIG 3.3 / The Keller business model

Figures 3.4 and 3.5 show the size of the ground engineering market in 2010, at a time when the industry was still badly affected by the economic downturn, and Keller's own market share by geography.

In 2001, I was approached by Peter Waine from the headhunting firm Hanson Green, who asked if I would be interested in joining the board of Keller. One of

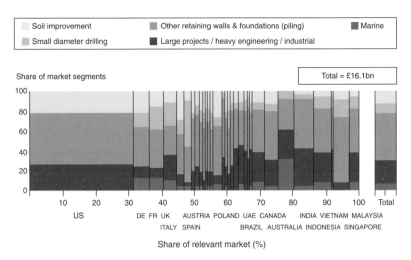

FIG 3.4 / **Total ground engineering market size**

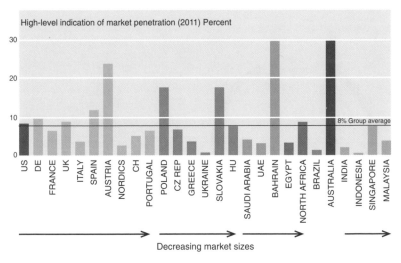

FIG 3.5 / **Keller's market penetration**

its independent directors had just retired, and they were looking for a replacement who had experience as a board member of a public limited company, as well experience as of international business and strategy. I fitted the bill, and joined the board later that year.

My stay as a board member was unusually long, and deserves comment. Independent directors are commonly appointed for terms of three years, and can be reappointed at the end of their term. Guidelines for independent directors suggest, however, that directors should not serve for longer than two terms (six years) and that three terms (nine years) should be the maximum.

By this rule, I should have stepped down in 2010, at the end of my third term. But this would have caused problems for the firm. A number of other independents departed at about the same time, and we also had a relatively new chairman, Roy Franklin, who had succeeded Mike West (Mike West retired in 2009 after forty-five years with Keller). The financial crisis was beginning to bite, and the company was facing a number of fairly formidable business challenges. I was the senior independent director, and it was felt that my departure on top of the others would have deprived the board of experience at a critical time. So, against the guidelines, I stayed on for another three years while the new board settled in, finally stepping down early in 2013.

Board Issues: Diversification, but How and Where?

Ground engineering, when I joined the board, was a heavily fragmented market. There were a couple of other big players, the Bauer Group being one of them, but mostly there were a lot of small companies bidding for contracts. Contracts tended to be small too; the vast majority of Keller's contracts were for less than £10 million, so in most parts of the world our divisions were managing a lot of little contracts, rather than a few big ones. An exception was North America, where we were involved in larger contracts.

However, there was a question in the board's mind as to whether the company had now become too dependent on North America for revenue: 70 percent of group revenue came from the North American division, and there was a clear risk should the North American economy run into trouble. The analysts who looked at Keller thought that its position in North America was strong enough to allow it to ride out any subsequent economic downturn. This proved not to be the case.

The construction industry is very vulnerable to economic fluctuations. Private companies that might be planning new construction projects will put these on hold if they think that a downturn is coming; and once it becomes clear that hard times are on the way, construction projects are the first things to be cancelled. Sometimes governments will pump money into the economy through construction and infrastructure projects, and in these cases the industry has an alternative source of income. But, after 2008, many governments, especially the American government, cut back on spending. The construction industry was thus hit from both sides.

From well before the downturn, it was apparent that Keller's position as a focused, specialist company was both a strength and a weakness. The fact that Keller was the biggest company in the business, plus its technical knowledge and skills base, made it a formidable competitor in almost any market where we cared to do business. At the same time, we were almost entirely dependent on an industry which, as we have just seen, is very vulnerable to economic fluctuations and cycles. One way to reduce the risk was to diversify, but how and where?

The idea of a "second leg," another business area to complement the core ground engineering business, had been discussed previously. The question of what that business should be, however, was difficult to answer. Part of the problem was that Keller itself was culturally very much attached to the ground engineering business. Most of the senior executives, and the chairman, were "Keller men" who had grown up with the company and risen through the ranks. As we saw at Vantec, when a company's executives share a very strong common culture, and have little any experience of any other culture, their worldview can become rather limited. They think from the perspective of their own business only, not from the perspective of the market.

In the end we did make one notable diversification, buying the American firm Suncoast which specialized in post-tension concrete products and services. Although Suncoast, like the rest of the industry, suffered in the downturn, on the whole this has proved to be a good investment. This apart, Keller stayed very much focused on ground engineering.

Rather than expanding into new services and products, Keller chose instead to expand geographically. This went well and existing markets such as Australia grew rapidly. We also moved into some new geographies such as Brazil, though we never did gain a foothold in China; however, India became an important market. At first it seemed that the Asian markets would help hold the company up in the aftermath of 2008, as Asia was at first less affected by the downturn.

By 2010, however, the decline had spread worldwide and Keller's turnover and profits were beginning to suffer. The Australian operations, which had been one of the best-performing parts of the business, were particularly hard hit and the business as a whole was struggling. The City began to get alarmed because Keller was no longer delivering on its forecasts. The company's excellent track record and prospects did not seem to matter; all that counted was the present and immediate future. The share price declined.

The independent directors saw this happening and began to ask questions about the company's response to the downturn. Was enough being done? Were the right things being done, and were they being done quickly enough? Roy Franklin, who had recently taken over as chairman, wanted to bring in consultants to conduct a strategic review, and the independent directors supported him, not without some initial opposition from the executives. Some of the independent directors were new, and some executives considered that they did not yet fully understand the company. After some discussion the strategic review went ahead with the appointment of strategy consultants LEK.

The strategic review looked at purchasing, management succession, our product and market portfolio and pretty much every aspect of the business. Our role as directors, after appointing the consultants and giving them their brief, was to allow them to do their work and then discuss their findings at board meetings. We did step in to encourage some of the more reluctant executives to open up and cooperate with the consultants.

One of the issues that LEK looked at was the structure of the company. While it is possible to be too centralized (as it could be argued that Quintiles was), equally it is possible to be too *de*centralized. Keller, when I first joined, was a lot smaller and the CEO could keep in touch with the divisions and manage opportunities. The divisions were run almost as independent businesses, with little contact with the board. When I told Mike West, the chairman, that I intended to visit Suncoast and view its operations while I was in the USA, he raised his eyebrows. "That doesn't normally happen," he said.

But as the company grew, this had to change. After Justin Atkinson became CEO, he began a programmed of twice-yearly meetings and visits where each subsidiary would present its business plan and strategy. It was a simple device, but it had two important outcomes: it put the board more in touch with the company, and it gave everyone else a chance to see what each company was doing and what could be learned from it.

The strategic review was a success, and we came out of it a stronger and better organized company than we went in. Central control was tightened up, but not to the extent that we lost the local focus. We decided against indiscriminate geographical expansion and instead decided, in Justin Atkinson's words, to "be bigger in fewer places." Keller became a more coherent company, and now has good prospects ahead with some major projects to sink its teeth into, such as Crossrail in London and the Gdansk Tunnel in Poland.

Another issue that demanded the board's attention was health and safety. Construction is, or can be, a dangerous business and over the course of three years Keller suffered a run of accidents, including several fatalities. Soon after he came became chairman, Roy Franklin, who had a background in the oil industry where health and safety is also a major issue, pressed us to make this a priority. A health and safety committee with board representation was established, and a number of recommendations for improvement were quickly made and implemented.

Lessons Learned: There Are No Substitutes for Knowledge

Several interesting lessons present themselves from the Keller experience. The first concerns the need for control. At the outset, too few people really knew what was going on around the company, and this led to some questionable decision-making. For example, when the American division began to perform badly, some of the directors criticized the head of the division. Justin Atkinson recalls that the latter was furious, accusing the board of not knowing enough about his business; and to a certain extent, he was right.

I had been to see the American operations on a number of occasions and I knew how good this man was. In my view, but he was the right person to help the American division turn around. I made this point strongly to the board, arguing that if we were going to have a change of executives in America, there had to be a proper succession plan; changing a competent executive in the middle of a crisis is just about the worst thing one can do. Cooler heads prevailed and we kept the head of division in his post, and the American division duly turned around. The first lesson, then, is to ensure that the board has the information it needs (which might be different from the information it wants).

The problems in America, and also Australia, did turn out to be worse than the board anticipated, and this was partly a result of lack of reporting and control. Not knowing enough about what was happening in the divisions and different geographies led to crisis when Keller started to miss its forecast income and profit targets. This, for a quoted company, is one of the worst things that can happen. Once companies start issuing revised forecasts, markets react very severely; indeed, they often overreact. Analysts and investors are not always logical in their decision-making. They scare easily, and revised forecasts are one of the danger signs that makes them take fright. The answer is, avoid re-forecasts. Get it right first time.

It is also important to have people on the board who have experience of other geographies and can help the company expand into new markets. At Keller, for example, we investigated opportunities in Korea, Qatar and Russia as a result of initiatives by individual board members. Even if those opportunities do not develop further, it is good to ensure that the board continues to scan the environment.

My own connections with Spain played a role in the acquisition of the Spanish ground engineering firm, Terratest. Terratest's chairman, Pedro Jimenez, then came onto the Keller board. Pedro was a flamboyant figure, who also sat on the board of Real Madrid football club and had been instrumental in bringing the football star David Beckham from Manchester United to Real Madrid. He was a very well-read and cultured man, and we got on well. However, he struck sparks off some of the other directors. The cultures of Terratest and Keller were quite different, especially in matters of corporate governance. Pedro found it difficult making the transition from a privately owned Spanish company culture to that of a public corporation in Britain. He adjusted in time, but there were some difficult moments during the adjustment process. This example is a useful reminder that sometimes the problems companies encounter when making acquisitions are more cultural than financial.

By necessity, Keller remains a highly decentralized company. One issue that falls out of this is the question of management succession. It is very hard, in a decentralized company, to grow people to take over top management jobs. There are very few people able to succeed the chief executive, for example, should he fall ill or be incapacitated at short notice. In centralized companies this is easier; there should be two or three people close to the CEO who know the business and can take over. In Keller, the senior division people know their own divisions but are less familiar with the rest of the company. There is no easy answer to this problem, but it does need to be addressed.

Among other things, I served as chairman of the remuneration committee for Keller. Being chairman of a Remco has become a more important and more challenging role recently. One of the jobs of the Remco is to ensure that people are paid fairly, but in a global business, what is "fair" can also become a subject for dispute. At Keller, some of the senior American executives had profit-sharing deals, negotiated when Hayward Baker and other companies were taken over. In good years, these executives could end up earning more than the CEO. Some thought this was unfair. After some debate, we opted not to establish a single global pay structure because it seemed that any attempt to do so might be equally unfair. How do you relate pay in Singapore with pay in Russia, or Spain? There seemed no equitable way of doing so. In the end we decided that pay would be related to the performance of each business. This worked for Keller; but each Remco has to establish what system and method will work best for its company.

Finally, a brief closing word on the independent director guidelines and my twelve-year stint at Keller. The restriction on independent directors serving more than three terms was imposed in the belief that, if they serve for any longer, there is a danger that they will come to identify too closely with the company and its executives, and will therefore no longer be independent. There is a danger that this can happen, of course. Institutional investors are very diligent on this issue, and will point out long-serving independent directors to the chairman and question whether they are still independent. But the other side of the coin is that when companies lose long-serving directors, executive or independent, they lose a great deal of accumulated institutional memory and knowledge. In the case of Keller, the near-simultaneous turnover of most of the independent directors and the chairman left the board crucially short of experience at a vital time for the company. Roy Franklin's view, and that of the board, was that I had to stay.

There is a need for continuity on boards, and in my view institutional investors should take a more nuanced view of this issue and not push quite so hard. Long-serving directors can of course continue to be independent; there is no reason why not. A case-by-case basis might serve the interests of corporate governance rather better than a hard-and-fast rule.

CH Jones Ltd

CH Jones was a fuel management company providing services to the commercial road transport industry. Founded in 1895, the company moved into diesel bunkering in 1977 and established a very solid business providing fuel services for both light and heavy commercial vehicles. Peter Vallis, the principal owner, was a skilful entrepreneur who anticipated both industry and technological trends. In 1989, he launched the Keyfuels prepaid fuel card, which customers could use to purchase fuel anywhere in the CH Jones network, and in 2000 the first online platform, eFuels, was established, allowing customers 24-hour access to their accounts. Turnover grew from £16 million in 2001–2002 to £36 million in 2006–2007, with profits increasing from £4 million to £9 million.

Fuel typically accounts for around one-third of operating costs in the road transport industry, where margins are very low. Bulk buying offers transport companies discounts of perhaps 3-4 pence a liter less than the price paid at the forecourt pump. When we consider that in the 1990s a typical forty-four tonne lorry used £35,000 worth of diesel in the course of year's operations—and that figure has risen significantly since—those discounts are very important.

However, bulk buying brings its own management and stock-control problems. Poor stock-control systems resulted in many companies "losing" between 5 and 8 percent of the fuel they bought; and, again with rising fuel costs, that loss represented a very significant additional cost. If hauliers were using several depots, it could take weeks to reconcile accounts between depots and find out how much fuel had been used. In practice, many companies didn't even bother to reconcile their accounts. A golden opportunity to control costs went begging.

CH Jones aimed to give transport companies the best of both worlds. It offered discounts to bulk purchasers but, instead of storing fuel at just a few sites, let customers draw on their pre-purchased stock of fuel at any of the company's bunker sites across the UK. The result was a total fuel management service that took the burden and cost of stock control and reconciling away from the haulage companies, while allowing them access to their fuel whenever and wherever they needed it. The Keyfuels and eFuels systems meant that drivers could refuel at any depot in the network, and CH Jones' IT systems automatically monitored stock and control accounts. Another service, Diesel Direct, allowed drivers to fill up at retail outlets, or "on the road," if they were not in easy reach of a bunker.

CH Jones also offered a vehicle-tracking system that calculated fuel efficiency for each vehicle. There is a lot of variation in fuel consumption among drivers, and a good driver can save his company as much as 15 percent in fuel costs by driving more efficiently. Vehicle tracking systems help to identify which drivers are less efficient, so that the company can offer training or take other corrective action as needed. Figures 3.6 and 3.7 respectively show the dynamics of the market and the range of the company's services and product offerings.

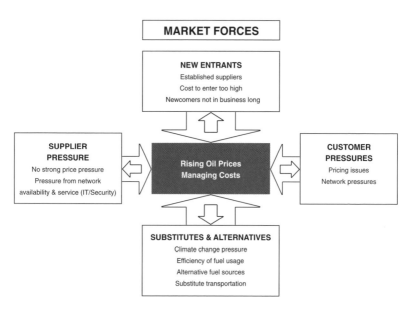

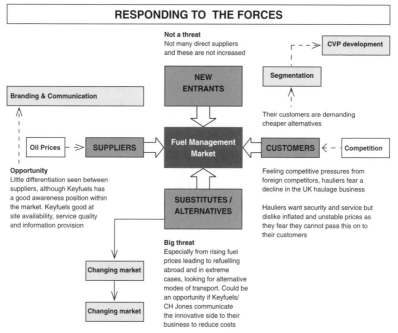

FIG 3.6 Dynamics of the fuel market

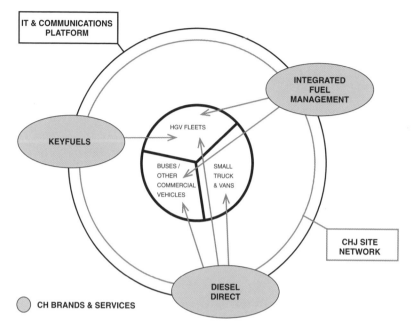

FIG 3.7 CH Jones products and services

The company faced considerable potential competition from the large fuel retail operators, such as BP, Shell and Esso. As road haulage became more and more of a cross-border business, with companies operating across Europe, our purely British operation also had a competitive weakness; a competitor offering a European-wide service could have made inroads into our business. However, CH Jones also had a number of competitive strengths. It had the largest bunker network in the UK, giving customers access to their fuel in more locations. It had its own bespoke fuel management software, Oasis, linking the network and providing very accurate stock management and reconciliation. The company was very customer-focused, and was constantly innovating and developing new services to help customers reduce costs and manage fuel more efficiently. Figure 3.8 shows how CH Jones continued to maintain a strong market share.

I joined the board in 2001, at a time when Peter was strengthening the management team. He had recruited Chris Welsh as CEO, and also a very good finance director, Cliff Cartwright. Sometimes relationships between entrepreneurial owners and professional managers are prickly, but in this case, as Chris says: "Within a year there was such a high degree of trust that board meetings

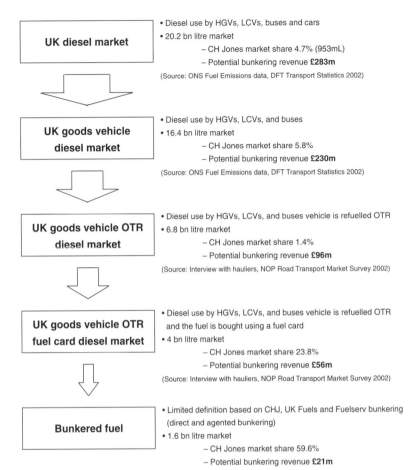

FIG 3.8 / CH Jones market

had become rather cozy. We were cash-rich, cash-generative, the most profitable business in our sector, and it was a nice place to be." There was clearly a danger of complacency and, says Chris, "the problem was to change the culture when it was not immediately obvious that change was needed."

After the team had made a couple of investments, which seemed like a good idea at the time, but which did not work out as planned, Chris went to Peter. "I said that I thought we needed to bring someone in who will challenge our thinking, and occasionally say no," he recalls. An outsider was needed to break up the "cozy" atmosphere and question previously held assumptions. Peter agreed and hired a headhunter, who approached me.

I knew a little about the company—at Exel we had used their services—but I had no experience of their business. I had been operations director of Exel, one of the largest commercial vehicle operators in the country. Therefore, I knew something about fuel management, and I could see how I could make a contribution. I also have a rule that one should never say no to such approaches until you have met the people involved, because you never know what you will find.

I met Peter Vallis and liked him; we got on well. I then met Chris Welsh, a very intelligent man with lots of ideas about the company. Chris Welsh recalls a conversation where he asked me how I worked with chief executives. According to him, I replied: "I support them, right up until the point where I tell the chairman that I think they need to be replaced." "As a chief executive, I found that incredibly reassuring," says Chris Welsh. "I knew then that I could talk to him honestly and have his support, until such time as it became clear that I had outlived my usefulness."

After having run the company for many years, Peter Vallis wished to exit. We looked at a number of options, and finally, in 2006, Peter Vallis accepted an offer of £53 million from the American fuel management company Fleetcor—a very good multiple bearing in mind that the company had recently been valued at £24 million. The company was integrated into Fleetcor, though the CH Jones brand continues in the UK. I stepped down from my post when the company was sold.

Board Issues: Charting a Course

When I joined the board, CH Jones was an excellent company with a solid foundation, but which had no very clear idea of where it wanted to go next.

From the start, it was clear that we had plenty of strengths to work with. Keyfuels was a good product with a strong brand. Knowledge of the market, robust information and stock control systems, and equally strong cashflow and financial management, all meant that CH Jones could deliver service on a par with, if not better than, any competitor. Importantly, too, we had strong management. Peter Vallis was a hands-on owner, a flamboyant character who rode almost everywhere on a motorcycle and was often in the office, talking to people and learning what was going on. He was complemented by Chris Welsh, an excellent chief executive. I felt we had little to worry about in terms of management quality.

Many of our weaknesses were internal. There had been a number of changes in management, meaning that there was a lack of continuity at the top, and this may have contributed to weaknesses in areas such as marketing and customer management. We were open to a potential competitive threat from the big fuel companies. They could choose to invest in the same kinds of technologies as CH Jones, and market directly to haulage companies, eliminating middlemen like us. (Fortunately, their strategic attention always seemed to be occupied somewhere else, and they never took the opportunity.) We needed some more and different ways of adding value for customers. In sum, we were technically very efficient, but we did not always manage as effectively as we might.

We also lacked a strategic focus. While Keyfuels had been a successful product, it was not in itself enough to sustain growth at the rate required. The fuel card itself was a pretty straightforward offering, easy to replicate. We had to diversify away from that core product and, as noted above, we were once again faced with the choice of whether to diversify into new markets, new products and services, or both.

One major market opportunity was in information technology. We could use IT as a platform for consultancy to help customers save money, such as fuel management information systems that showed fuel efficiency by vehicle and driver. Operators of commercial vehicles needed this kind of information, and CH Jones was well placed to provide it. Today, operators can capture this kind of data themselves through existing software, but my feeling is that most still are not very good at analyzing this data, and even less good at knowing what to do about it. Companies like CH Jones are still needed.

Among other strategic options, we discussed ways of strengthening relationships with fuel providers, and with operators of light commercial vehicles (up to this point, as the Figure 3.7 show, we had been more focused on heavy goods vehicles or HGVs). We also looked at expanding the client base, for example by bidding for outsourcing contracts with large fuel consumers in the public sector such as the Ministry of Defence or the National Health Service. We made a couple of acquisitions along these lines, notably the fuel dealer Croft Fuels, and a liquid natural gas provider, Keygas; in the latter case we were aware that alternative fuels might be coming onto the market and wanted to give ourselves a position. We looked at new markets both domestic and foreign; we were probably not large enough to expand by acquisition overseas, but partnerships with companies like European fuel management firm DKV offered interesting possibilities.

At the same time, we had to make sure the firm stayed focused. Peter and Chris were both entrepreneurial men who had keen eyes for an opportunity. From time to time one or the other would come up with a new idea, such as an acquisition of a company in a related business or rights to a new technology, and then we would drop everything to discuss this in detail. This was a small firm with a small executive and, unlike large companies like Keller or Quintiles where the board was not involved in day-to-day operations, here the board tended to get involved in everything. Life at CH Jones was never dull.

Peter had given his senior executive incentives in the form of equity in the firm. In my view this was a very wise decision; many owners try to keep everything for themselves, and this can make executives resentful. When it came time to sell the firm, the executives were naturally pleased and worked together with Peter to bring about the sale. An investment bank, HawkPoint, was appointed as advisor in 2004, and thereafter we set to work doing what was necessary to get the company ready for sale.

First on the list was a clearly defined strategy and business plan. The board consulted management through the company, developed a business plan and then measured progress against the plan on an annual basis. The second issue concerned corporate governance. We had to have properly run board meetings with minutes and records, and more generally the company had to work to accepted corporate governance standards. Sometimes in small, entrepreneurial organizations the rules of corporate governance, if not actually flouted, get pushed somewhat to one side. But any potential purchaser would require transparency and want to know that all our operations were on board. We started thinking about a "data room," the collection of information such as asset registers that any purchaser would want to see before proceeding with an offer. Finally, we started thinking about the kind of company that we would want to buy us, and began to make potential purchasers aware of the opportunity.

CH Jones was a well-managed and profitable company with strong financial controls where, unusually in my experience, the financial results always met the forecasts. Although there were occasional shocks, for the most part we were able to concentrate on planning for the future. Why? Because we had a strategy, and stuck to it.

Lessons Learned: There Is No Substitute for a Good Strategy

There is no substitute for a highly focused well-thought-out strategy. At CH Jones there were a number of options we could have pursued, acquisitions we could have made, expansions we could have undertaken, which would have led us onto sidetracks and byways, and taken our focus off the company. We avoided these, and we maintained our focus.

In any company, the most important thing strategically is to decide what *not* to do, and in small companies where resources, including management time and attention, are very limited, this becomes even more important. But we worked out what we did not want to do and stuck to what we did want, and that is one of the reasons why we were so successful and got such a good price for the company.

I believe firmly that all our success flowed from the company having a good strategy. Datrontech, by contrast, did not have a good strategy, and ultimately it paid the price. The same was true of Michael Gerson, which we shall come to shortly.

From a personal perspective, I enjoyed helping Peter and his team make this business successful right through to the exit. I enjoy working with people and seeing a business run well. I like helping people to be successful, and this was a success. All of this gave me a great sense of satisfaction.

And that leads me to another lesson. I believe that it is critical that an independent director should enjoy the experience. If he or she does not, if the fit between director and company is not right, then both sides will be unhappy. I have met people and felt that the chemistry between us was not right, and in those cases I wanted nothing to do with it no matter how much money was involved. There is, after all, a matter of opportunity cost. If you take a job with a company and do not enjoy it, you are almost certainly denying yourself a chance to work with a different company where you would enjoy it. Money really isn't everything. If there is not a sense of pleasure and satisfaction that comes with the work, then maybe it is not worth doing.

Forth Ports plc

Forth Ports is descended from the state-owned Forth Ports Authority, which managed all five seaports on the Firth of Forth in Scotland from 1967 onward. In 1992, the company was privatized and listed on the London Stock Exchange. The Forth Ports of today includes the original five ports:

Leith, the port of Edinburgh. It has the largest enclosed deep-water port in Scotland and can handle ships of up to 50 000 tons. Cruise liners call here, and the port also handles general cargo, dry bulk and grain. The company also owns 400 acres of land along the Leith waterfront.

Grangemouth, further west at the head of the Firth of Forth. It is Scotland's largest container port, handling up to nine million tons of cargo each year. Grangemouth is also the site of a major oil terminal.

Rosyth, northwest of Edinburgh. As well as dry bulk, forest products, grain and general cargo, Rosyth is the terminus for Norfolkline's thrice-weekly ferry service to Zeebrugge, Belgium.

Burntisland, in Fife on the north bank of the Forth, northeast of Edinburgh. Burntisland is a major service center for the North Sea oil and gas industry.

Methil, further east in Fife, again on the north bank of the Forth. The port specializes in the distribution of timber and wood pulp.

In 1995 Forth Ports acquired two more ports:

Dundee, on the Firth of Tay on the east coast of Scotland. This major port handles general cargo but also specializes in forest products, including paper pulp, and agricultural products. It also services the North Sea oil and gas fields, has a ferry terminal, and is a port of call for cruise liners.

Tilbury, one of the most important ports serving London. The London Container Terminal at Tilbury can handle more than half a million containers per year. Tilbury is also the UK's leading paper-handling port, and handles grain and a wide variety of bulk cargo; it also has an important cruise ship terminal. Forth Ports also owns 760 acres of land at Tilbury.

In 2007, Forth Ports acquired the Nordic Group, which manages the cargo terminal at Chatham on the Thames Estuary. Forth Ports also invested for a time in the cargo terminal at St Petersburg in Russia.

Forth Ports employed around 1,200 people. It reported revenues of £182 million in 2010, with pre-tax profits of £56 million.[2] Figure 3.9 shows how income was fairly evenly spread across five broad business sectors, although there are differences between the Scottish ports and the two English ports, Tilbury and Chatham.

There were then around 130 commercial ports in the UK, but traffic was heavily concentrated; just thirteen ports handled 75 percent of all goods shipped by sea into or out of the country. London's ports accounted for about 20 percent of all port traffic in the UK, followed by Liverpool with about 10 percent. Other major port operators included Associated British Ports, Clydeport, and Mersey Docks and Harbour. Figure 3.10 and Table 3.4 show the distribution of major ports and owners, and the largest ports by volume.

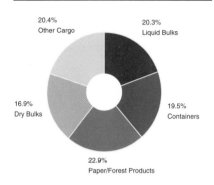

FORTH PORTS INCOME

- Broad spread and security of income
- Resilient performance

20.4% Other Cargo

20.3% Liquid Bulks

16.9% Dry Bulks

19.5% Containers

22.9% Paper/Forest Products

TILBURY	SCOTLAND
Growth from:	**Growth from:**
Ro-Ro	Coal
Grain	Ferry traffic
Dry bulks	Steel pipes
Nordic Forest Terminals	
Decreases in:	**Decreases in:**
Containers	Containers
Paper volumes	Liquid bulks
(not revenue)	(marginal effect)

- Operating efficiencies
- Profit decrease mainly from container handling and storage revenue

FIG 3.9   **Forth Ports Income**

Growth in port traffic roughly paralleled growth in the UK economy as a whole, with average annual growth of about 3 percent (not including oil traffic). Much of this growth was in unitized or containerized cargo, and containers represented about 25 percent of all port traffic. This relatively slow rate of growth had several consequences for the industry. Firstly, it left some companies with just one port, or a few ports, exposed to cyclical downturns in whatever commodities happen to ship through their ports; Mersey Docks and Harbour, for example, ran into trouble when port traffic declined at Liverpool, as it had no other streams of income. Secondly, there was a trend towards consolidation with more and more traffic running through a few large ports such as London. Finally, port operators diversified into other businesses in order to compensate for the slow growth in port traffic.

Diversification for Forth Ports meant finding better ways of using one of its key resources: the land it owned around the ports. In 2007, the 400 acres at Leith were independently valued at £218 million. Forth Ports had raised revenue by selling off parcels of land for residential development at Western Harbour and Granton. A partnership was also set up with the Bank of Scotland to build a shopping center, Ocean Terminal, at Leith, and another partnership was established with a property company to develop residential housing. (After the 2008 crisis, when Bank of Scotland ran into trouble, we were able to buy the whole of Ocean Terminal at a very good price.) The policy of land sales was subsequently changed and Forth Ports prepared its own plans for the development of the Waterfront area and for the harbor at Leith Docks.

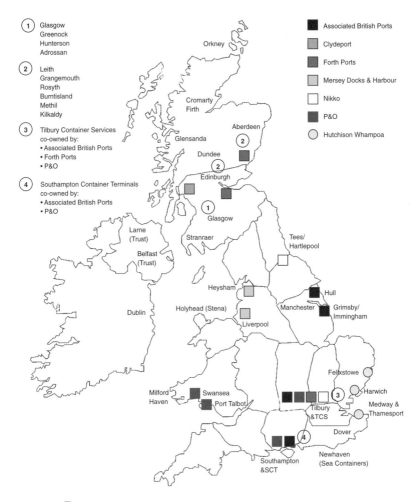

FIG 3.10 / **Distribution of UK ports and owners**

At Tilbury, under the leadership of Perry Glading, logistics and warehousing facilities were developed and leased to a wide range of clients. One early partnership was a fifteen-year contract with a major international paper company, Stora Enso. Using the latest innovations in supply chain technology we provided the world's first port-based, fully integrated, automated paper handling and storage facility. We also worked with Cemex on the creation of a new cement blending and grinding plant as part of Tilbury's strategy of becoming the preferred supply chain route for the London 2012 Summer

TABLE 3.4   UK top 10 ports by non-oil tonnage (2000)

Port	Owner	Non-oi (mt)	Percentage of Non-oil total
Felixstowe	Hutchison	29.7	11.4
London	Various	28.7	11.0
Grimsby & Immingham	ABP	20.6	7.9
Dover	Dover Harbour	17.4	6.7
Liverpool	Mersey Docks	16.4	6.3
Tees & Hartlepool	Nikko	15.3	5.9
Medway	Various	11.9	4.6
Hull	ABP	9.5	3.7
Belfast	Belfast Harbour	9.1	3.5
Southampton	ΛBP	8.5	3.3
		167.1	64.2%

Olympics. Another example of diversification was a specialized grain store for an importer.

Discussions as to whether to spin off a separate property arm were shelved in 2008 when the financial crisis brought the value of property crashing down. Forth Ports responded to the downturn in several ways: by reducing costs by about £3 million on an annualized basis, by improving port-handling efficiency, building stronger links with key customers, and improving IT and operating systems.

We also looked at further diversification. Recycling and green energy generation were two key areas of focus. A major paper recycling center was opened at Tilbury, and plans were developed for wind farms and biomass power plants both there and in Scotland. Some of these efforts were more successful than others. The recycling business never yielded the revenue or profits expected from it. There had been high hopes for this, as London generates an enormous amount of waste paper which has to be collected and recycled; this looked like a business with a future. However, as we quickly learned, the price of waste paper is cyclical and volatile, and can drop unexpectedly. The same was true of other recyclables.

We lacked the expertise and experience to run this business, and as chairman David Richardson points out, there were many competitors in the market who could read the market trends better than we could. "In theory this diversification looked quite good," he says, "but in practice it proved very difficult to execute." The recycling business did not lose money, but it did underperform. Whether diversifying in this direction was the right thing to do remains an open question.

By 2010, Forth Ports was the last independent port operator in the UK. Despite the economic downturn, its financial results were healthy enough to make it an attractive takeover target. We were approached that year by a consortium led by Arcus Capital, offering to purchase the company for £12.85 a share. We rejected the offer. We had weathered the crisis. We had a sound strategy and plans in place that we knew would add value to the company. We took a firm position on the value of the company and held to it, refusing a further offer of £14 per share. At this point several members of the consortium pulled out, but Arcus Capital came back on its own, and after further negotiations, in early 2011 Arcus' European Infrastructure Fund offered £16 a share, valuing the company at £751 million. This equated with the future value we had put on the company, and was a very good premium on the existing share price. We accepted the bid in March 2011.[3]

I joined the board of Forth Ports in 2003, having first been approached by the headhunters, Hanson Green. Another director was retiring, and the company was looking for someone with experience of property and logistics to take his place. I served until 2011, stepping down after the sale.

Board Issues: What Kind of Business Are We In?

Forth Ports were very good at thinking about strategy. This is not always the case with companies, and it is not uncommon to find board members who do not get involved in strategy. Research published by McKinsey suggests that some 60 percent of board members simply nod strategy through. Not at Forth Ports; there, all of the board were involved.

We held an in-depth strategic review every year, spending two days off-site usually at either Gleneagles or St Andrews. Every board member attended these, and Chris Collins, who was chairman when I joined, made certain that everyone contributed, executive and independent directors alike, and that their views were heard. That was very much Chris' style. He did not impose his own opinion; instead, he sought a balance of views from everyone, and led an intelligent debate and discussion in which all options were considered. The strategic deliberations, as CEO Charles Hammond confirms, were of a high standard.

We also held board meetings at one of the ports, rotating around all the sites in turn. Thus, board members could see the ports and become more familiar with the business. However, getting close to the business could sometimes have unintended consequences. In January 2007, on a bitterly cold and dismal day, the board toured the port of Leith on a tug. I can still recall the harsh wind blowing from the Arctic across the bleak grey water, and the damp feeling in my bones. A photograph was taken of the board on the tug, which appeared in the annual report. The Forth Ports annual general meetings were always held at the Caledonian Hotel in Edinburgh, and many small shareholders often attended and asked interesting questions. On this occasion, however, a stout, fierce-looking woman of a certain age rose to confront the board: "Mr Chairman, in these difficult economic times, what were the board doing going on a cruise?"

Charles Hammond makes some very good points that are worth repeating here. Firstly, he says: "The board acted almost like a team," with little difference in opinion between executive and independent directors. Secondly, the diversity on the board was a positive force. All of the independents had different backgrounds, some from finance, some from oil and construction, some like myself from logistics. Some were strong on finance, others were strong on people issues. This meant that debates over strategy were wide-ranging and covered many different points. The chief value of these discussions to the CEO, Charles says, is that "they made you go away and think. Have we covered all the issues? Have we addressed them properly?" He sums up the board's contribution as "a collective group of minds that made us think and then address fundamental issues."

David Richardson, the former non-executive chairman, believes that this is the most important thing that independent directors can do. "The board can genuinely help the CEO by giving him the wherewithal to be robust in decision-making," he says. "At Forth Ports, none of us were brought up in the ports industry. We brought our different experiences to bear on problems and helped the executives to think more clearly. It can be difficult, when in an industry, to think outside traditional lines. Non-execs can gently nudge executive directors into ways of thinking outside the paradigm."

All this said, there was a fundamental strategic issue that occupied us throughout my time on the board, and ran like a fault line down the boardroom table. What kind of business were we in?

Ports are usually in a monopoly situation, with a single port serving a single geographical area (there are exceptions, for example, the competition between

Tilbury and London Gateway). They are very much tied to their geography and, if a shipping company decides to withdraw its business and go somewhere else, there is not much that you can do about it. Growth in actual port traffic is slow, and affected heavily by economic cycles. Port companies need to diversify, by acquiring other ports, by developing their property portfolios, or by expanding into related areas of business, such as logistics and supply chain management.

In terms of port growth, there was no appetite at Forth Ports for growth outside the UK. Chris Collins, chairman until 2009, felt that management had enough to do running a UK business, and he recalls that while the executive looked at a number of overseas opportunities, "I was always rather relieved when these fell by the wayside." We did make one investment in Russia, which I supported. Russia was a growing economy with a rising demand for imports, and to me, investment in a cargo port seemed to make sense. Forth Ports held this investment for about three years during which time, as Chris' successor David Richardson says: "The investment did not go the way we expected," and the company began thinking about an exit. Our share of the business was sold at a profit, but this experience did little to enthuse the board for further international investments.

If we were to grow, then, it would have to be through diversification outside of ports. There were certainly opportunities to develop the property portfolio, and earlier I described successful developments at Leith and Tilbury. The question was, how to proceed? Struan Robertson, my fellow independent director, and I had the view that running a property business was very different from running a port. We felt that Forth Ports should look at the possibility of spinning off its property management into a separate company.

On the other hand our CEO, Charles Hammond, felt that it was important to keep port and property closely related, and was opposed to the idea of a spin-off. He believed, as he says, that property had to be looked at "as a total business, not just tacked onto the end of the ports business." Charles Hammond felt that the property business was not mature enough: it had major assets in its land, but lacked the experience and management skills to exploit that asset fully. Chris Collins, during his time as chairman, was also unsure whether it was a good idea to split the ports and property businesses. "I didn't quite see the value of separating them into two smaller companies, which might be below investors' radar screens," he says. "I was reasonably satisfied that the two businesses were working well together. The port side supported property with cash flow and its relationship with Edinburgh authorities, which was probably helpful on the planning front."

We concluded that we needed to manage the property portfolio more effectively, and we conducted a full strategic review of the property division. We also appointed James Tuckey, who had a strong background in property, to the board as an independent director. A senior property executive was appointed who, although not a director, did attend board meetings. We also strengthened the management of the Ocean Terminal shopping center.

Unfortunately, in 2008, that asset lost a lot of its value very suddenly when the financial crisis struck. In the course of a matter of months in 2008, our property portfolio was revalued sharply downwards, from £218 million to £80 million. This was a tricky moment, as we had to explain to shareholders why the company's assets had been downgraded so severely. The idea of the spin-off, and other property initiatives, had to be shelved for the time being, but even after property prices began to recover, the idea was not revived. We still lacked a consensus on the board as to whether in the medium term property should be run separately from ports, or whether the two should be combined into a single business.

Diversification also led us into fields, such as supply chain management and logistics, and here we did have some success, especially at Tilbury. This seemed to be a natural form of diversification, ports and logistics complementing one another, and here we did have management expertise. Again, though, we did not move quickly enough to exploit the opportunities. Instead, we chose to diversify into "grass is greener on the other side of the fence" opportunities like recycling, which never quite lived up to expectations.

This sounds as if I am being critical of the company's strategy. In fact, although I am critical of some elements, there is no doubt that the process of strategic review and thinking worked very well on the whole. We had directors who were committed to and engaged with strategic thinking and ideas. The fact that we did not always move quickly enough to seize opportunities is probably more a reflection on the company's culture and background than on the strategic abilities of the board.

Lessons Learned: Choose Your Chairman Carefully

There are several lessons from the Forth Ports experience, including the need for a coherent strategy, the need for directors to be involved in strategy, the need for board diversity and the role of the chairman. We have covered these in other chapters, however, and here I want to focus on one lesson in particular: the process of choosing a chairman and why this must be managed very carefully.

When I joined the board of Forth Ports, the chairman was Chris Collins, a former jockey who had gone on to a very successful business career. Among other things, he had been chairman of the Hanson conglomerate. He was very good at getting the best out of people, and I regard him as a model chairman in many ways. In 2007, Chris informed the board that he intended to retire in two years' time, when he turned seventy. That gave us plenty of time to recruit a new chairman and orchestrate the handover process. As senior independent director, leading this process fell to me.

Among the vast and wide-ranging literature on leadership and management, there are no books that tell you how to recruit a new chairman. And yet, getting the right person is absolutely vital. The consequences of recruiting the wrong chairman can be very serious indeed.

We had three candidates: David Richardson, chairman of the audit committee who had previously been finance director of Whitbread; Struan Robertson, a South African who had been a senior executive at BP; and James Tuckey, our property specialist non-executive director. I drew up a specification describing the job and listing the ideal qualities for a chairman to use as a template, and developed a scoring system. I then interviewed each board member, executive and non-executive, and we scored each of the three candidates. David came out ahead, in large part thanks to his experience with the City and investors. (We were, by this point, expecting that a takeover bid for the company would be made at some stage in the future.)

The most difficult part then was to break the news to Struan and James. I explained to both that rejection did not mean they could not do the job; it was clear that both could. The board had decided to offer the job to David for specific reasons connected with his experience and the current situation of the company; he was judged to be the right chairman at the right time. We needed Struan and James on the board, and my task was to ensure that they were satisfied that the process had been fair and remained with us. They understood and both stayed, but I learned that the job of senior independent director is often not a very easy one. Without a fair and equitable process for the appointment, I am not sure that I would have succeeded.

U-POL Ltd

U-POL was one of the world's leading makers of automotive refinish products, primarily for the repair of cars that have been damaged in accidents. Its primary markets were in the UK, continental Europe and North America, but it

TABLE 3.5   U-POL's products and revenues

Year to 31 December	Actual 2002 £'000	Actual 2003 £'000	Actual 2004 £'000	Forecast 2005 £'000
Fillers	12,209	13,446	14,143	13,959
Coatings	5,358	6,209	7,156	7,494
Aerosols	2,657	3,169	3,764	4,130
Adhesives & Sealants	374	499	375	309
Others	2,902	3,315	3,639	4,129
Sales	**23,500**	**26,638**	**29,077**	**30,021**
Adjustment to normalise			(800)	800
Normalised sales	**23,500**	**26,638**	**28,277**	**30,821**

sold into markets around the world. U-POL was founded by the David family in the mid-1950s, and remained in family ownership until 2002 when it was the subject of an MBO led by Graphite Capital, a private equity house. In 1964, the company opened its factory at Wellingborough in Northamptonshire, where all of its products continue to be made (the sales and design office is in London). The factory underwent considerable expansion and alteration over time to keep up with new technologies and the introduction of new products. It demonstrated a consistent record in growing sales (from £23.5 million in 2002 to over £30 million in 2005) and profitability. Table 3.5 shows the range of the company's products and its revenues.

In 2004, sales of all categories totaled just over £29 million worldwide. Ninety-five percent of sales were to the professional market, i.e. garages and body shops, with the remaining five percent going to the do-it-yourself (DIY) market. The company developed two separate brands: U-POL for the professional market and ISOPON for the DIY market. ISOPON became very popular in Africa. As well as its own branded products, U-POL made private label products for third-party customers, including Brown Brothers and Kent Industries in the UK and Förch in Germany.

U-POL had a strong customer orientation, and its products had a good reputation for quality and value for money. Packaging played an important role in making the brands distinctive, and U-POL was very innovative in its approach to packaging. It pioneered and patented a number of new packaging systems, for example, the use of bag technology for certain filler and hardener product lines. These innovations also helped the company to cut costs. Unusually for a manufacturing company, U-POL handled all design functions in-house,

TABLE 3.6   U-POL's markets

Year to 31 December	Actual 2002 £'000	Actual 2003 £'000	Actual 2004 £'000	Forecast 2005 £'000
UK	9,795	10,383	11,133	11,918
USA	2,920	3,103	3,283	3,535
France	1,816	2,212	2,441	2,800
Ireland	743	877	969	1,155
ROW*	7,320	8,683	9,742	9,071
Outsource	906	1,380	1,509	1,542
Sales	**23,500**	**26,638**	**29,077**	**30,021**
Adjustment to normalise			(800)	800
Normalised sales	**23,500**	**26,638**	**28,277**	**30,821**

including packaging, advertising, promotions, and website design. This led to a consistency and control of image that have served the company very well in its relations with customers. CEO Jean-Charles Julien describes U-POL as "a sales and marketing company that happens to make its own products," which fairly summarizes how U-POL saw its relationship with customers.

U-POL did not generally sell directly into the retail market. Instead, it marketed its products to approximately 2,200 account customers—distributors, wholesalers and importers—in eighty countries. About 750 of these customers were based in the UK. In the UK, U-POL employed a sales team of nine field representatives and four back office staff, all focused on the UK wholesale trade. There were also six sales representatives in France, four in Spain and three in the USA, plus representatives in Germany, Portugal, Ireland, Australia and South Africa. Table 3.6 shows the geographical spread of U-POL's markets.

Although U-POL did not sell directly to end customers, it kept in close touch with the people who used its products. U-POL ran its own training center which, as well as training its own sales staff, hosted groups of customers from around the world and offered sessions that explained the company and its products. This was considered an important and valuable part of U-POL's marketing strategy with both existing and prospective customers.

Customers in this market often expect deliveries to be made on very short lead times, which means that logistics are extremely important. U-POL invested heavily in warehousing and distribution and won several "best supplier" awards in its industry. Along with strong customer relationships, U-POL also had good long-term relationships with its key suppliers and worked closely with them to ensure both competitive prices and an efficient and reliable service. Alternative suppliers for all key products were identified in case a key supplier should suddenly no longer be able to provide a needed product.

The market for U-POL's products was stable and relatively recession-proof; as long as there are cars on the road, there would be accidents. Compulsory car insurance means that damage from these would always be repaired. However, the market landscape had changed. In 2000, there were about 6,000 body shops in the UK, but by 2005 that number had declined to around 4,800. Ownership had become more concentrated, with smaller shops being bought up by groups and chains. In 2004, Factor Service Group (FSG) consolidated a large portion of the market into a single group that controlled about 10 percent of the UK market. These larger customers used their buying power to put pressure on wholesalers to bring down prices, and that pressure was in turn passed on to U-POL. As well as its direct competitors, U-POL faced increasing competition from large multinational paint companies, which introduced low-cost, generic products.

However, U-POL had an excellent brand, a dynamic management team led by Jean-Charles Julien who, between them, had more than one hundred years' experience of the industry, excellent financial management and high profitability, and a proven policy of investing in innovation and new product

TABLE 3.7　U-POL's strengths and weaknesses

UK / Ireland	
Strengths	**Weaknesses**
Dominant brand with strong marketing reputation	Lack of future product lines
Innovative existing product lines	Distribution politics in coatings
Knowledge and understanding of the market	Management skill level
High profitability.	Management stretched
Established customer base	
Dominant position in fillers	
Established sales force	
Product pull-through capability	
Opportunities	**Threats**
New products' consolidation	Mature market
Growing generics coatings market	Customer consolidation
Filler market still receptive to new products	Environmental legislation
Ancillary range	Powerful competition
Aerosols offer excellent growth potential	Paint companies moving into generic market
Growing private label market	Paint companies' vertical integration
	Customers becoming competitors

(Continued)

Table 3.7 continued

USA	
Strengths	**Weaknesses**
Brand with good reputation	Distribution politics
Innovative premium product lines	Manufacturers' reps are difficult to motivate
Knowledge and understanding of the market	Limited product-pull capability
Established customer base	High service cost
Established sales force	
Light organisation structure	
Opportunities	**Threats**
Dynamic and responsive economy	Mature and very aggressive market
Huge market potential	Powerful competition
Growing generics coatings market	Paint companies moving into generic market
Aerosols offer excellent growth potential	Currency fluctuation

EXPORT	
Strengths	**Weaknesses**
Brand with good reputation	Sales force thin on the ground
Innovative product lines	Some distribution politics
Knowledge and understanding of the markets	Personnel stretched
Established customer base	Limited product pull capability
Established sales force	
Light organisation structure	
Opportunities	**Threats**
Huge market potential particularly in continental Europe and the Far East	Mature and competitive market
Small market share in coatings	Paint companies moving into generic market
Growing generics coatings market	Currency fluctuation
Aerosols offer excellent growth potential	

generation, which kept the company a step ahead of its competitors. Table 3.7 shows some of the company's strengths and weaknesses in different markets.

One strategic response was to move into areas, such as tools and consumables associated with the repair business, including spray guns, sanders, wipes, masking films, abrasive pads and paint filters. This diversification enabled U-POL to expand its business within a consolidating market. The company also began investing more in its export markets, hiring more sales people in the USA and continental Europe and investigating the potential for markets in India and China. Despite market pressures, by 2005 with support from Graphite Capital, management were confident that they could achieve significant growth over the succeeding years. That confidence was borne out. Graphite Capital sold U-POL to ABN AMRO in a secondary buy-out in 2006, and has since reacquired the firm.

I was approached by a headhunting firm, Directorbank, working on behalf of Graphite shortly after the original MBO. Graphite wanted a non-executive chairman who could represent its interests and help the company to a successful exit three to four years down the line. U-POL also had no experience of working with private equity, and thus a chairman was needed who could manage the transition to this new culture and ways of working.

I was invited to meet John O'Neill from Graphite, who in turn invited me to meet Jean-Charles Julien, the CEO. Jean-Charles was a veteran of U-POL, who had built the company's market in France from nothing and then served as export manager before becoming managing director a few years before the buy-out. I found the company interesting because it was a manufacturing company with niche products and a strong distribution system. There was also another chance to work with private equity, and both these things were useful to me in developing my own portfolio. I felt I could offer them expertise in international business. I accepted the offer and served as chairman for four years until the sale at a very attractive premium to ABN AMRO, when I stepped down.

Board Issues: Managing towards an Exit

U-POL had been a family owned company from its foundation up until the sale in 2002, and that had consequences for the company's culture and ways of making decisions. This is not to say that the company had been badly managed; on the contrary, it had been managed very well indeed and this was one of the reasons why Graphite had found the company so attractive. "A fabulous British gem" is how one of the Graphite team described U-POL to me. But family owners have their own agenda, and like all of us they are constrained by their past experience and reasons for founding the company in the first place. Family owners can, for example, be quite cautious and risk-averse in their outlook; they tend to stick to what they know and can do well.

One of the jobs of an incoming chairman is to take a look at the company as completely and objectively as possible, and use all of his or her experience to think about what can be done and explore the possibilities. At U-POL, we needed to ask ourselves questions, not so much about what we were doing, but what we could do in future, where the potential lay. We needed to look at the factory and supply chain arrangements, the product portfolio, and the markets. This strategic review was, of course, driven by the needs of the major shareholder, Graphite. The big issue for them, too, was not so much what the business was doing now, but what growth potential there was for the future.

Demonstrating growth potential would be a key factor in helping them get the exit price they wanted.

It was clear that, for the reasons discussed above, we needed to broaden the product range. Once the key decisions had been made as to what the range should be, Graphite was happy to support investment in research and development (R&D). Table 3.8 shows the range of new projects that the company began to work on.

One important subject for discussion was international expansion. This was an area where the family owners had been quite cautious, aware of the risks and unwilling to invest heavily in an export sales force because they were concerned about the consequences for overheads. But it seemed clear to us that there was clear potential for international growth. Jean-Charles Julien had already demonstrated this in the way he had built up the French business in the years before he became CEO.

We needed to keep control of overheads, of course, and so we managed the subsequent international expansion carefully. Importantly, we identified savings in buying and warehouse efficiency, for example, which freed up money to invest in overseas development. Nor did we need to invest in large numbers of people all at once. We were not starting from scratch; we already had a presence in some of our key international markets. For example, we were already selling products in the North America. The problem was that we were

TABLE 3.8 **New products at U-POL**

2003—2005	2006 and beyond
Dolphin High viscosity filler	Orbital sanders
Water-based panel wipe	Abrasive pads
Solvent-based panel wipe	Aerosol foam barrier cream
Guide-coat aerosol	Plastic masking film
Color-match primers	Painters overall
Solid black paint	Paint filters
2.1 VOC clear and primer (California)	Respirator masks
Tintable stonechip	Tack cloth
High 5 primer dark grey aerosol	Fish-eye eliminator
Bumper colour paint aerosols	Contact adhesive aerosol
Copper weld through aerosol	New generation 2007 VOC clears
Range of convenience wipes	4:1 and 2:1 economic primers and clear
Spray guns	
Truck bed liner coating	

supporting that huge market with just three sales people. If we were to grow there, we needed to put more people on the ground. It was a relatively easy matter to cost this expansion and build it into the business plan, and we went on to expand our presence quite significantly in North America and Europe.

In other markets where we were not already represented, however, growth was slower. To enter India or China we would have needed to build a direct sales force from scratch, and this would have required investment which would take three or four years, at least, to recover. There were also problems with payments in some area; there was one agent in West Africa, for example, to whom we refused to ship products unless payment was received in advance. Our best strategy was to build relationships with local distributors, which would share the risk with us. However, finding those reliable local partners as a slow process, and we had still not made much progress when I left the board.

As chairman, I served as the link between the executives and Graphite. There were two quite different cultures at work here. Private equity houses have, on the whole, little or no experience at running a business; they are interested in results and potential. Companies like U-POL in turn have little experience of the world of private equity. Jean-Charles recalls that he had "no clue" about how private equity worked before the Graphite buy-out in 2002, and had to learn very rapidly the technicalities of PE. "You can have people who are very good at running companies, but who have very little awareness of the financial world and private equity," he says. Sometimes this relationship can be very difficult with each side failing to understand the other and the chairman can get caught between competing interests.

At U-POL, however, the task of managing and guiding that relationship was pretty straightforward. I tried to make sure that the board was close to the company, and I spent a lot of time getting to know the business, going to trade fairs and so on. We held some board meetings at the Wellingborough factory, with a factory tour as part of the meeting. Executives and independents got to know each other quickly, and got on well. Jean-Charles Julien had a very good management team around him, and I found it a pleasure to work with him. Once the management understood what we wanted, they bought in very quickly and came up themselves with many of the new ideas that were needed to take us towards our goal.

On the other side, Graphite were very supportive and willing to invest in anything that would give us growth potential; and at that time, that was not always the case with private equity firms. We formed a partnership that worked so well that Graphite eventually bought back into the firm.

Lessons Learned: Understanding Private Equity

Graphite invested in U-POL with a view to making an exit after three or four years. After about three years, we started to think seriously about the exit process. We appointed investment advisors and studied the market, considering prospective buyers and what price they might be willing to pay.

Partway through this process I received a telephone call from John O'Neill of Graphite, with some startling news. ABN AMRO wanted to buy the firm, and were prepared to move quickly and pay an excellent price. The reason? They had been following the progress of U-POL and saw it as a hot prospect. John's view was that the offer was such a good one that we did not need to look at any other prospective buyers. The deal was accordingly done. ABN AMRO paid a good price and everyone was happy.

Private equity houses have "stages" in their funds, and their behavior is very often driven by what stage their fund is at and how well it is invested. I learned subsequently that although private equity houses all use much the same model for valuing companies, the amount they will pay for an investment can vary by anything up to 20 percent depending on, for example, what stage their fund is at.

Private equity plays a huge role in business today, and it is important for independent directors to understand how it works, and why it works the way it does. Having experience of working with a PE house is very important when it comes to building a portfolio, and also to managing the cultural differences between PE and management. Of course, not all PE houses are the same; each has its individual characteristics, reflecting the ideas of the partners and their specific mandates. Private equity has itself undergone a dramatic change over the past five years. It used to be that PE houses had a reputation for not doing a lot beyond financial re-engineering: selling off assets, or "asset-stripping," refinancing, taking on debt and so on. They had little to do with strategy, for example. Today the emphasis is much more on "buy and build" and more PE houses will invest substantial amounts in the companies they buy.

Private equity houses are much more active investors than they once were, and that has consequences. They are more likely to support businesses to build in capability for value creation and growth, because they realize that this will enhance the price they receive at exit. They are also much more closely involved in strategy and boardroom issues. This can have both positive and negative consequences. Jean-Charles Julien feels that the experience PE houses have of working with different companies in different industries can be a positive force. "They make suggestions based on things they have seen elsewhere, and these can be very useful," he says.

On the other hand, the pressure to achieve results can be even more intense, with more scrutiny of strategy and key decisions. Here is where the lack of experience of hands-on management can become an issue, and if the PE investors and the executives do not understand and trust each other, then the relationship becomes much more problematic. The cultural differences between private equity and business management that I have described must be managed. If they are not, then the resulting tensions can pull a company in two ways, to the detriment of everyone involved. The independent chairman has a very important part to play in bridging this gap.

Michael Gerson Ltd

Michael Gerson Limited was a high-end removals firm specializing in corporate moves, i.e. helping corporate executives to move themselves, their families and belongings from one location to another. The company was founded in 1961 by the entrepreneur Michael Gerson. In 1978, the company established a major operations center at Whetstone in North London, expanding that facility four years later. From this London base Michael Gerson built up a network of international clients including Citibank, HSBC, Merrill Lynch, ABN AMRO, Fidelity, BP, Procter & Gamble, Unilever and Pfizer, among others. Fifty percent of European corporate removals passed through London, and Michael Gerson was well placed to exploit what was, at the time, an expanding and dynamic market.

The industry was highly competitive, with other players including IDX, TEAM and Sterling offering strong competition. (Sterling had expressed an interest in buying Michael Gerson in 2001, but withdrew after 9/11: the September 11, 2001 terrorist attacks on the USA.) However, Michael Gerson performed well, thanks to several strengths. The first was quality of service, provided by committed staff and backed up by very good facilities. "They had good people who were prepared to work very hard," recalls Francis Peck, who became chairman in 2004. There was a strong culture built around the values that Michael had built into the company when he founded it, including a belief in service. Michael Gerson did not have a high staff turnover; it was the sort of company where people got a job and then stayed.

The second strength was a strong brand with a high public profile. One of Michael Gerson's most prominent clients was Margaret Thatcher, who had a long relationship with the firm. Michael Gerson moved her into 10 Downing Street when she became prime minister in 1979; eleven years later, the company moved her out again when she resigned. She even visited the company several times, which gave Michael Gerson very good free publicity. The firm also had other prestigious customers, including the Royal Armouries, handling the removal of a collection of 40,000 items of arms and armor from the Tower of London to the new Royal Armouries Museum in Leeds. In 1983, the company received a Queen's Award for Exports, the first time such an award had been made to a removals firm.

In December 2002, the founder-entrepreneur, Michael Gerson, sold the firm to his management team, executive chairman Brian Charles and managing director Niall Mackay. Gerson and his family retained a minority stake in the business. They also retained ownership of the buildings from which the firm operated, including its headquarters in London, so the Michael Gerson firm rented its premises from its former owner. The buy-out was financed by Bank of Scotland's Integrated Finance division, an operation set up by the bank in 2000 to allow it to invest in companies in a manner similar to private equity. Mike Innes of the Bank of Scotland led the buy-out team.

I say "similar to private equity," but there were more important differences. As an investor, Bank of Scotland continued to behave like a bank rather than a private equity house. Its main concern was to ensure that the company could meet its loan repayments and, so long as it could do so, there was little pressure on the board to change or behave differently. With a true private equity house, on the other hand, there is great emphasis on the future exit. Everything that is done, is done to ensure that the company creates value, which will be reflected in the final sale price. That means a very different approach to issues such as strategy, new product development and so on. Bank of Scotland also paid a great deal more money for Michael Gerson than a private equity house might have. With hindsight, Francis Peck believes the right price would have been about £8.5 million; instead, the price paid was £19 million.

The MBO took place at a time when the corporate removals sector was at a low ebb, thanks in part to the 9/11 terrorist attacks. Many companies, especially American firms, were reluctant to relocate executives overseas. One competitor firm remarked that trading conditions were the worst they had seen in thirty-five years. From 2001 to 2002, the overall volume of trade in the sector fell by 24 percent.

In 2001, Michael Gerson had a turnover of £15.8 million and earnings before interest and tax (EBIT) of nearly £3.9 million. It was clear, however, that the

TABLE 3.9   Overall removals tonnage shipped outbound worldwide

Year	(all figures shown in '000 lbs) Tonnage	+ / – % on Previous
2001	47,338	–24%
2002	38,186	+1%
2003	38,840	+11%
2004	43,218	

company would not meet its targets for 2002. Bank of Scotland agreed to reduce the company's debt in order to help it through what most analysts—including those who carried out industry due diligence for the bank—believed was a temporary downturn. The analysts described the situation in 2002 as a "wait and see period," where clients were waiting for the recovery and postponing decisions until they could see the future more clearly. Once they began to relocate staff once more, the industry would pick up.

However, continuing worldwide political volatility and terrorist attacks in Madrid, London and Mumbai continued to dampen the market. International companies began to reduce the numbers of expatriate managers they sent to overseas subsidiaries, preferring to hire larger numbers of local managers instead. Finally, as Mike Innes says, client companies became more effective at procurement and identified relocation and removals as an area where they could cut costs, putting pressure on industry margins. Both these factors cut into the market for international corporate removals. Tables 3.9 and 3.10 show how the market continued to suffer.

Following the MBO, several strategies were introduced with the aim of diversifying and strengthening the firm. The company was too dependent on its London base and needed more connectivity in Europe. Before the MBO, Michael Gerson had been instrumental in setting up the One Alliance network of thirteen independent removals firms. Now the firm tried to move from straight forward *removals*—the physical transportation of goods and possessions—into *relocation*, a more complex bundle of services which included physical removal and transport, helping executives find new homes for themselves and their families and schools for their children, arranging documents such as identity papers and green cards, and so on. Providing relocation services required highly specialized expertise in each of the geographies where the company worked, and this required the building of a network of agents who could be brought in to help manage a relocation, sometimes at fairly short notice. A relocation services business unit was created in 2003, though Mike

TABLE 3.10   **UK inbound tonnage**

Company	2001	2002	2003	2004
Team	2,379	1,372	1,446	999
Sterling	n.d.	1,035	725	665
M.G.	1,562	714	724	646
Masons	722	794	501	610
Robinsons	459	495	426	454
Whites	628	300	457	435
Davies Turner	156	187	286	325
G.B. Liners	76	72	146	123
S.H.W	162	131	82	86
Morgan	2	40	44	48
Total (all figures shown in '000 lbs)	6,145	5,140	4,837	4,391

Innes comments that the development of this business was slow and poorly executed and Francis Peck notes that the business "consistently failed to pay its way."

As well as targeting new sectors, we looked at a variety of other issues, including developing the existing customer base more fully, providing more training and upgrading systems, including IT and financial management systems, and reviewing the size of the workforce. In the latter case, we did not find many opportunities for rationalization, as the company was well organized around its two key depots, at Whetstone and Daventry.

Although these moves brought some improvement, Michael Gerson as a company remained heavily reliant on the corporate removals market, and that market continued to shrink. By 2007, the writing was on the wall and, in 2008, the company was sold to the Swedish firm, ICM Kungsholms, for £950,000, a very small fraction of its value at the time of the MBO. The deal also preserved the jobs of the company's workers, none of whom were made redundant.

I joined the board of Michael Gerson in 2003, shortly after the MBO. Bank of Scotland Integrated Finance were looking for someone with experience of working with private equity firms and I had also worked for NFC, one of whose subsidiaries was the removal firm, Pickfords, one of the oldest and best-known international removals firms. I was interested in this model of integrated finance and wanted to see how it compared to private equity. Michael Gerson and I also had acquaintances in common, and he agreed with Bank of

Scotland that my presence on the board would be useful. Accordingly, I was invited to come onto the board.

Not long after I joined, the executive chairman, Brain Charles (who had been Michael Gerson's right-hand man), announced his retirement. It was agreed that the new chairman should be an independent. I introduced Francis Peck, whom I had known for some years and, in April 2005, he was offered the post of non-executive chairman. It had become clear, however, that Michael Gerson also needed an independent director who could give it and its problems a great deal of time and attention. I felt I did not have the time; I was already working with six other companies, and I knew I could not be effective in this role. It was time to make way for someone who could, and I stepped down as a director in 2005, soon after Francis was appointed.

Board Issues: Getting out of the Comfort Zone

The board of Michael Gerson had a number of issues to deal with after the MBO, some of which were outlined above. However, there were two particular issues that dominated all others: how to respond to a declining market, and how to change the culture and mindset of the company and management as a whole. Both these issues interconnected, and affected everything else that we did or tried to do.

Prior to the MBO, Michael Gerson had concentrated almost exclusively on high-net-worth individuals and corporations, especially in financial services. These were its clients, and it was among these that its brand recognition was strongest. But that market, as we saw above, began to decline in 2002 and never recovered. The financial crisis of 2008 exacerbated what was already a worsening situation.

It was clear from the beginning that we had to diversify. We carried out a strategic review and identified a number of sectors to attack. We also initiated a comprehensive plan for developing new business. Outsiders like Mike Innes, the Bank of Scotland representative on the board, and myself, gave them the same message over and over: "The market you are in is shrinking. How will you diversify?" It was this constant push that led to the development of a relocation business but, in the early days at least, this business was burdened with costs—it employed five people, when probably one would have been enough—and struggled to make headway in a competitive market.

Francis Peck put his finger on it: the management team lacked the experience and confidence to think outside the box. Michael Gerson had been a very hands-on owner-manager, supported by Brian Charles. This meant that his managers lacked experience of thinking about strategy and other "big issues"; they were used to Michael and Brian handling these matters themselves. "Management had been conducted on a need-to-know basis," Francis says. "Everything at the top of the business had been strictly controlled by Michael and Brian."

Now, "getting them to open up their minds and think strategically was difficult … All they tried to do was carry on doing what Michael had been doing." Mike Innes observed much the same thing. "Most of the board had been with the company for decades," he says. "They had worked for Michael Gerson man and boy. Michael himself controlled what happened at the top."

Soon after taking over as chairman, Francis discovered that the sales team did not have targets for generating new business. The company was heavily focused on its existing customers, and was making little effort to bring in new business. At board level, each director concentrated on his or her own department and did not get involved with other areas of the business; thus the finance director reported on the company's finances, but did not get involved in costs or pricing, which other departments set at whatever level they liked. Senior management lacked coordination and integration, which made planning and change management even more difficult.

The executives, and indeed the entire company, were locked into their own narrow comfort zone. Michael had carved out a very successful business; management continued to believe that if they stuck to the tried-and-tested methods, everything would come out all right. But, it did not. In 2005, Francis Peck estimated that, unless there was a major change of direction, the company would run out of money in about three years' time. Events proved him right.

This is an issue that I have encountered many times and in many places. Despite all the evidence placed before them, executives have a blind faith that if they just wait long enough, things will go back to the way they used to be. Everything is due to the market, but we know the market is cyclical; if we wait, the market will come back. Sometimes this is true; at Keller, for instance, we had every confidence that the market would come back, and we were right. But the decline in the removals business was not linked directly to economic activity. This had always been a very specialized service, and now, as times changed, the demand for this service was declining.

How could we get Michael Gerson staff and management to change their mindsets? The question was a difficult one, and the answer in the end eluded us all. One of Michael Gerson's greatest strength was its deep-rooted corporate culture, but now that culture also turned out to be a weakness. It rooted management into previous ways of doing things, and made them resistant to change. We found that it was quite easy to get them to talk about change, and people would understand the issues and discuss new moves that could be made. But when it came to making change actually happen, not enough was done.

Change management requires that someone in leadership within the company, the executive chairman or managing director, has to buy into the change movement wholeheartedly and then take the rest of the staff with him or her. That never happened at Michael Gerson.

And, of course, the execution of change management, like any other strategy, is an executive issue, not a board issue. Independent directors can do only a limited amount in these cases, as responsibility lies with the executives. That may sound like I am passing the buck, but that is not the case. There have to be defined lines, limits of responsibility, over which one does not step. The term *independent* director was invented for a reason; we are independent from the company, and our role is to advise, question and scrutinize, not to manage.

Lessons Learned: A Good Brand Is Not Enough

Michael Gerson had a very good brand. It was at the high end of the removals business, with blue-chip clients like international banks and the British prime minister. (The company continued to handle Thatcher family removals even after Margaret Thatcher left office.) It had a history of good service, was liked and respected by its customers, and had performed well financially.

However, none of this meant anything once the crisis of 2002 arrived. The executive team at Michael Gerson can perhaps be forgiven for initially assuming that this was a temporary blip and the markets would recover; that was after all the advice it and Bank of Scotland were getting from outside. But it quickly became apparent that the predicted recovery would not happen. At this point there were two choices; diversify into other markets, or sit still and wait for the roof to fall in. In the end, the firm's great brand and track record of excellence meant nothing because fewer and fewer customers were buying what Michael Gerson had to offer; and the company failed to change its offering in time to ward off its own decline.

Bank of Scotland's integrated finance model complicated the issue too. Had the bank behaved more like a traditional private equity house, it is likely that more would have been done sooner. Changes in management, for example, might have instituted cultural and strategic change more quickly. Mike Innes, who went on from the Bank of Scotland to join private equity house Graphite Capital, confirms this. "A private equity house, with majority control, would probably have made changes to the senior management team more quickly," he says. But the bank had different priorities from a PE house. As long as interest was being paid on the loan note, the bank was satisfied. It did not place sufficient emphasis on long-term change in the company; it was not, as Mike Innes says, an activist investor. This loose approach did Michael Gerson no favors in the end, and it could be said that, in this case at least, the integrated finance model failed.

I think there is also a lesson to be learned from the final point in the previous section, about the limits of the role of the independent director. Independents are sometimes, and rightly, blamed when things go wrong for failing to exercise sufficient scrutiny and act diligently. That was not the case at Michael Gerson. We *knew* what had to be done, and gave our advice and made our views known repeatedly. But as Francis says, "you have got to make sure that you don't try to run the show. You've got to stand back and let people make their own decisions. You can guide them on those decision, but the only way things will get carried through is if they feel themselves that it is the right thing to do." Sometimes, that means letting people make mistakes. But, forcing other people to do things they do not want to do almost never works.

Biocompatibles plc

Biocompatibles International was a medical technology company based at Farnham in Hampshire. Its core products were a range of drug-eluting beads used in the treatment of liver and other cancers, but the company was actively engaged in R&D in a number of other product lines as well.

As well as its Farnham research center, Biocompatibles had operations in the USA and Germany, the latter through its subsidiary, Cellmed. It had collaborative agreements with AstraZeneca, Bayer HealthCare Pharmaceuticals, Medtronic and Merz Pharma, as well as distribution and licensing agreements with a number of other companies including Angiodynamics in the USA, Terumo in Europe and Eisai in Japan. Its products were used in more than thirty-five countries.

Biocompatibles was founded in 1984 by the late Professor Dennis Chapman. Working out of the Royal Free Hospital, Professor Chapman and his team of researchers had conducted groundbreaking research in the area of *biocompatibility*, that is, creating materials that interface with body tissues without creating an adverse biological result. They identified phosphoryl-choline, a substance present in cell membranes within the human body, as one of the primary natural materials that enables biocompatibility. It was discovered that phosphoryl-choline could be used to make a coating that would allow medical items to be inserted into the body—for example, into an artery—without the body's defence systems being activated to reject it. Professor Chapman founded the company in order to commercialize the use of phosphoryl-choline.

In 1989, the Rothschild Bioscience Unit invested in the company and Jeremy Curnock Cook, head of the unit, joined the board as an independent director. Professor Chapman later stepped down from the board, remaining as emeritus director and consultant. The first task of the new board was to give the company some focus. Jeremy describes the business at that point as "a technology looking for an application." "At the time I joined," he recalls, "we were looking at applications for the product ranging from coatings for boat's bottoms to food for fish farms. We needed to pull out of most of these activities and choose one or two themes on which to concentrate."

One early brainstorming session led to the realization that the product could be used to make contact lenses that would not stick to the eye, thus reducing inflammation and irritation. Biocompatibles launched its first product, the Proclear contact lens, in 1994. In 1998, the company launched a coronary stent, BiodivYsio. The stents were made of metal but coated with a polymer based on phosphoryl-choline, which ensured that they would not be rejected by the human body.

Both these businesses were sold in 2002 and the company then began research into embolization therapy, a form of minimally invasive treatment for tumors and vascular malformations (which can affect the circulation system in key areas, such as the brain or the spine). The company went public in 2002 and Rothschild Bioscience Unit exited, though Jeremy Curnock Cook remained on the board (he served as independent director of Biocompatibles for more than twenty years).

The company's first drug-eluting beads were launched in 2006. These are tiny microspheres that can be inserted into tumors using a catheter (meaning there is no need for an operation). Inside each bead is a drug, which is then eluted (absorbed) into the tumor. The first drug to be used in this way was doxorubicin, a well-established drug for treating tumors. If taken orally, doxorubicin had a number of side-effects. However, if the drug eluted straight into the tumor, these side-effects could be avoided; and at the same time, the concentration of the drug in the tumor gave it a much more powerful effect. The drug-eluting beads were marketed directly to oncologists, with Biocompatibles also providing ongoing technical support. Later, in Japan, the bead technology was licensed to Eisai, who were themselves responsible for technical support in that country.

Biocompatibles went on to enter other areas of research and product development. A few examples will suffice:

- Cellmed, Biocompatibles' German subsidiary, had developed a drug-eluting bead product for the treatment of strokes, and had also developed proteins for the treatment of diabetes and obesity in partnership. In 2011, Cellmed began a programmed of pioneering research into stem cell products for the treatment of brain tumors.
- In 2007, Biocompatibles signed an agreement with Abbott Laboratories to supply materials for the Endeavor drug-eluting stent being developed by Medtronic (the product was launched in the USA the following year).
- In 2008, the company acquired the US-based BrachySciences, which makes and distributes brachytherapy products (radiation-delivering seeds, or pellets) which are used in the treatment of prostate cancer.

The medical technology sector is a very tough one, characterized by high levels of risk, and many companies never succeed in making a profit. In 2007–2008, of the forty-three medical technology companies listed on UK stock exchanges, only twelve saw their share price rise, while fourteen saw declines of 75 percent or more (Figure 3.11). Many medical technology firms were, like Biocompatibles, founded by scientific entrepreneurs who were very good at development and even initial stage commercialization, but not so good at gaining traction in their primary markets. Nor was it easy to get funding in Europe (thought it was somewhat easier in the USA). Some funding came from the corporate venture arms of big pharma companies that were looking to buy outright rather than invest. These funds scoured the universities and research labs looking for molecules and other technologies that could be bought outright (Novartis has been particularly successful at this). Thus, if they wanted to see their inventions developed, most entrepreneurs had little option but to sell their business early on.

The few success stories included companies such as Immunodiagnostic Systems, Lidco, Lifeline Scientific and Abcam. Each of these has a strong niche, which it dominates: Lidco supplies cardiac monitors; Lifeline Scientific specializes in organ recovery and preservation; and so on. They do not usually compete with

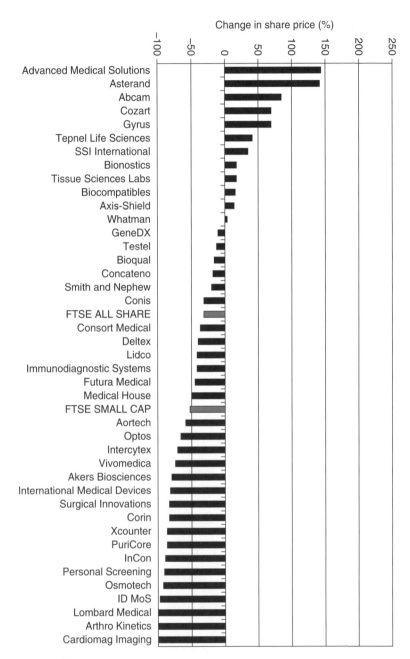

FIG 3.11 / Share price movements of UK medical technology companies

each other directly. The challenge they face is to find products where there is sufficient demand for them to be commercially viable, and then provide those products at a very high quality standard.

Biocompatibles was one of the success stories, for several reasons. First, it had a strong niche market in oncology, where it had considerable expertise, and this gave it a base for developing both products and customer relationships. Early penetration of the US market for drug-eluting beads was key to financial and commercial success. Strong partnerships with pharmaceuticals companies increased resilience; for example, Biocompatibles has a long-standing relationship with Abbott that has spanned several projects. The acquisitions of Cellmed and BrachySciences gave the company a necessary diversification into other niches. Finally, there was good management: Biocompatibles set strategic priorities, exercised tight control of cash flow through a very good finance director, Ian Ardill, and controlled quality. Figures 3.12 and 3.13 show how revenue increased in different product categories, and outline the company's strategic thinking.

By 2010, Biocompatibles had passed through its purely entrepreneurial stage and had matured as a company. This made it attractive to those buyers who were interested in buying an existing stable business, rather than merely the promise of a mature technology. Specialist healthcare company BTG made its first approach in 2010, and after further negotiations, in 2011 made an offer of £177 million, which the shareholders accepted.

I was recruited to the board of Biocompatibles in 2006. I wanted to gain more experience of listed companies, and I thought that I had some experience that might be helpful. I emphatically was not a medical technology specialist, but I had by that point spent eight years on the board of Quintiles and understood the life sciences market; in particular, I knew quite a lot about clinical trials, and also had experience at working and partnering with big pharma companies. But I think my experience in strategy and commercial operations, and my general board experience, were valuable too as we took Biocompatibles through the transition from entrepreneurial venture to mature company. I stepped down in 2011 when Biocompatibles was sold to BTG.

Board Issues: From Scientific Breakthrough to Profit and Value

Biocompatibles is an interesting company in that it is located midway between biotechnology and medical devices. Through extensive R&D, Biocompatibles created a great deal of intellectual property. The drug-eluting beads were pioneered at the British firm; new stem cell technology was developed by the

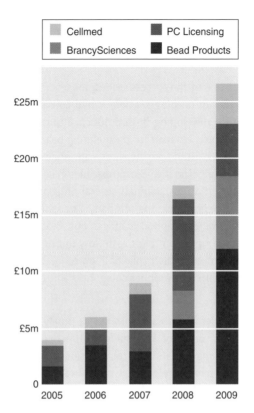

FIG 3.12 / Revenue progressiony

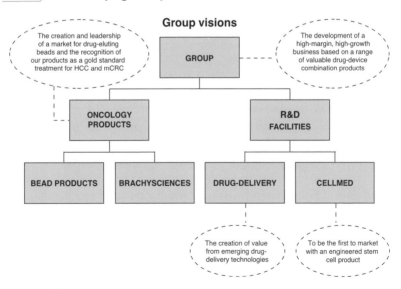

FIG 3.13 / Biocompatibles' Strategy

German subsidiary, Cellmed; and BrachySciences had its intellectual property in brachytherapy. Once intellectual property had been developed and legal title to it had been established, however, the next question was: what to do with it?

One of our biggest strategic debates at Biocompatibles concerned the kind of company we wanted to be. Did we want to be purely an R&D business that came up with new ideas and then sold them to pharmaceuticals companies? Or did we want to become a commercial business, one that made profits and paid dividends out of revenue achieved from selling our own products?

The shareholders clearly had one eye on an exit, i.e. they wanted to sell their shares at some point down the road for an attractive premium. As Figure 3.11 in this chapter shows, Biocompatibles' share price had risen, but not by as much as some others. Thus, the next question became: how could we best create value? Some members of the board believed that the value at exit would lie in the strength of the R&D products, but others felt that those products would be valued more highly if they had already been commercialized. After intense debate, we chose the latter course.

We began the process of turning Biocompatibles into a profit-making commercial enterprise. Revenue from Abbott for the Endeavor project enabled us to pay dividends to shareholders, and also enabled us to fund further R&D. We began a process of strategic reviews, to each of which we invited a panel of outside experts and people who had been successful in the industry. We asked them to tell us what they had done and what they thought we should do. Through these reviews we were able to gain insights from right across the industry, and to consider a variety of different viewpoints, not just those of the CEO, commercial director and R&D director (which is what often happens). Sifting through all these different views and debating them enabled us to think more clearly about the direction we should take.

Even with revenue coming in, the resources we had available for commercialization were limited. We took several strategic decisions. Firstly, we agreed that we would commercialize where we could, but commercialization nearly always meant clinical trials. If the cost of these was too high, then we should form partnerships with pharmaceuticals companies, like Abbott or AstraZeneca, rather than selling the product outright. This enabled us to keep control of the intellectual property, and the value it would ultimately generate once the products went to market. Secondly, we decided against setting up our own sales force and decided to license products wherever possible. This again generated steady revenue and transferred risk away from us.

Turning back to those products that we could commercialize, we knew that we needed to get involved in clinical trials. In the mid-2000s, it was not common for medical device makers to do clinical trials (the practice is now much more widespread). However, we knew that clinical trials would play an important role in convincing the medical community of the value of our products. Oncologists would be much more likely to use our bead technology to deal with tumors, for example, if they could see the results of clinical trials.

If we were to conduct clinical trials, then we needed someone on the board with expertise in this area. We were fortunate to recruit Anne Fairey, an oncologist and former medical director of Novartis, as an independent director working with Peter Stratford, the excellent executive director responsible for R&D. Anne oversaw the clinical trial operations and made sure that we got our products approved and adopted by the market. The drug-eluting beads were increasingly adopted, and are now a standard technology for dealing with liver tumors and several other kinds of cancer. We were also able to bring in expertise from Quintiles. In some cases, we ran clinical trials in partnership with pharmaceuticals companies; at Cellmed, the stem cell trials were run in partnership with AstraZeneca and the skin polymer product was developed along with Merz. Anne's presence on the board put us in a much stronger position when negotiating these alliances, and made us credible in the eyes of the pharma companies.

Penetration of the US market was key to our long-term success. This was partly because of the size of the market, and partly because of its structure. Getting approval from regulators in the USA is very difficult, but once you are in, selling medical technology is easier. For one thing, there is a much higher propensity to pay. Patients, or their insurers and health maintenance organizations, are more likely to pay for life-extending drugs than in other markets. Our first clinical trials and licensing agreements were focused on getting us into this important market.

On top of this, there were the day-to-day board issues that never go away. We were an R&D-based company and so there was no shortage of good ideas in circulation. But which ones should be taken forward? Where should our limited resources be directed in terms of both research and commercialization? We set up a quality committee, chaired by Anne, which oversaw the whole process of research, clinical trials, manufacturing and the distribution chain to the patient. As can be imagined, the manufacture of these products is highly regulated, as is the supply chain, and both require continuous and detailed oversight.

And, finally, there were people issues. When I joined the board we had an excellent CEO in Crispin Simon, formerly of Rothschild and McKinsey. John Sylvester, the commercial director whom we appointed, was also very good, but was his opposite in temperament and character. We helped to smooth over some of the rough edges of the relationship until the two men could work together. In my experience, these people issues are every bit as important as purely business issues. Most people can make a contribution in any situation, but sometimes as a director one has to step in and find ways to help them.

Lessons Learned: Knowing Your Own Worth (as a Company)

The first lesson to be learned was that it is possible to be an R&D company and make money. Many R&D companies don't make money, and this has led to the investment community looking on them with disfavor. But in fact, the combination of a strong R&D capacity and a strong commercial management team can be a winning one.

During my tenure as chairman we received a number of approaches from companies interested in buying Biocompatibles. All these were rejected because we did not think that they valued the company highly enough. BTG's first approach in 2010 offered a premium of about 20 percent, and our brokers recommended that we accept. But, after considering the issue thoroughly, we rejected this offer too.

This may seem strange, given that our brokers were specialists in the field and should have been in a good position to know the true value of the company. But there are a couple of issues to be considered here. Firstly, brokers and other intermediaries only receive fees if the company exits, so they have a vested interested in ensuring a sale. But also—as we found at Forth Ports and Quintiles—markets don't always value companies accurately. In the case of Biocompatibles, we felt that the external valuations did not fully value the future potential of the company.

When considering an exit, it is important, first, to determine the future value of the company and, second, to convince shareholders, investment banks, and markets that your own valuation is the correct one. There will always be pressures from other parties to sell at a lower price. Shareholders may want to realize their investments, intermediaries may want to clear the deal and move on. But for the good of everyone, including—especially—shareholders, it is important for the board to make its position clear and persuade others of its case.

At Biocompatibles, there was no pressure from shareholders to sell, and as a board we were quite happy to carry on indefinitely until the right offer was made. We had a good pipeline of products, which we were commercializing successfully, a strong brand, and good relationships with partners and customers. We did not need to sell, and we were certainly not going to sell for the sake of it. We made our case, and made it well. In particular, we were honest with shareholders (remembering always that it was their company and they could sell if they wanted to), telling them our plans and making it clear what we believed the real value of the company to be.

Then BTG came back with its offer of £177 million, the premium now about 40 percent rather than the original 20 percent, and the picture changed. This seemed to make sense, in terms of value for shareholders and the future of the company. Some of the board disagreed at first, wanting to carry on, but they soon realized this was a deal which would secure the immediate future of Biocompatibles. The board recommended acceptance of the bid and the shareholders concurred. The financial press at the time thought this was a win-win acquisition, and I have since spoken with both our original shareholders and the chief executive of BTG, all of whom are extremely happy.

Getting the value of a company right is not easy, and it cannot be assumed that analysts, even specialists, are very good at it. External valuation experts can help and advise, but in the end it is down to the board members themselves to decide on the future value of the firm. Only then will the interests of all stakeholders be served.

There is a secondary lesson, which I have touched on before but will allude to again. To what extent can you be on the board of a specialist biotech company without being a scientist? Of course, scientific expertise is important, and at Biocompatibles we had two independent directors who were scientists, Anne Fairey and Jeremy Curnock Cook. But that does not mean that everyone has to be a scientist. In fact, very often in these companies there is no shortage of scientific experience: the founders themselves are usually scientists, who find it difficult to move from a purely scientific perspective to that of the general manager of a business. These entrepreneurs need help, and they need it to come from outside the scientific community. Jeremy Curnock Cook agrees that "it is very important to have a blend," and recalls that, over the years, the board has included scientists, healthcare professionals, people from commercial backgrounds and a former commissioner from the Food and Drug Administration (FDA): all people who could provide useful skills and knowledge. "You need the push of the scientific entrepreneurs," he says, "but you also need the tempering views of those who know what the world is like and what the challenges will be."

Biocompatibles, Jeremy feels, has always had "a more balanced blend of executive and independent directors than you normally get in this field." My feeling is that this is one of the reasons why the company has been successful.

I believe that one of the lessons of Biocompatibles is that the boards of these companies need a mixture of specialists and generalists (though the generalists, of course, have to learn as much as they can about the sector, as quickly as they can, if they are to make a meaningful contribution). Both perspectives are necessary. But we will discuss this issue in more detail later in the book.

NFT Ltd

NFT was the UK leader in primary chilled food distribution, transporting products from manufacturers to retailers. It had its origins in Dronfield Foods, a small transport operation set up by Northern Foods in 1979. In 1983, Northern Foods bought a large chilled food distribution operation from Lowfield Distribution and merged it with Dronfield Foods, renaming the company NFT. The new company now had distribution facilities around the country and picked up contracts with Sainsbury's.

Growth was steady and, by 2006, NFT employed 1,450 people, had a turnover of £112 million, and was delivering 85,000 pallets of products per week through four trading divisions: Sainsbury's dedicated primary operations (that is, delivery of goods from factories and plants to regional distribution centers; secondary operations consists of onward delivery from distribution centers to stores), Asda's dedicated primary operations, the Sainsbury's regional distribution center at St Albans, and a shared user network.

Its status as a wholly owned subsidiary meant that NFT could not work directly with other food manufacturers competing with Northern Foods. Its captive status meant that there were clear limits to growth. In order to expand further, NFT needed to acquire more manufacturing customers. David Frankish, CEO of NFT, could see real possibilities for growth if NFT could be decoupled from Northern Foods. "That was the only way we could get the necessary investment to become a total logistics company," he says.

In 2006, NFT was the subject of an MBO led by David Frankish and backed by Phoenix Equity Partners. I knew David from before the buy-out, and when Phoenix approached me and asked if I would serve as chairman, I was interested. However, I was still on the board of Vantec and did not feel I would be able to give this new post enough time, and therefore regretfully declined. Phoenix discussed the matter with David, and then came back to me and said they would be willing to wait. That clinched matters and six months later, once I had resigned from Vantec, I took up the post of non-executive chairman of NFT.

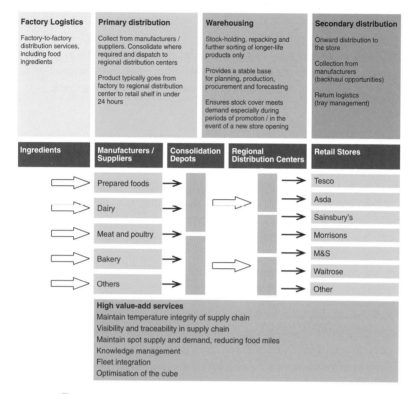

FIG 3.14 / **Fresh and chilled food supply chain**

NFT described itself as "the intelligent link in customers' supply chain management." Figure 3.14 shows how the chilled food supply chain functions. NFT worked in the primary distribution sector, moving goods from manufacturers and suppliers to depots and distribution centers, and it had warehousing operations as well.

The fresh food market in the UK was large and growing. The market was estimated to be about £40 billion per annum, with forecast growth of more than 6 percent over the next four years as consumers turned increasingly to fresh foods on the one hand, and chilled products, such as ready meals, on the other.

Delivering these products from supplier to market requires highly specialized operations. Delivery is, of course, highly time-critical, and there are tight regulations on how long foods can exist in warehouses or on shelves before they must either be consumed or thrown away. Health and safety issues are paramount, not just during production but during transit as well. Legislation on this issue has become progressively tighter over the years, and it is necessary to

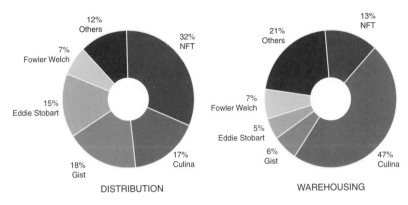

FIG 3.15 / **Competitor analysis and market share**

have equipment that records and maintains precise temperatures so that every product has a "temperature footprint," a record that can be traced back to the source.

New entrants into this market are rare. Any company aspiring to enter this market would need to invest heavily in technology—including IT systems capable of linking all parts of the distribution network—and skills. That heavy investment would require the company to grow rapidly and acquire a significant market share in order to recoup the investment. New competitors would need to know the market well and be able to develop quickly a track record of success that would impress retailers and manufacturers. All of these factors mean that barriers to entry are high. As a result, with limited competition inside the industry, margins are good. A fairly small number of firms currently share the industry. Figure 3.15 shows how the markets for warehousing and distribution are divided.

Within the distribution sector, NFT had a number of strategic strengths. It had a fine track record stretching back more than thirty years, and its excellence in the area of chilled food distribution is widely acknowledged. Many of its staff were long-serving men and women who understood the chilled food business, especially the health and safety aspects, and know their own duties very well. NFT had a good network of distribution centers and an IT system that linked retailers, manufacturers, and other parts of the supply chain, thus ensuring timely distribution and minimizing waste.

This was critical, because in a network operation like NFT, supply and demand have to be balanced exactly for each individual vehicle, not over a month or even a week, but every day. If there was too much demand, the company had to hire in expensive sub-contractors; too little demand, and it was left with surplus capacity and had to pay drivers to stand idle. NFT used its customer relationships to build up a number of long-term open book contracts, whereby the retailer paid for resources and NFT delivers. These contracts gave NFT a base volume, on the back of which it has built other relationships with other, high-value customers. Very few companies make profits out of network businesses—even fewer in chilled foods—but NFT succeeded in large part because it understood the dynamics of networks.

Another area where NFT led the way was in the intelligent use of sub-contractors. Inevitably there were times when sub-contractors had to be used, but too much sub-contracting could have led to loss of control over quality. What NFT did was to build an information system that told management who the sub-contractors were, what trips they made, what rates they charged, and what their capabilities were. That meant we could match sub-contractors to requirements much more efficiently and effectively.

That "intelligent link" manifested itself in other ways too. NFT worked with both manufacturers and retailers, and could serve as advisor to both sides. Thus, if a manufacturer developed a potential retail client, thanks to its knowledge of the industry, NFT could advise the manufacturer about how this client works, and even make introductions for key account holders. If a retailer wanted to know more about a manufacturer and their capabilities, then we could provide that information too.

David's vision of growth proved correct and, after the MBO, the company grew dramatically. By 2013, the company had seven depots and employed 1,900 staff; its transport fleet included 430 tractor units and 560 trailers of various sizes. The company delivered 136,000 pallets a week to its clients, which included almost every major UK retailer; the total value of goods delivered was over £11 billion per annum. NFT itself had an estimated turnover of £175 million (to March 2014) with and earnings before interest, taxes, depreciation and amortization (EBITDA) of £9.5 million over the same period.

As with U-POL and Vantec, this growth strategy had one simple aim: to increase the value of the company so that Phoenix and management could make a profitable exit. In fact, Phoenix held onto the company longer than anticipated. In late 2013, Rothschild were retained as the investment bankers and a price was determined, but it was clear that Phoenix would not be interested in selling for anything less than a very good premium. As Richard Daw, Phoenix's representative on the board, says, from their point of view there was absolutely no pressure to sell. NFT was finally sold to the Asian PE fund, Emergevest, in April 2014, for a very attractive return for the shareholders.

Board Issues: The Art of Focusing

NFT, when I joined the board, was in a position very typical of former subsidiaries of big firms that have recently become independent. As Richard Daw says: "NFT needed to be separated both physically and culturally from the mothership. It needed to change from being an inward-looking supplier of services to a parent company to an outward-facing provider of those services to the world at large."

The MBO freed NFT from the shackles, so to speak, but it was clear that the top management team needed strengthening. The company was being run by David and his technical director, Charles Stephens. They were very capable people, but they had no experience of running an independent company and there simply were not enough of them.

At first, too, they were strategically uncertain of what to do with the business now that it was independent. NFT as it stood after the buy-out was essentially a transport company working in the chilled food business. Should the company try to expand in that market, or should it broaden out and diversify? Should it go into warehousing? What about secondary distribution, to retail outlets? Were there opportunities in related sectors such as ambient, frozen food, produce? And what about other markets, such as servicing restaurants? Were there opportunities in international markets such as continental Europe? Figure 3.16 shows the strategic options we considered.

The company was now in a very different strategic situation from before, and effectively we had a blank sheet of paper. The first task was to determine what the strategy should be; the second, to determine what kind of top team would be needed to carry out that strategy; and the third, to recruit the team and get started.

But, in order to do these things, we also had to get the management team used to working with private equity owners. David had no prior experience of working with PE. I had a number of private conversations with him, passing on what I had learned. There was also the issue of adapting to a new role. As CEO, David no longer had to do everything. He had a team now, and his job was to lead, manage and motivate that team. He could also spend more time with customers, building relationships with them, and that has been one of the major factors in NFT's success. We appointed an experienced coach, Fran Moscow, to help David with all these changes.

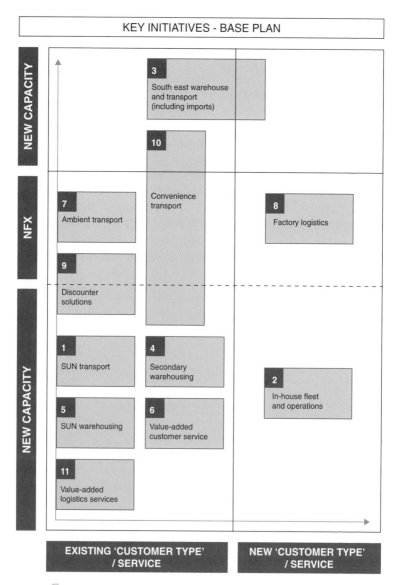

KEY INITIATIVES - BASE PLAN

NEW CAPACITY

3
South east warehouse
and transport
(including imports)

10

NFX

7
Ambient transport

Convenience
transport

8
Factory logistics

9
Discounter
solutions

NEW CAPACITY

1
SUN transport

4
Secondary
warehousing

2
In-house fleet
and operations

5
SUN warehousing

6
Value-added
customer service

11
Value-added
logistics services

EXISTING 'CUSTOMER TYPE'
/ SERVICE

NEW 'CUSTOMER TYPE'
/ SERVICE

FIG 3.16   **Strategic options at NFT**

One of the biggest challenges we faced was getting that team together. "We
spent a lot of time working with David to pick the management team that
would take NFT forward," Richard Daw recalls. We were fortunate to be able
to make some very good appointments, including Steve Dennison as finance
director. We created the post of sales and marketing director and recruited

Dale Fiddy from a competing firm; he had excellent market knowledge. We appointed Mark Davis as company secretary and in-house lawyer Maria Ferguson as head of human resources. Our head of IT, Stephen Szikora, came from Exel and proved to be worth his weight in gold; he played a very important role in the transformation of the company and the building of the end-to-end IT systems that became one of our competitive strengths.

On the operations side, things were more difficult. There had been a strong "Northern Foods culture" among the staff, and this carried on after the MBO. Northern Foods had been the priority customer, and when the parent company asked for something, it got it—irrespective of cost. Now, Northern Foods was still a customer, but it could not get special treatment to the detriment of other customers (it took a while for Northern Foods to realize this too). "We had to go all the way down through middle management to front-line staff," Richard says, "and get them to understand that, while we wanted them to continue giving fantastic service, they had to do so in ways that made commercial sense." We brought in people from outside the company in the hope of changing the culture, but we made mistakes with a couple of appointments; instead of changing the culture, the new executives got people's backs up and created resistance. In the end we had to replace these people, promoting Tom Starkey and Alex Fisher and recruiting Andy de Vere. These proved to be very good appointments.

As for the strategy itself, we used much the same process as at Biocompatibles and Forth Ports. There were annual strategic reviews attended by all of the board and we brought in specialists from outside. Lawrence Christensen, supply chain director at Sainsbury's and the UK's leading expert on supply chain management, was one of these. We brought in specialists on HR and also Straycat, a specialist company in marketing and public relations. On one occasion we invited an advisor from Phoenix to talk us through the issues around an exit. All of this got people thinking and stimulated discussion. As a result, all of the members of the board and the senior management team got involved in the strategy and everyone bought into it. There was no question of strategy being imposed on anyone.

We ended up with a strategy that was rigorous and highly focused, and which had the support of the entire top team. Over the years, that strategy has hardly changed at all. This has allowed management to get on and do what it needed to do, which was to grow the business and profits. We saw improvements in operations, the introduction of state-of-the-art systems and a series of excellent relationships with customers, all because management knew exactly what needed to be done and were free to get on and do it. There was no chopping and changing, no veering off onto new courses. The company, like its strategy, became focused on the job in hand and on its strategic goals. That is one of the reasons why Richard Daw and Phoenix liked the company so much, and why there was no pressing hurry to sell it.

Lessons Learned: Relationships Make a Business

The first lesson to come out of the NFT experience is that, following MBOs, boards need to move swiftly to ensure the transition from being a subsidiary of a corporate to being an independent business, and that requires two things: the swift determination of the strategy the company will follow, and the equally swift recruitment of a senior management team. We did this quickly at NFT, but with hindsight perhaps not quickly enough. In particular, the two senior management appointments that went wrong set us back, as we had to recruit new people and repair the damage that had been done.

The second lesson follows from the first: it is vital to get the right people into senior posts. If the wrong person is appointed and has to be replaced, the comings and goings create confusion and send the wrong signals to staff. In this case, we had two people come into posts, do a certain amount of damage, then depart to be replaced by a second person with different policies and different idea. All this created uncertainty, at a time when we really needed to have everyone focused on moving the company forward. It took time to get the top team together in a properly functioning relationship.

And it is important that the members of the top team *have* a relationship, trust each other, and can work together. Within that team, the most important relationship of all is that between the chairman and CEO. David and I got on extremely well and understood each other. It helped that I had experience of both logistics and chilled food distribution, so I understood the company and its business; I was not an "outsider" in this instance. Once David realized that he had a chairman who knew how operations functioned and how the market worked, he felt more comfortable. I have noted before the need for both specialists and generalists on boards, but this was a case where having specialist knowledge was useful. CEOs should ideally see chairmen as people who can help them.

Relationships with business partners are vital too, and we saw above how relationships and market knowledge played a big role in NFT's success. Here again, the chairman has a very important role to play in building relationships with clients. On one occasion, NFT and Sainsbury's had a dispute which appeared to have reached deadlock. I had personal connections with Sainsbury's CEO Justin King and was able to talk with him and ensure we got the matter resolved. Making and maintaining those kinds of senior-level relationships is part and parcel of the chairman's job.

The third important relationship is, of course, with investors. Phoenix understood this from the beginning, as demonstrated by their policy on shared equity. In most cases, private equity houses give equity to the CEO and finance director, but the rest of the board members receive nothing. This creates inequalities, and can be demotivating for other directors. Phoenix, on the other hand, gave equity to every executive director, making them all owners of the company. Thus when our terrier-like sales and marketing director went out to wipe the floor with our competitors, he knew that both he and the company would benefit.

The relationship with Phoenix was impeccable throughout, and NFT was very fortunate in its owners. Phoenix invested £20 million in NFT after the buy-out to fund expansion; not something every private equity house would do. "NFT wanted to focus on value creation," says David Frankish, "and Phoenix was willing to invest in that. This has been a real success story in terms of growing the business and growing value." Phoenix's representatives attended every board meeting and always made their views known but, having done so, left it up to management to run the business; they never interfered. Richard Daw is very specific about where the boundary lines of involvement lie. "We don't manage any of the businesses we invest in on a day-to-day basis," he says. "We are not experts in the business. We ensure that the board appoints the right people to run the business and then leave them to it." That kind of relationship is to be cherished.

NovaQuest Capital Management

NovaQuest Pharma Opportunities Fund 3 was created as a spin-out from Quintiles (it was formerly the corporate venturing arm of Quintiles). Dennis Gillings was one of the original investors, and other "anchor investors" included private equity investors in Quintiles such as Bain Capital, Temasek, TPG and 3i. The Japanese bank Mitsui also became an anchor investor. NovaQuest specializes primarily in investments in pharmaceutical products that are either in late-stage clinical development or commercialization. This is a very specialized niche, in which NovaQuest is one of the few players.

NovaQuest managed the two corporate venture funds established by Quintiles in 2001 and 2004 in which, over the course of ten years, they invested $879 million in twenty-two specific projects. Other investments were made in both companies and funds, and the total invested over that ten-year period was over $1.5 billion. The remnants of these investments, valued in excess of £200 million, were spun off into PharmaBio, which I chaired and which Dennis Gillings subsequently acquired. Fund 3 was an independent private equity fund structured on conventional PE lines, and registered in the Cayman Islands. It was launched in the USA in 2010 and closed in 2013. It raised a total of $459 million, in the most difficult fundraising environment in the history of private equity. By mid-2014 it had invested over two-thirds of this money.

The decision to spin off from Quintiles was taken for several reasons. Quintiles' shareholders were contemplating taking the company public once again, and knew that the issue of valuation would once again rear its head (see the earlier case study of Quintiles in this chapter). Analysts were no better at valuing corporate venturing operations in 2010 than they had been in 2000. Spinning off the corporate venturing operation would be one way of getting around the problem and ensuring a fairer valuation. There were also benefits to Quintiles itself. The company had decided on a strategy of partnering with pharma companies, but it was clear that as part of any partnership those companies would want to see "skin in the game" in the form of risk capital. Directly providing risk capital to these ventures would mean that Quintiles would have less money to invest in its own core business. However, NovaQuest could provide this investment at arm's length.

However, Dennis Gillings' ambitions did not end there. He and I had already discussed the idea of a "family of funds" uniquely focused on life sciences and covering every asset class from product investing to buy-outs, growth equity, venture capital, and debt. We believed it was possible to raise perhaps as much as $3 billion over time. The establishment of NovaQuest was to be a first step towards that goal. Following the success of NovaQuest, the first GOH Capital private equity fund was launched in London in May 2014, with Dennis as chair (I was involved in creating the mandate and planning the fund). The mandate of this fund is much broader, covering equity investments in management buy-outs and growth equity across the biopharma, medical devices, and med-tech sectors. GOH Capital, the umbrella organization, is now in place and more funds are planned. Dennis has also invested in Huya, a venture biotech company focussed on developing products from China and run by Dr Mireille Gillings, his wife. PharmaBio invested in this company, where I am an observer director.

"Big pharma" is facing severe pressures. The so-called "patent cliff," the simultaneous expiry of a large number of existing patents on drugs, is looming. Those who buy pharmaceutical products are increasingly resistant to paying high prices; the NHS in the UK and other nationalized healthcare services are under severe budget pressures and are capping their spending on medicine. Tighter regulations mean that fewer drugs are being approved, and the process is longer and more costly than ever before. Figure 3.17 shows some of the costs and pressures the industry is facing.

At the same time, this is a very exciting time for pharmaceutical and biotechnology research. Demand is rising, particularly in BRICS and MINT countries where rising prosperity means there is more demand, and more ability to pay, for advanced medicines. Scientific advances in genetics and proteomics (the study of the structures and functions of proteins) have opened up fascinating prospects, for example in stem cell research, which offer the prospect of treatments for diseases such as cancer and dementia. A new generation of drugs is waiting to be developed, and the rewards for those who can manage the development process successfully will be very high.

However, the research process must be resourced. Banks will not lend money to fund this kind of R&D work. Stock markets no longer attach value to products in the pipeline of pharmaceuticals companies, no matter how strong the market potential might be; the billions spent every year on R&D are worth nothing unless and until the regulator (for example, the FDA in the USA) gives approval for the drug and commercialization begins. Back in the early 2000s, venture capital funds were willing to invest in start-up firms with new products, but their appetite for investment is less than it once was. Besides, by definition venture capital only invests in companies at a start-up stage. Mature companies really have only two choices; they can ally with each other to share expertise and spread risk, or they can turn to private equity for support.

Why would pharma companies seek investment from NovaQuest? The answers are basically twofold. Firstly, NovaQuest investment helps pharma companies to share the risks of these incredibly long and expensive development processes. The fact that we only invest in late-stage projects means that the risk is not spread over the whole lifetime of the project; on the other hand, it is also the late stages (full clinical trials and so on) where the expense is greatest and where, having already invested to get the product this far, companies are most anxious to see a positive result.

It is important to note that unlike conventional PE houses, which invest in equity in companies, NovaQuest invests primarily in products. More

The "Patent Cliff" will see big pharma
lose $92 billion in revenue

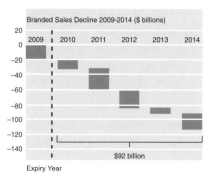

Source: IMS

The cost of developing a new
drug has increased to $1 billion

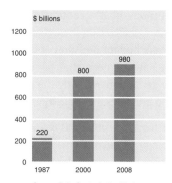

Source: Tufts Center for the Study
of Drug Development

Number of new drugs approvals
continues to decline

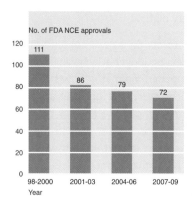

Source: Burril & Co. www.phrma.org, 2006 PhRMA
annual report, Datamonitor, E&Y Convergence:
The Biotechnology Industry Report 2000, Tufts
Center for the Study of Drug Development News
Release (11/06/06). Representative of drug
approval in the United States.

The drug development process
is long and risky

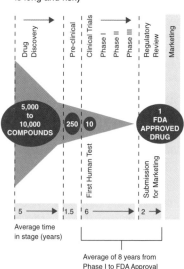

FIG 3.17   **Pressures on the pharmaceuticals industry**

specifically, it invests in a range of products, seldom one product only. For example, if a company with ten molecules in late-stage development were to come to us and ask us to invest in just one of those molecules, we would usually refuse. Investing in three, or four, or five molecules spreads the risk (and, from experience, the one the company most wants us to invest in is also probably the most risky!). Having identified a range of products, we would then ask a series of questions. What is the history of these molecules and their development? What barriers are there to getting FDA approval, and how hard will it be to overcome those barriers? What are other companies doing in terms of research in these areas? These and other questions help us to determine the likely risks and whether this represents a good investment.

Thus, as well as providing risk capital, we can also help companies benchmark their work and make better decisions about prioritizing products for development. Heads of R&D traditionally work very hard to protect their pipelines. If a product runs into trouble, their solution can be to invest more money in it rather than stopping any further investment. Some products clearly should not proceed beyond Phase II; the likelihood that they will be approved and commercialized is very small. But, having come so far and devoted so much effort to these products, R&D directors are reluctant to abandon them. An outsider like NovaQuest, with a wider knowledge of the industry, can help companies to identify which projects to stop, and which to take forward. "Pharma companies work in a very trying environment," says Ron Wooten, managing partner at NovaQuest. "Our style of investing solves a lot of their problems."

Secondly, NovaQuest has, through its ongoing connection with Quintiles, the world's largest pharmaceuticals development company, access to expertise in every stage of development from clinical trials to marketing and distribution. For example, if an Australian company wants to sell its products in Europe, we can not only fund the venture but also introduce Quintiles. The latter can provide consultancy advice, even a sales force on the ground. There is no compulsion to use Quintiles, and the company is free to look around for a better deal; but the support is there if they want it.

NovaQuest's funds represent attractive opportunities because, perhaps surprisingly, the risk levels are low. The investment is very specific, in a particular range of products. If we were to invest in companies, then we would face a wider range of strategic, operational, financial and other risks. But if we invest in products—provided that we understand the products, and we would never make an investment unless we *did* understand the products—then the range of risks is narrower and easier to understand. When we invest in a product at the beginning of Phase III, for example, there is a clear plan for clinical trials, which is agreed with the company. If the company departs from that plan, or if trials begin and it is at once apparent that the product will not succeed, then we halt the investment. This reduces risks for investors, and is one of the reasons why we have been successful at attracting funds, even in a very tough market.

Never in the course of my career had I expected to end up as chairman of a private equity house! But when Dennis announced his intention to spin off NovaQuest, he asked me to chair the new venture. He and the other investors needed someone who understood both private equity and Quintiles and its business. He also needed someone who could work with the managing partner of the funds, Ron Wooten, and the partners, John Bradley, Will Robb and Jonathan Tunnicliffe.

I accepted for two reasons. Firstly, this sounded like a very interesting challenge. There was a chance to learn more about managing private equity funds, and I felt my skills and experience could be of use. The second reason is that Dennis asked me. He and I have been friends for many years, since we were at university together. I became non-executive chairman of NovaQuest in 2010, and remain in that post today.

Board Issues: Building a Team

The team that led NovaQuest after the spin-off was led by Ron Wooten, who acted as managing partner for the third fund. Ron and all the members of his team were very experienced at corporate venturing, and most of them had worked together at Quintiles for the past ten years. I had plenty of experience in this field too and had managed investments for a number of private equity houses. "We had the financial rigor and the skills to make investments," says Ron, "and we had the infrastructure of the global company that had employed us to tap into." But not one of us had any experience of managing a fund or raising private equity money to go into the fund. We were used to being part of Quintiles, and the transition from running the corporate venturing arm of a multinational to running a standalone private equity fund was hard, much harder than we had imagined.

We had a fortunate beginning compared to most first-time funds. The launch of a private equity fund is the most critical point. One needs investors, and needs them quickly, to get money flowing in. Once the first investors are in board, others are more likely to follow, but getting those first investors to commit can be painfully hard. However, we had no problems in this respect; we had money coming straight in from Quintiles, including the remnants of the old corporate venture fund, which we were able to take over. We also had support from the PE houses that had stakes in Quintiles, TPG, Bain Capital, Temasek and 3i, who gave us valuable advice and helped to design the fund and make sure it was set up properly. As well as these four, the Japanese bank Mitsui was persuaded to come in as an anchor investor.

But there were plenty of other issues to occupy our attention. One of the big ones was the legal and regulatory framework. We had secured the services of a top-flight legal team from Proskauer, which specialized in private equity funds, to set up the legal framework, but we still had to get to grips with the maze of regulations that surround all private equity operations, especially in the aftermath of the Dodd-Frank Wall Street Reform and Consumer Protection Act of 2010. We had to learn quickly how to operate in this environment and remain compliant and, as noted, none of the management team had any prior experience of doing so. Ron Wooten makes the point that the regulatory changes were a new experience for all PE houses and so to some extent we were all in the same boat. Even so, the learning curve was very steep.

Having set up the fund and attracted our anchor investors, we then had to get the rest of the money in and find institutions that were prepared to invest. We faced a number of difficulties. There was the perception that we were a first-time fund, therefore no one knew anything about us. There was the very specific mandate of investing in pharmaceuticals products, which not everyone understood or was prepared to invest in. And, finally, there was the very difficult fundraising climate in the aftermath of 2008.

The support of the anchors helped us to be credible in the eyes of other investors, and TPG, 3i, Bain Capital and Temasek all helped to make some introductions. Otherwise we relied on working our networks, introductions from other third parties, and placement agents. The latter are an interesting class of firms and people that have sprung up as the private equity industry has grown; they make introductions between investors and funds, and if the investor then chooses to put in money, they receive a percentage. We also learned that placement agents do not have a lot of appetite for first-time funds because they are perceived—not always accurately—as being more risky. In the end we had a contact database of over 500 potential investors, and we ended up actually making contact with over 90. As I noted earlier, the market was very tight and many PE groups struggled to raise money. "Investors were very wary of PE groups that had made big promises but not delivered, and were reducing allocations," says Ron Wooten. But we raised $469 million in three years which, given the conditions, has to be seen as a great success.

Then we had to get the money invested. For the third fund, we have so far looked at over 250 potential investments, but so far only 10 percent of them are within the mandate of the fund: that is, investment in late-stage clinical development and commercial development, for multi-products rather than single products. We learned that sometimes the best way to develop a partnership is to go first to the finance director of the company where we are making the investment and only later to bring in the R&D director. This might seem counterintuitive, but in fact it is better to understand the financial structure of the investment first, and then decide what—if any—products are suitable for investment. We have sufficient of the fund invested now that we can raise a follow-on fund with the same mandate for investing in products.

And, inevitably, there have been cultural issues. As I said earlier, all of the NovaQuest team came from Quintiles. Most have worked there for many years, and have imbued the values of the Quintiles culture. Additionally, apart from one Briton, all of the management team are American. This has several consequences. Firstly, a culture has developed where what the managing partner says, goes. Secondly, in terms of investments the focus so far is very much on the USA and the Japan.

NovaQuest needs to take a worldwide view. One of my current priorities is to encourage the partners to plan for the future, especially in terms of the structure of the next fund and strengthening the team.

Lessons Learned: Get the Experts on Board Early

You will have gathered that starting a private equity fund is a very difficult business. I can only say that you have no idea how difficult it is until you have done it!

The first lesson concerns strategy. The global mid-sized private equity sector is full of general funds, so we needed to have a very specialized fund to differentiate ourselves. Fortuitously, the corporate venture fund had invested broadly in funds, in companies, and in products. The latter had been some of the most successful investments, and this was an area where the team had a lot of experience. We also had the strategic advice of the Quintiles investors, all of which were private equity funds.

The second lesson from my experience is that if you are moving into this field, it is essential to have an experienced private equity professional on board from the beginning. The complexities of private equity and the tough regulatory environment mean that you must have people with experience who know how to navigate their way through the regulations and build relationships with key investors. Ron Wooten and I knew how to make investments, but the rest was new to us. As I noted above, when setting up GOH Capital a managing partner with wide experience of private equity was appointed.

General
- Focussed strategy
- Upgrading the offering or service
- Strengthening the team
- Investing in people management and development
- Operational efficiency
- New sectors
- New geographies
- Downsizing and disinvestment
- M&A
- Organic growth
- Systems improvement
- Developing existing customer base

Biocompatibles
- Much more emphasis on the use of clinical trials
- Development of the commercialisation of drug eluting beads to generate revenue
- Penetration of the USA market
- Prudent cash management
- Obtaining the Medtronic stent payment
- Controlling R&D and setting priorities
- Publishing the annual team objectives for the coming year
- Paying a dividend
- Partnering with pharma companies
- Acquisitions of Cellmed and Brachytherapy
- Sector expertise, notably oncology
- Patent protection
- Quality controlled manufacturing capacity for medical devices
- Handling of exit to maximise price

Michael Gerson
- Premier international corporate mover
- Strong brand
- Blue-chip customer base
- Quality of service
- Quality of international partners
- Quality of physical assets
- Financial control
- Family business philosophy

Keller
- Acquisitions to broaden product offer successfully implemented
- Deep expertise in ground engineering
- Disinvestment of property maintenance and refurbishment business
- Strength of operational line management
- Decentralisation philosophy
- Geographic expansion in Europe, Asia, Middle East, Brazil
- Investment in technology
- Highly specialised equipment high barrier to entry
- Design capability to tailor value-added solutions
- Organic growth
- Risk management

U-POL
- Widened product range
- Strong brand
- Geographic expansion
- Manufacturing flexibility to expand
- Manufacturing efficiency
- Supply chain improvements
- Team strengthened in USA, UK, export
- Long-term relationships with suppliers
- Cash management
- Experienced team used to working together
- Investment in R&D
- Investment in IT systems improvement
- Network of distributors

NFT
- Only national network for chill food logistics
- Open book contacts with Sainsbury and Asda to underpin the volume
- Upgrade product offer by offering warehousing
- Investment of £20m in facilities and IT
- Blue chip customers both manufacturer and retailer
- Organic growth
- Strengthened management team
- Operational excellence in operating a network
- State-of-the-art management information systems

Forth Ports
- Strategic locations, e.g. Tilbury
- Property assets for development
- Acquisitions of assets
- Widen product offer, e.g paper, renewables, recycling
- Financial control
- Reduction of cost base
- Improvement in productivity by investing in latest technology
- Investment in IT systems
- Improved utilisation of port assets
- Handling of exit to maximise price
- Very experienced management

NovaQuest
- Partnering agreement with Quintiles
- Excellent track record of investing
- Very focused fund mandate that was also very differentiated
- Market opportunity
- Support of PE houses who were Quintiles investors (TPG, Bain, 3i)
- Experienced team

Quintiles
- Breadth of product offer
- Development of global coverage
- Range of therapeutic expertise
- Track record in improving productivity
- Information systems
- Partnering capability with pharma companies
- Access to risk sharing capital via NovaQuest
- Blue chip customers providing organic growth
- Increasing regulation leading to larger clinical trials
- Very experienced management team

CH Jones
- Development of product offer into integrated fuel management
- Growth of customer base
- Information systems and the development of fuel cards
- Network of fuel bunkering facilities and its expansion
- Cost conscious / financial control
- Cashflow
- Open minded exec team on strategy development
- Handing of exit to maximise price

Vantec
- Upgrade product offer from transport to supply chain management
- Development of new sectors away from automotive
- Organic growth in automotive
- Maintain excellent relationship with Nissan
- Geographic expansion, e.g. China
- Invest in people development
- Strengthen the team and appoint CEO
- Improve efficiency
- Rationalise network and asset base
- Cost control

FIG 3.18 / Critical success factors

	Chairman	SID	NED	Audit Committee	Remco	Quality Committee	Health & Safety	Nomination Committee
Biocompatibles	✓		✓	✓	✓	✓		✓
CH Jones			✓	✓	✓			
Datrontech	✓		✓	✓	✓			✓
Forth Ports		✓	✓	✓	✓			✓
Keller		✓	✓	✓	✓		✓	✓
Michael Gerson			✓					
NFT	✓		✓	✓	✓			✓
NovaQuest	✓		✓	✓				
Quintiles			✓	✓				
U-POL			✓	✓	✓			
Vantec			✓	✓	✓			

FIG 3.19 / **Summary of roles played**

Thirdly, and this returns to one of the running themes in this book, it is important to have a board with a wide range of backgrounds and skills. A variety of perspectives leads to dialogue, debate, and consideration of options that might otherwise get overlooked. We were fortunate to have people such as Fred Cohen and Jim O'Brien from TPG, Chris Gordon from Bain and Todd Dantsuka from Mitsui on the board to provide that variety and diversity. Had we not had their support we might have struggled to adjust to this demanding new environment.

That concludes our eleven case studies. As a reminder, I have included two figures (Figures 3.18 and 3.19). One lists the critical success factors: what made each company successful (or in the case of Datrontech, the factors that had to be managed in a time of crisis). The second shows the summary of roles played by me as an independent director in each company. It will be useful to keep this list in mind as we begin to explore the key themes that are critical to the work of the independent director and help to determine their own success.

Themes

Boards

> It is not the strongest of the species that survives, nor the
> most intelligent that survives. It is the one that is the most
> adaptable to change.
>
> — Charles Darwin

Independent directors do not work in isolation. They are part of a team, the board of directors, which has overall responsibility for governing and steering the larger organization. They need to work closely with the other team members, both other independent directors and the executive directors, so that the whole board functions together. I will come to the specifics of the role of the independent director later, but before that we need to look at the role of the board as a team, and how that team can discharge its responsibilities effectively.

A great deal has been written about boards and how they function, and for those interested in more detail on this subject I recommend *Boards at Work* by Ram Charan, *The Effective Board* by Neville Bain, *Boards, Governance and Value Creation* by Morten Huse, and *The Future of Boards* by Jay Lorsch; there are other good works out there as well.[1] The purpose here is to provide an overview that will be useful in guiding independent directors to better understand their own roles as team members.

It is hard to over-emphasize the importance of the role of the board. Companies—especially large, publicly owned companies, those owned by private equity, and private companies—have a powerful impact on the world around them. They make the goods and services that we consume, and their actions have a direct impact on the world economy, which means in turn that they have an indirect impact on our personal welfare and prosperity. Some of these companies, the very largest, have such an impact that they have become "too big to fail," so damaging would the consequences of their failure be. Those companies, whether publicly or privately owned, are run by boards. It follows that boards of directors have, through their words and actions, a very powerful impact on us all.

Given this importance, it will probably come as no surprise that, following a spate of corporate governance failures in recent years, boards have been sharply criticized. Richard Koch, in *The Financial Times Guide to Strategy*, remarks acidly that "most firms get bogged down in far too much operational detail and discuss strategy infrequently. Most board meetings are therefore largely a waste of expensive time."[2] Professor Andrew Kakabadse of Cranfield Business School agrees: "Non-executive director posts … have become 'status roles' of little or no value to the business, with research showing that management teams around the world don't respect their boards and don't feel they are getting value."[3] Samuel Malone, in his book *Greed, Fraud and Corruption*, argues that "the concept that the board of directors represents shareholders and the CEO reports to the board is sometimes a myth. In practice the board often reports to and represents the CEO."[4]

A contrary view is that of Simon Massey, tax partner with Menzies, who observes that over the last twenty years, "the quality of boards has definitely improved, even in SMEs. There used to be a lot of self-made people who did not have a lot of education, but now the standard of education is quite high." William Underhill of legal firm Slaughter & May concurs that the standard of experience and expertise is improving steadily. Their view is backed up by a recent report from McKinsey, which suggests a strong link between the engagement and commitment of board members, and overall corporate performance.[5]

Of course there are still examples of firms whose boards have failed to act as they should. But there is also a great deal of ignorance about the role played by boards. In this chapter, I want to try to dispel some of that ignorance and clarify what boards can, and cannot, do.

In business corporations, boards report to the shareholders and are accountable to them. However, boards are responsible for much more than just creating and delivering shareholder value. They also have responsibility for the long-term health of the company. That means, among other things, that they are responsible to, and for, their employees, and that they have obligations to the wider community. Indeed, it can be argued that there is a direct connection between these things and shareholder value. A company that is well managed and meets its responsibilities to other stakeholders is more likely to create lasting shareholder value than one that is not.

That may sound quite simple, but in fact, the work of boards is very demanding, and is getting harder. Boards must consider a wide array of ethical and governance issues, any one of which could have an adverse effect on the company and its stakeholders. Here are just some of the issues that boards routinely face:

- Should the company do business in or with countries that have oppressive regimes, the policies of which are anathema to employees, shareholders and the general public? Do they metaphorically "shake hands with the devil" in the hopes that their actions in those countries will create jobs and help people on the ground, or do they consider the ethical risks so high that they should walk away?
- When operating in countries where bribery is commonplace, should the company follow local customs and pay bribes, or attempt to keep its hands clean?
- How should the company make sure that local subsidiaries, suppliers and so on are not behaving in unethical ways, such as exploiting child labor or failing to provide a safe working environment? For example, at Keller we realized that in order to ensure safety in all the countries where we operated, we would need a global health and safety policy rolled out across the entire firm, rather than letting local business units make their own policy.
- What stance should the company take with regard to tax avoidance, conflicts of interest, and insider dealing? Some executives behave as if corporate assets were their own private property to be used as they wish for personal aggrandizement. Some companies think there is nothing wrong with using tax havens to reduce taxes and maximize earnings. But are these things right?
- What policies should the company have with regard to executive pay and stock options? How will shareholders and the public view bonus schemes that provide excessive reward, or are even seen to be apparently rewarding failure?

• What stance should the company take with regard to its customers? Will it engage in price fixing, price exploitation or dumping in order to grab market share, regardless of the long-term impact on customers?

• How safe are the company's products? At Quintiles and Biocompatibles, we took safety very seriously indeed, well aware that any mistakes in product development and clinical testing could result in harmful side-effects for customers. At Keller, too, we were aware that unless we produced work of the highest possible quality, we would be putting the people who used our clients' buildings at risk.

• Is the company behaving in an environmentally responsible manner? For example, at NFT we developed a fuel-economy initiative and reported on this to shareholders so that they understood clearly what we were doing and why. Some of the issues faced by boards in the 11 case studies are shown in Table 4.1.

And this is just the beginning. A full list of the responsibilities of boards could span a book as long as this one.

What happens when boards fail in their duties? At the very least, companies will see their reputations damaged. Regulators can issue fines, and recently the scale of those fines has increased. Fines of more than a billion dollars have been levied, especially in the financial services sector. We have also seen a rise in the number of criminal and civil prosecutions of companies; and never forget that individual directors can also be prosecuted if they are seen to have been derelict in their duties. Companies can be put out of business, like Enron,

TABLE 4.1   Issues faced by boards in the 11 case studies

Biocompatibles:	should the company focus on research and development or become a fully integrated business?
CH Jones:	should the company become an integrated fuel management solutions business?
Datrontech:	should the company go into liquidation?
Forth Ports:	should the property business be divested?
Keller:	should the company develop a second leg?
Michael Gerson:	how could the service offering best be diversified?
NFT:	should the business expand outside of the UK?
NovaQuest:	how narrow should the fund mandate be?
Quintiles:	how should the business be organised globally?
U-POL:	how much should be invested in international expansion?
Vantec:	which countries and sectors should be targeted in order to grow the business?

Arthur Andersen, and SwissAir, or reduced to shadows of their former selves, like Royal Ahold. And in financial services in 2008, we saw an example of mass failure by boards right across the financial services sector. Some banks, like Lehman Brothers in the USA and Northern Rock in the UK, collapsed; others required multi-billion dollar bailouts.

Boards, and their actions, are coming under ever-tighter scrutiny from regulators, the press, and the general public. Failures that might once have been concealed are now brought out into the open, with consequent damage to corporate reputations. Think about some of the following issues and how they have damaged companies:

- Mis-selling of services by banks, for example the massive mis-selling of payment protection insurance by UK banks, which has cost them billions of pounds and damaged their relationships with customers.
- Tax avoidance by international firms such as Amazon, which routes income through low-tax domiciles in order to avoid paying tax, and led to them being pilloried in the international press.
- Anti-competitive behavior, such as the persistent rumors of collusion between energy firms.
- Unethical behavior, such as the phone-hacking scandal, which threatened the stability of the entire News International group.
- Corruption, for example, the payment of bribes in countries where the rule of law is weak in order to secure contracts.

In all of these cases, failures of corporate governance have damaged companies, entire sectors, and sometimes entire economies. The responsibilities of boards are heavy indeed. Let us look at one further example, the demise of the Royal Bank of Scotland (RBS). Here is how Iain Martin describes the causes and consequences in his book, *Making It Happen*:

> The collapse of the bank was not just a corporate catastrophe for those who worked at RBS or owned shares in the company. It also presaged a severe and sustained downturn in the economy that has had adverse consequences for the prosperity of Britons. In January 2013, five years into the crisis, the UK economy was still 3.4 percent below its pre-peak slump. The living standards of millions of families have declined ... A member of the management team put it this way. "When you write this book, you must tell everything about Fred [Fred Goodwin, CEO of RBS] because he has so much to answer for ... But there is a lot more to it than that. We on the management team should have stopped him. We failed."[6]

But the members of the management team were not the only ones responsible. Where were RBS's independent directors during the crisis? What were they doing?

Boards and Shareholders

We will discuss shareholders in more detail later in the book, but it is important to remember the relationship between boards and shareholders when considering the work of boards. In particular, as the case studies presented earlier clearly show, that relationship is very different depending on whether the company is publicly or privately owned. Private equity houses are interested in medium- to long-term growth; as long as they can see that the company is sticking to its growth plan, they tend not to interfere in the day-to-day running of the company. Good PE houses encourage the independent directors who represent them to get involved in thinking and decision-making on strategy and other topics of importance, and focus on key issues facing the company. If the company is publicly owned, on the other hand, it can be more difficult to get independent directors sufficiently involved.

Indeed, some commentators argue that there is a general trend for shareholders to become less involved and to delegate key decisions to management. That may sound like a good idea from management's point of view! But in practice, there are important decisions—like those discussed above—where shareholders should, and must, become involved. I have never believed that the total separation of ownership and control is a good thing, and there are times when shareholders must step up and recognize their responsibilities. Yet, some investors—the big investment funds and hedge funds being cases in point—often do not give sufficient priority to having a dialogue with boards and management. They sit silently until something goes wrong and only then raise their voices; too late, after the damage has been done.

Shareholders sometimes put pressure on boards over issues such as the remuneration of directors and dividend policy, but usually again only in the aftermath of some sort of problem or scandal which puts the issue into the public spotlight. The rest of the time they carry on passively. At Keller, we had fourteen significant shareholders and getting a consensus among them was not always straightforward.

Board Composition: Executive and Independent Directors

Boards create competitive advantage by using the collective skills of the board members. Independent directors are part of that team, and they and the executive directors must work closely together in order to succeed. If they are not part of the team, then the CEO and the other executive directors will be seriously constrained in what they do. At NFT the private equity owner, Phoenix, was well represented on a board that worked very solidly together. When the board asked for £20 million in investment, Phoenix was willing to provide it. But if Phoenix had not been part of the team, then that money may not have been forthcoming and NFT would have missed a major chance to invest in and upgrade its service offering.

We saw something similar to this at Keller, where independent directors wanted a strategic review but some of the executives at first rejected the idea. Fortunately, the two sides came together and the conflict did not last. If it had, it could have been very dangerous for Keller to be disunited at a critical moment.

The ingredients for a successful board will vary, sometimes quite widely, from one organization to another. Different jurisdictions and different cultures have a significant impact on the ways that boards function. Many continental European companies have a two-tier board system, usually with a governing board that handles direct management issues and a supervisory board providing oversight. Stakeholders—including employees—are represented on supervisory boards in an attempt to ensure that wider responsibilities are met.

Single-tier unitary boards are the norm in the UK, and these very rarely feature worker representation. Unitary boards are also the prevailing practice in the USA.

The head of the board is the chairman. In the USA it is not uncommon for the roles of chairman and CEO to be held by the same person. Alternatively, a company might have an executive chairman, a full-time member of the executive team. In the UK, on the other hand, the Combined Code demands that the roles be split, and exceptions to this are very rare.

In theory, the independent director should give a greater level of independent oversight. However, as Geoff Beattie and Beverly Behan point out in an article in the *Ivey Business Journal*, that depends on the chairman. An ineffectual independent chairman can be an obstacle, and even in some cases a compliant tool in the hands of the CEO.[7] There are also concerns that some independent chairmen lack sector expertise—this was certainly one of the accusations leveled at the former chairman of the Co-operative Bank, Paul Flowers, in a recent high-profile case—and that as "part-timers" they lack the authority to deal effectively with the CEO. The American solution to the problem is to appoint "lead directors" who lead the independent directors and have the authority to act as a counterweight to the chairman/CEO. But again, as Beattie and Behan point out, whether this works depends on the personalities of those in these roles, and their relationships with each other.

Beneath this level, the number of variations in boards is nearly as great as the number of variations in companies. Each board must develop structures, processes and practice that fit the needs of its business. There is no "one size fits all" solution. The number of directors and their backgrounds varies widely. When we look back over the examples described earlier in this book we can see vast differences. Big companies with global reach, like Keller, required more directors to handle different areas of responsibility. On the other hand, companies such as CH Jones and Michael Gerson had small, tightly focused boards with just a handful of directors to look after their smaller, tightly focused businesses. CH Jones also required fewer directors as it was privately owned and shareholder interests were much simpler. U-POL, owned by private equity, had a different board structure, and publicly owned Forth Ports was different again. Different geographies also have an impact. Quintiles (USA-based), Biocompatibles (UK-based) and Vantec (Japan-based) all had boards that differed in terms of numbers and background of directors. There is no model solution for board composition. Each company must have a board that meets its own needs.

Boards also have their own cultures and ways of doing things, and very often these evolve out of both past practice and the immediate pressures on the company. Morten Huse divides these board cultures into four categories: barbarian boards, aunt boards, clan boards and value-creating boards (see Table 4.2).[8]

Barbarian boards are focused on monitoring and control. They maintain their distance from management, and there are no bonds of trust between them. An *aunt board*, by contrast, is largely passive. It acquiesces in whatever management does, not because it trusts management *per se*, but because it cannot really be bothered to do anything else. Huse comments that people become members of aunt boards largely because they like to see their name in print. They let management get on, and do not rock the boat. *Clan boards* see the company as one big family, one big collegiate enterprise in which all are involved. Board members are more closely involved with management and exercise more direct oversight. Finally, *value-creating boards* are proactive in a way that aunt boards are not, but they strike a balance between service and control. All members of the board are fully engaged, and there is a good relationship and dialogue with management too.

Huse favors the value-creating model as an ideal, and it is clear that aunt boards are something to be avoided. However, it is important for independent

TABLE 4.2   Board typology

Barbarian board	Value-creating board
Rationale from finance	Integrated rationale – strategy
Monitoring board	Participative board
Control tasks	Balances control and service
Distance and hostility	Balances distance and closeness
Independent – external	Balances independence and interdependence
Do not trust the management	Both integrity and competence-based trust
Is not trusted by the management	
Aunt board	**Clan board**
Rationale from law	Rationale from sociology
Passive board	Collegial board
Formal tasks	Service tasks
Dependent – dominated by management	Closeness
No competence-based trust – no expectations	Interdependence
	Trust by the management

Source: Morten Huse, *Boards, Governance and Value Creation*, Cambridge: Cambridge University Press, 2007, p. 310

directors to observe the line that separates them from the executives and not become too involved in day-to-day management. Ensuring that the right board culture is created is part of the role of the chairman, but all board members have a role to play.

What Do Boards Do, and How Do They Do It?

"Being on a board today isn't for the faint of heart," wrote John R. Engen in an article for *Corporate Board Member*, "and it's certainly not for those lacking energy or inclined to live in the past."[9] It is generally agreed that the role of the board is becoming more complex. Boards are under greater scrutiny than ever before. Since 2008, the regulatory environment in most developed economies has become even more complex. Globalization, technological developments, and the increasing size of companies is complicating the task too. The demand for more, and more effective, corporate governance, has risen steadily (see Table 4.3).

TABLE 4.3   Board effectiveness, dynamics, and value creation

	Decision-oriented (practice and codes)	Process-oriented (observed at TINE Corporation, Norway)
Board effectiveness		
Criteria for board effectiveness – main board tasks	Controlling managerial opportunism and ratification of decisions	Embedding and participation in strategic decision-making
Effective boardroom culture	Independence	Criticality
		Creativity
		Cohesiveness
		Openness and generosity
		Preparedness and involvement
Board dynamics		
Decision-making speed	Fast	Slow
Length of meetings	Short	Long
Time spent by board members	Little	Much
Director number	Small	Large
Director background	Homogeneous	Heterogeneous
Director personality types	Crusaders / barbarians	Strategists
Board-management relations	Distance	Closeness
Board-management relations	Distrust	Trust
Boardroom norms influence	From finance	From leadership
Board leadership	Decision-maker and chairperson	Coach and leader
Decision-making	Information and voting	Communication and negotiations
Dynamics	Vicious circles	Virtuous circles
Results and value creation		
Decision outcome	Pre-determined	Open
Decision consequences and ownership interests	Short-term	Long-term
Value creation definition	Narrow	Comprehensive

Source: Morten Huse, *Boards, Governance and Value Creation*, Cambridge: Cambridge University Press, 2007, p. 234

Responsibility for corporate governance rests squarely on the shoulders of the board. Board members must realize this, and must not try to duck out of that responsibility. Directors are responsible—and in many jurisdictions this means personal, legal and financial responsibility—for the operations of the company. Some of the most important tasks of the board are:

- *Strategy*. The board is responsible for overseeing and directing the activities of the business. Here again there are differences depending on where one operates. In the USA, the more usual practice has been for management to take the lead role in defining the company strategy. The board then assesses the strategy's soundness and either rejects or approves it. In the UK, it is more common for boards to become directly involved in strategy, as they did at Forth Ports, Biocompatibles and NFT. Either way, it is not enough for a few directors to consider strategy and the rest to sit by passively. The entire board needs to become involved in both understanding the strategy that is being adopted and then monitoring the strategy over time to ensure that it is being executed correctly.
- *Succession*. The board appoints the senior team, which is responsible for executing the strategy. Getting the right people into top executive posts is another critical part of the board's role, and there are enormous consequences for getting it wrong. Only a handful of companies have maintained top quartile performance for more than a decade. One common feature of firms that have done so is that they have managed succession well. CEO turnover rates are increasing as the job becomes harder. My own view is that, if possible, it is often best to develop and promote CEOs from within, but this is a time-consuming process and candidates need lengthy mentoring and grooming before they are ready to step up. And when it does become necessary to recruit from outside, great care must be taken to get the right person who can fit in quickly and develop an understanding of the company, its business, its employees, its culture, and its technology. This, too, is not a simple or quick process.

Hiring the wrong people can be disastrous, as I saw at NFC, but a good appointment is a great source of value and competitive advantage. Boards need to think about succession, especially to the key roles of CEO and chairman, well in advance so that they can make informed decisions and achieve the best fit between person and role. This was very well illustrated at Forth Ports, where the chairman, Chris Collins, gave us two years' notice that he intended to step down. As John Engen pointed out in his article, most companies tend to leave succession until the last minute, and then scramble to get the right person.

• *Audit and compliance*. The board must ensure that the company is fulfilling its legal and financial responsibilities. This includes, of course, the auditing of financial accounts, but also extends to areas such as legal compliance, ethics, and health and safety. Again, the exact focus depends on the company and its business. At Keller, workplace health and safety was a major concern. At Biocompatibles, the emphasis shifted to areas such as medical ethics and the safety of the medical devices we made.

• *Remuneration and reward*. People go to work for a complex variety of reasons, but money is still one of the key motivators. Providing people with the right level of reward that compensates them fairly for the work they have done and motivates them to carry on, while at the same time protecting the company's financial interests, is a key part of the board's task. The resources available to the board to remunerate depend on the ownership structure: if the company is owned by a private equity house, then the money comes from them, or if it is publicly owned then the money comes from shareholders. If the company is experiencing financial constraints, then the board's ability in this area may be severely limited.

• *Risk management*. Everything that a company does entails risk, but what levels of risk are acceptable? How can risks best be laid off? When considering all of the issues above, the board needs to think about the potential risks, analyze the presence of risk and then make informed decisions. Here the need for different points of view comes into play, as boards need to consider many options before making the right choice. "The collective will of the board allowed us to manage our way through three quite major situations," says Charles Hammond, CEO of Forth Ports.

• *Communication*. "A lot of this business is about managing shareholder expectations," says Crispin Simon, CEO of Biocompatibles. Boards need to communicate with stakeholders and explain what they are doing. Strategy has to be explained, and shareholders also want to know about levels of risk, remuneration, compliance, and so on so that they can assess their own risk. Boards need to explain their actions, clearly and in a transparent manner. According to the Eversheds Board Report of 2013: "The relationship between the board and its shareholders is changing with increasing dialogue between them … Shareholder engagement is having an impact on board strategy and remuneration."[10]

One of the rising issues at the moment is social media, which poses a risk to companies but can also in the right hands be a potent communications tool. A study by Korn/Ferry International in 2013 found that three-quarters of directors believed that social media will have a major impact on their roles, yet less than a quarter felt that they understood social media well enough to give advice and oversight on the issue.[11] It can be hypothesized that this is an age issue and that as a younger generation of directors, more fluent in social media, arrive in boardrooms this problem will lessen. But that day is still some way off, and it is incumbent on directors to get to grips with social media and learn how to use it.

These are some of the tasks that boards face, but how do they carry them out? One answer is to set up committees (of which more below), and these do play a valuable and important role, but they are not the sole answer. To repeat what I said earlier, board members must work together as a team. In today's tough business environment, companies must use every available resource to the fullest. Boards are—or should be—composed of men and women with a great range and depth of experience and wisdom. That experience and wisdom needs to be brought out into the open through discussions and conversations that involve everyone. There is sometimes a tendency to leave everything to the CEO, who has these conversations with the directors on a one-to-one basis, but that is not good enough.

Chris Collins, my first chairman at Forth Ports, was in this respect a model chairman. He ensured that the board worked together as a team. Unlike some chairmen, he never imposed his own view on the board. Instead, at board meetings he made certain that every member spoke and made his or her views known. Out of the distillation of all those views and ideas, our strategy emerged. At NFT, for example, we brought in outside experts such as Lawrence Christensen (a very experienced supply chain director of retail companies) to provide us with fresh ideas. The successful strategies developed at both of those firms could not and would not have emerged without those discussions and exchanges.

And those discussions and exchanges in turn were only possible because we had a good set of relationships within these boards and were able to talk freely and frankly with each other. As I said of Forth Ports, there was a long-standing debate about how best to manage our property arm. Some of us took one view, others took another. In another board, this might have caused dissension and rifts. At Forth Ports, the difference of views became a subject for healthy debate. Whatever strategy we chose in the end had been thoroughly and completely discussed.

"Boards that work have broken boardroom norms and protocols," says Ram Charan. "They engage in an exciting exchange of ideas on the topics that matter most to the business. Directors ask incisive questions, constructively challenge management's assumptions and express honest opinions. Management shares information freely."[12] Alfred P. Sloan, the legendary chairman of General Motors, once asked his directors whether they were all agreed on a certain course of action. When all indicated that they were, he suggested that they go away and think of some reasons to disagree, so that at the next board meeting they could have a proper discussion of the plan. Sloan's point was that conformity is not a good thing. Board members must feel free to discuss their differences of opinion, albeit in a civilized and respectful way.

It also needs to be recognized that the role of the board is not limited to board meetings. Executive directors, of course, have their on-going "day jobs," but the role of the independent director is a continuous one as well. Independent directors cannot do their job by reading the board papers and turning up at meetings. They need to get involved with the company. They need to get to know the management, the market, the key advisors, analysts, and above all the investors. For example, at Quintiles, I spent a considerable amount of time traveling around the various geographies where we worked, to meet staff and understand their different business issues. At Keller, there were two overseas board visits every year.

Boards also need to be clear about their purpose and how they will achieve it. "The starting place in running an effective board is no different than running a good business—it begins with a plan," say Geoff Beattie and Beverly Behan. "And most boards don't have one. They largely react to management's priorities or whatever seems to be the 'pressing issue of the day'—be that a regulatory matter, a shortfall in profitability, etc. Arrows are shot, targets are painted around them and victory is declared."[13] Above, I cited Morten Huse's work on board cultures. Boards must seek to develop a forward-looking, proactive, value-creating culture, built around a plan.

Board Committees

What committees a board should have will depend on the nature of its business, the size of the business and the board (a board with only half a dozen members, or less, can end up with committees all composed of the same members), and the key risks and pressures that the business faces. As well as formal standing committees there are also temporary working groups to consider issues of a transient nature.

The two most high-profile committees in most companies—and which are present in almost every company—are the remuneration committee and the audit committee. Remuneration committees, or Remcos, are often in the spotlight when the media decides to take an interest in executive pay, particularly when a chief executive or board are awarded what seem to be excessively large pay rises or bonuses (and especially when the companies they run are not actually doing very well). Remuneration committees were created mainly to avoid situations whereby directors set their own salaries and bonuses, and were intended to bring a measure of objectivity to the compensation-setting process. Remcos composed of independent directors also allow shareholders to have direct input into levels of executive compensation.

Remcos primarily do two things: they determine overall policy on executive compensation, and they review compensation arrangements on a regular basis. (The illustration below, from KPMG's guidance notes for Remcos, shows how these tasks break down in more detail see Table 4.4.) The chair of the remuneration committee reports to the chairman and works closely with him or her, and with the CEO and HR director, to ensure that the remuneration policy is the right one for the circumstances. Executive compensation needs to be fair and transparent: executives should be rewarded for their achievements, but shareholders also need to be treated fairly as it is in effect their money which is being paid out to the executives.

Remuneration committees function well so long as the committees keep these principles of fairness and transparency in mind. Being a member or chairman of a remuneration committee is in fact a difficult and very responsible job, and it can involve making tough decisions that will annoy members of the executive team.

At Keller, the remuneration company was involved in two difficult decisions. One concerned whether to pay a bonus to executives at a time when the company financially constrained. The second concerned pay in the company's US subsidiary, where it was realized that senior executives were earning rather more than those in the UK and elsewhere. This was a reflection of local market conditions; Keller had expanded in the USA through acquisition, and had honored the previous contracts of its executives, which awarded a lower basic salary but the opportunity to receive high bonuses depending on the performance of the subsidiary.

The other important committee is the audit committee, which is responsible for overseeing the financial controls of the company. Ernst and Young recommends that audit committees should have at least three independent directors as members (two in the case of smaller companies) in order to ensure truly

TABLE 4.4 Duties of the remuneration committee

1. The Committee shall:

1.1   determine and agree with the board the framework or broad policy for the remuneration of the company's Chief Executive, Chairman, the executive directors, the company secretary and such members of the executive management as it is designated to consider. The remuneration of non-executive directors shall be a matter for the Chairman and the executive members of the board. No director or manager shall be involved in any decision as to their own remuneration;

1.2   in determining such policy, take into account all factors which it deems necessary. The objective of such policy shall be to ensure that members of the executive management of the company are provided with appropriate incentives to encourage enhanced performance and are, in a fair and responsible manner, rewarded for their individual contributions to the success of the company;

1.3   review the ongoing appropriateness and relevance of the remuneration policy;

1.4   approve the design of and determine targets for, any performance related pay schemes operated by the company and approve the total annual payments made under such schemes;

1.5   review the design of all share incentive plans for approval by the board and shareholders. For any such plans, determine each year whether awards will be made, and if so, the overall amount of such awards, the individual awards to executive directors and to other senior executives and the performance targets to be used;

1.6   determine the policy for, and scope for, pension arrangements for each executive director and other senior executives;

1.7   ensure the contractual terms on termination, and any payments made, are fair to the individual, and the company, that failure is not rewarded and that the duty to mitigate loss is fully recognised;

1.8   within the terms of the agreed policy and in consultation with the Chairman and / or Chief Executive as appropriate, determine the total individual remuneration package of each executive director and other senior executives including bonuses, incentive payments and share options or other share awards;

1.9   in determining such packages and arrangements, give due regard to any relevant legal requirements, the provisions and recommendations in the Combined Code and the UK Listing Authority's Listing Rules and associated guidance;

1.10   review and note annually the remuneration trends across the company or group;

1.11   oversee any major changes in employee benefits structures throughout the company or group;

1.12   agree the policy for authorising claims for the expenses from the Chief Executive or Chairman;

1.13   ensure that all provisions regarding disclosure of remuneration including pensions, as set out in the Directors Remuneration Report Regulations 2002 and the Combined Code are fulfilled; and

1.14   be exclusively responsible for establishing the selection criteria, selecting, appointing and setting the terms of reference for any remuneration consultants who advise the committee and to obtain reliable, up-to-date information about remuneration in other companies. The committee shall have full authority to commission any reports or surveys which it deems necessary to help it fulfil its obligations.

TABLE 4.4   Continued

2. Reporting Responsibilities

2.1   The Committee Chairman shall report formally to the board on its proceeding after each meeting on all matters within its duties.

2.2   The Committee shall make whatever recommendations to the board it deems appropriate on any area within its remit where action or improvement is needed.

2.3   The Committee shall produce an annual report of the company's remuneration policy and practices which will form part of the company's annual report and ensure each year that it is put to shareholders for approval at the AGM.

3. Other

3.1   The Committee shall, at least once a year, review its own performance constitution and terms of reference to ensure it is operating at maximum effectiveness and recommend any changes it considers necessary to the board for approval.

4. Authority

4.1   The Committee is authorised by the board to seek any information it requires from any employee of the company in order to perform its duties.

4.2   In connection with its duties the Committee is authorised by the board to obtain, at the company's expense, any outside legal or other professional advice.

Source: Report of the Remuneration Committee Institute, sponsored by KPMG

objective scrutiny. EY's guidance note lists the duties of the audit committee as including:

- Monitoring the integrity of financial statements and any formal announcements relating to the company's financial performance.
- Reviewing internal financial controls and the company's internal control and risk management systems.
- Monitoring and reviewing the effectiveness of the company's internal audit function.
- Recommending the appointment of an external auditor and approving the terms of engagement of the auditor.
- Reviewing and monitoring the external auditor's independence and objectivity.
- Reporting to the board any matters concerning the above points where action or improvement is needed.

Membership of the audit committee is definitely not a sinecure. The audit committee is directly responsible for ensuring the financial health of the company and the safety of its financial assets. Audit committee members need to work as a team. They need to understand the firm and its operating environment, the key issues confronting the sector and the strategic response taken by the business. They should, of course, have financial expertise; one of the charges leveled at Enron's audit committee was that its members lacked the skills to understand the data presented to them. They should be able to manage the relationship between the external auditor and the rest of the board. Finally, they should be prepared to commit substantial amounts of time to the tasks listed above, and be prepared to take on other tasks as well. For example, at Quintiles we were faced with a sudden set of very disappointing trading results, which came as a surprise to the board and caused a reduction in share price (Quintiles was listed on the NASDAQ at the time). As chairman of the audit committee, I was then tasked with undertaking a detailed enquiry into the financial control of the company.

Other important committees include the nomination committee, the health and safety committee, and the quality committee. The exact work of these depends on the nature of the company and its business. The nomination committee exists to find candidates for key posts, such as the chairman and chief executive. At Keller and again at Forth Ports, when the chairmen stepped down, it was up to the nomination committee to come up with a shortlist of candidates to replace them.

Health and safety committees sometimes deal with fairly mundane matters relating to workplace environment, but where the company works in high-risk environments its work becomes much more important. At Keller, we had several fatalities in the workplace, which put health and safety issues in the spotlight. It was up to the health and safety committee to identify the key faults and problems that needed solving, and to recommend a comprehensive health and safety policy that would prevent similar accidents in future. Similarly, the quality committee's work takes on new importance if there are high levels of risk. At Biocompatibles, the quality committee was directly involved in the setting up of clinical trials and monitored their progress throughout.

Board Evaluation

As well as overseeing the company, boards also need to scrutinize and examine themselves. This process, known as board evaluation, is something that every company needs to do on a regular basis.

Board evaluation used to be a largely informal matter, in which the chairman would have a series of one-to-one conversations with other board members and ask them whether they thought the board was running okay. If they all did, no further action was taken; if there were issues, the chairman would try to deal with them.[14] This kind of informal monitoring is actually very useful.

When I took over as chairman of Biocompatibles, one of the first things I did was to sit down with each board member individually and, in effect, gauge the temperature of the boardroom. I found this a valuable exercise, which helped me to understand the board and its dynamics.

However, there is now a growing trend towards more formal evaluation of boards carried out by external parties, usually consultants. Headhunting firms such as Hanson Green often provide this service. In the UK it is now a requirement for public companies to have an external board evaluation carried out every three years. At Keller, we used Spencer Stuart to conduct a board evaluation (a list of the issues covered in the evaluation is shown in the display box below, and is a very good example of an evaluation checklist see Table 4.5). Although different companies work in different ways, the usual procedure is for a consultant to interview each member of the board individually. Opinions are then collated and provided, on an anonymous basis, to the chairman in the form of a report. The process usually takes from four to six weeks.

The quality of the evaluation depends crucially on the quality of the consultant. I was involved with one board where the consultant was, I fear, rather useless. He was not very good at asking questions or listening, and he had already formed an opinion before he began the evaluation process. On the other hand, good consultants are able to tease out deep, underlying issues and bring them to the surface. At Keller, for example, the evaluation made us realize that we needed to think seriously about succession to the post of chairman. The matter had never been openly discussed; but during the evaluation, everyone raised this as an issue.

Good evaluation also serves as a way of sharing best practice. Consultants who are experienced at board evaluation will make recommendations based on what they have seen elsewhere. For example, they may advise on new ways of thinking about strategy, or suggest methods for handling management succession, based on their observations. This kind of advice can be very valuable. Once again, though, everything depends on the quality of the consultant and my advice is: choose your consultant wisely.

What Can Go Wrong

The worst things that can happen to a board are either a breakdown in relationships that leads to the board fragmenting into fractions, or a descent into collective complacency and inaction, the "aunt board" scenario described by Morten Huse. Either can be equally disastrous, leading to the board taking its eye off the ball and making mistakes.

TABLE 4.5 Board evaluation: topic guide

1. Overall Impression of the Board
  – Dynamics of the board
  – Culture and climate in the boardroom
  – Sense of teamwork
  – Quality of discussion / balance of debate

2. Organisation of the Board
  – Agendas, and formation of agendas; coverage of the right topics
  – Reporting, including of board committees
  – Meeting frequency and length
  – Formal processes and duties
  – Informal processes (including board dinners)
  – Strategy sessions
  – Information and support materials; company secretariat and support

3. Committee Organisation: Audit, Remuneration, Health, Safety & Environment, Nomination
  – Agendas
  – Meeting frequency and length
  – Membership, internal attendees and adviser attendees
  – Information and support materials
  – Topics for the board versus topics for the committees

4. Board Composition
  – Size
  – Balance (including number of executives)
  – Skill sets
  – Independence
  – Rotation

5. Board Involvement and Engagement
  – Directors' knowledge of the business
  – Relationships with management
  – Contact outside the boardroom
  – Strategy development
  – Induction and training for new directors

6. Communication with Shareholders/Stakeholders
  – Shareholder messages
  – Analyst meetings and reports
  – AGM
  – Chairman's role with shareholders/stakeholders
  – Other Directors' role with shareholders/stakeholders

7. Looking Forward
  – Succession planning (Executive and Independent)
  – Directors' development needs

(Continued)

Table 4.5   Continued

8. Overall Board Effectiveness
- Progress since last board evaluation
- Fulfilment of fiduciary duties
- Ethics, Corporate Social Responsibility and Environment
- Compliance with UK Corporate Governance Code
- Expectations placed on directors including their responsibilities for governance and remuneration
- Support to the business
- Checks and balances
- Short- and long-term health of the business

9. Colleagues
- Chairman
- Senior Independent Director
- Chairmen
- Independent Directors
- Executive Directors

Failures of this sort are usually the result of some sort of underlying tension or pressure. Breakdowns in relationships often stem from tensions between members of the board. Jay Lorsch in *The Future of Boards* describes six tensions and how they arise:

1. Social cohesion tension. All boards need some social cohesion to enable them to work together, but too much is definitely a bad thing. Social cohesion can pressure people into conforming with the majority point of view. Conformity itself is held to be a good thing, "in the best interests of the team." Some non-conformity, a degree of irritant, is still required.

2. Dissension tension. On the other side of the coin, if there is too much dissension, the board can disintegrate into infighting and chaos.

3. Psychological safety tension. According to Jay Lorsch: "This is the shared belief that the group is a safe place for risk-taking, sharing unpopular ideas, and admitting errors. However, too much safety creates unhealthy 'social loafing'."[15] Certainly boards should be encouraged towards creative thinking, but an element of realism is needed too. Board members need to remember that actions are not free of consequences. Too much safety, says Lorsch, and there is a tendency to forget the need for accountability.

4. Collectivist-feelings tension. Again to quote Lorsch: "It is critical to create a balance between operating and feeling a group and still valuing individual contributions."[16]

5. Diversity of thought tension. Boards need diversity in order to help them overcome the tendency towards excessive social cohesion. As I noted when discussing Quintiles, it can be of real benefit for a board to have people from

different background offering different points of view. However, diversity cannot get in the way of decision-making. There must be a mechanism for reconciling different points of view and achieving a rational consensus.

6. Strong leader tension. The board is a team, and every member of the team must be encouraged to contribute. Encouraging people to speak up and make contributions is one of the roles of the chairman. However, this can be difficult for some of the executive directors. It is hard for an operations director to speak freely in front of the CEO—especially if his honest view clashes with that of his boss. Leaders, especially CEOs, need to sublimate their own egos to a degree.

Many, if not all, of these tensions are present, or potentially present, in most board relationships and need to be managed. There is no perfect solution, and the balance will change depending once again on the composition of the board and the pressures the business faces. Board members need to manage a series of trade-offs in order to keep the right balance in all six cases. If they fail, then as Lorsch explains, the board runs the risk of one or more of the following pathologies manifesting itself:

1. *excessive conformity*, or groupthink.
2. *negative group conflict*, or factionalism based on differences either in basic values and beliefs, or in personalities.
3. *politicking*, or people manipulating others in order to acquire more personal power. This can be a defensive mechanism if the power-seekers perceive that their own position is under threat.
4. *habitual routines*, or "that's the way we do things around here." People become ingrained in certain practices and actions, and cannot or will not change, even if a threat emerges. A certain amount of this pathology was on view at Michael Gerson.
5. *shared information bias*, or "we know what we need to know." This pathology concentrates on knowledge that is already known and shared among the group, and does not seek to look any further and find out if anyone else has any further information to bring to the table.
6. *pluralistic ignorance*, where people have important opinions and views but will not voice them because they fear to be seen differing from their colleagues. The "ignorance" results once again from a failure to share knowledge.
7. *social loafing*, where people work less hard when part of a team than when on their own. This phenomenon was first noticed in 1910 when a sociologist found that teams of men engaged in a tug of war would, as individuals,

pull less hard than if left to pull the rope on their own. On boards, this manifests itself in a "why should I get involved? Someone else will do it" mentality.

8. *group polarization*, which in some ways is the opposite of groupthink. In group polarization, members of the group encourage each other towards more extreme thinking. Those members who have doubts are encouraged to set them to one side. The collective decision, which is finally reached, is thus more risky than any of the group's members would have made if left on their own.

When boards fail, corporate governance breaks down and the company is at risk. I saw this happen at first hand at Datrontech, where the company ultimately ran out of money. At that point, the only responsible course of action was to wind up the company. That, if you like, was good corporate governance. On the other hand, the board also has to bear a share of responsibility for the mistakes of the previous months and years, which had put the company in this position. The decisions may have been taken by the executives, but it was up to the board to scrutinize those decisions and call the executives to account.

Best Practice for Boards

In conclusion, let me set out six rules that I believe are essential to follow if boards are to function effectively.

Boards must be of a suitable size and diversity. Asking how large a board should be is a bit like asking how long is a piece of string, but there are some rules to follow. Firstly, the board should not be too large; it needs enough members to cover all the tasks that the board faces, but there should not be any supernumeraries. Secondly, there needs to be a balance of executive and independent directors. Executive directors need the advice, contacts, scrutiny, and questions that independent directors bring, but they should not feel swamped by these. The right number of directors to make a functioning team should be the basic rule of thumb.

On diversity, the issue is much more clear-cut. Boards should be diverse. This is partly to avoid the drift towards groupthink and conformity, but it is also a matter of common sense. Peter Waine, an experienced headhunter who has advised on the recruitment of many independent directors over the years, maintains that "three-quarters of the useful experience of a good independent director is generalist skills; sector experience is only the bottom quarter."

At Quintiles, Keller, Biocompatibles and Forth Ports, in particular, I saw how a diverse board, a "ministry of all the talents," can work together in a much more creative and exciting fashion to create and deliver a sound strategy. Diversity is essential.

Board members must contribute to every aspect of the board's work. Board members should be energetic, inquisitive and attentive. They should be prepared to devote sufficient time to carrying out their duties, not just attending board meetings. They should be well informed about developments in their sector. They should participate fully in all discussions, expressing their views in a constructive way. Independent directors should, as Lawrence Christensen says, "be a guiding hand to develop the board to realize its full potential." Of course, their ability to contribute depends on the culture of the board itself and whether the executive and independent directors work well together. "It is easy for executives to keep non-executives in the dark, if they want to," says Peter Waine of Hanson Green. "It is up to the chairman to create a climate where everyone can make a contribution."

Boards must have strong leadership. In the UK, that means a strong independent chairman who is both an able diplomat and a superb organizer. He or she should also know the business very thoroughly. In the UK at the moment there is some discussion as to whether the chairman should be a sector specialist, especially in very technical and complex industries, such as banking. There are arguments both ways, but I would add that I chaired Biocompatibles, an extremely specialized company in a highly technical sector, and I did not find my own background to be any great hindrance. What mattered was my ability to learn quickly what the company was and how it worked. Crispin Simon, CEO at Biocompatibles, agrees. "I take the view that the chairman should be more detached and work to bring out other people's views rather than expressing their own," he says. "You could even argue that sector experience is a disadvantage, because you cannot help yourself from having views." Lawrence Christensen also cautions that "the chairman should not get too close to the chief executive."

Boards must have effective and functioning committees. Committees take the strain off the main board by dealing with specialized issues such as audit, remuneration, quality, safety, and so on. Their members must have at least a certain level of technical expertise in their particular subject; for example, it is mandatory that the chairman of the audit committee should be a qualified accountant.

Directors must be clear about their roles. Board members need to be clear about their individual roles and responsibilities. They need to be aware of the areas of expertise that they bring to the board, but also of the areas that others bring. Importantly, too, independent directors need to be aware of the roles and responsibilities of executive directors. I will say more later about the distinction between them.

The board should evaluate its own performance. Evaluation of the board as a whole and its individual members should be undertaken on a regular basis using individual consultants, and feedback should be used to improve performance. In the past this has been a contentious issue, and a number of critics have attacked board evaluation as being effectively a box-ticking exercise, which resulted in little real change. The competence of some of the external consultants has also been questioned. Fortunately, on this last issue there has been some progress and standards for board evaluation consultants are being introduced in the UK.

Summary

Boards are powerful institutions, but they can be hampered or hindered quite easily if their members do not work together constructively. Independent directors play a very important role in ensuring that boards function effectively.

I mentioned above that the composition of a board is in part dependent on its ownership structure. Different kinds of owners, public and private, will have different agendas, and this can and very often does affect both the number of board members and the nature and background experience of directors, especially independent directors. With that in mind, let us now turn to look at ownership.

Ownership

> Small opportunities are often the beginning of great enterprises.
>
> — Demosthenes

The ownership structure of a business has a very strong effect on how the business is run. That might sound like a truism, but this simple statement is just the tip of the iceberg. Ownership structures and the relations between the owners and managers of a business are an increasingly complex subject, governed by a mass of regulations and encompassing a wide range of complex technical and cultural issues.

Standing squarely between owners and managers—and, sometimes, caught between their competing interests—are the independent directors. Their task is both to ensure that the business is run as effectively and efficiently as possible, and to represent the views of the owners to the rest of the board, including the executive directors. So long as the owners and the executive team agree on the future direction of the company, that task is a fairly smooth one. When conflicts occur, however, then the task becomes very hard indeed.

There are many different types of business owner. Writers on this subject usually distinguish between public ownership and private ownership, but that distinction is only the beginning. Publicly owned companies nearly always have a significant number of investors holding shares; at Keller, for example, we had fourteen major shareholders and many smaller ones. They can include individuals (ranging from small investors with a few hundred shares to super-rich individuals with tens of millions invested), insurance companies, pension funds, investment funds, banks, sovereign wealth funds, governments, and other types of investors. "Private ownership" is likewise a catch-all term that can include ownership by a person or family, employees (such as was the case at National Freight Corporation), another company, a private equity house, a hedge fund, a sovereign wealth fund, a government, or any combination of these.

Ownership also changes, and these days it changes increasingly often. Yet when companies change from one type of ownership—from private to public, for example, or from family ownership to private equity ownership—they also have to change themselves. Governance structures must change. The size and shape of management teams must usually change. And, most importantly, cultures must change. I have seen at first hand how hard it is for companies such as Datrontech, Michael Gerson, Quintiles, Vantec and NFT to change cultures when they transitioned from one ownership type to another.

Each of the eleven companies profiled earlier has, or had, a different ownership structure see table 4.6. In some cases the differences were slight; in others they were vast. Even those companies with similar-looking profiles were in fact very different. NFT and Vantec, for example, were both spin-offs from parent companies financed by private equity, but there the similarity ends. The strategic aims, the cultures and the relationships between owners and executives were very different.

TABLE 4.6   Ownership structures for the 11 case studies

Biocompatibles:	publicly owned and quoted on the London Stock Market, then sold to another publicly quoted company, BTG plc.
CH Jones:	privately owned by the founding entrepreneur and partners, then sold to a US private equity fund.
Datrontech:	publicly quoted on the London Stock Market, but the two founding entrepreneurs who had sold the company remained on the board.
Forth Ports:	publicly owned (formerly government owned), then sold to a private equity infrastructure fund.
Keller:	publicly owned.
Michael Gerson:	family owned, MBO backed by the Bank of Scotland; founding entrepreneur was a board member.
NFT:	spinoff from Northern Foods plc, MBO backed by Phoenix Equity a private equity house.
NovaQuest:	spin-off from Quintiles, backed by a consortium of private equity houses including TPG, Bain Capital, 3i and Temesek.
Quintiles:	publicly owned quoted, on the NASDAQ exchange in the USA, then taken private by the founder with private equity backing, then taken public again, this time on the NY Stock Exchange.
U-POL:	family owned, then MBO backed by Graphite Capital, a private equity house.
Vantec:	spin-off from Japanese automotive company Nissan, backed by a private equity consortium of PPM Ventures and 3i, then sold to the investment arm of the Japanese bank Mizuho, then floated on the Nikkei exchange.

What Do Owners Want?

When dealing with the owners of businesses, independent directors face two key variables. Firstly, *how aware are the owners of what is happening in the business?* Some institutional investors barely seem to notice what is happening in the businesses in which they own shares. This is not surprising. Fund managers look after huge portfolios of investments, and literally do not have the time to familiarize themselves with every aspect of those portfolios. So long as the companies in which they have invested deliver the expected results, they tend not to break the surface. Individual investors sometimes have little knowledge of the true state of affairs of the business, not unless they have time to do a great deal of research, which many don't. Some private equity houses are famous, or infamous, for buying companies and then leaving them alone, to sink or swim on their own. On the other hand, some PE houses and other investors in public companies pay close attention to the businesses in which they have invested, and monitor events on a regular basis. This was certainly the case at U-POL, NFT, and Quintiles.

Whatever the case, independent directors serve as the link between owners and executives. Part of their job is to represent the interests of the former to the latter. If the owners are aware of what is going on in the company and have a clear idea of what it does and how it works, then this task becomes easier. If the owners know little about the business and, indeed, do not appear to want to be much involved with the business, then the task becomes much harder. It can be tempting for the independent director to simply throw in with the executives, "go native" and acquiesce to whatever management decides to do. This is the point at which it becomes very important for the independent director to remember that he or she really is *independent*, and has a duty of care towards the company and its shareholders, regardless of the attitudes of the latter.

Secondly, *how far do the owners want to be involved in the business?* This is a contentious issue. There is a school of thought, especially prevalent in the USA, which argues for the separation of ownership and control; that is, owners should step back from the business and let professional managers get on and do their jobs without interference. This opinion, which goes back to 1932 and the publication of *The Modern Corporation and Private Property* by the American scholars, Adolph Berle and Gardiner Means, has contributed to the view that independent directors should confine themselves to auditing and compliance issues rather than getting involved in strategic decision-making.[17]

It is important to make some distinction between owners and managers. Richard Daw of Phoenix Equity Partners, the owners of NFT, and himself an independent director of NFT, makes it clear that it is not his job to run the business. "At Phoenix we are very clear about where the boundary is from an operational perspective. We monitor whether the executive team appointed by the board is doing a good job of running the business, and whether that executive team is the right team to deliver on the strategic plan." There are, he believes, real dangers in crossing that boundary. Firstly, Phoenix is not an expert in the chilled-food distribution business, not in the way the executive team are. "We don't have the capability to have a view on day-to-day issues," he says.

Secondly, he believes that if the independent directors get too close to the executives, this can lead to a blurring of responsibilities. If independent directors start getting involved in operational management, then where does authority lie? Who makes the decisions? Richard thinks that in some cases the issues falls between two stools, everyone thinking that they are someone else's responsibility, and in the end decisions do not get made at all. Lawrence Christensen, himself an experienced independent director, agrees but makes the point that the line between executive and independent directors is different in different cases. In private equity-owned companies independent directors can end up being more hands-on than in publicly owned companies.

At an operational level, then, it is good to have a separation. At the strategic level, however, the separation of ownership and control makes less sense. As discussed elsewhere in this book, the best strategies are made when the executive and independent directors work together as a team. Crucial to the process is knowing the answer to this question: what do the owners want? Are they primarily interested in income, profits from privately owned companies or dividends from public ones? Or are they primarily interested in growth? And if so, what sort of growth? Turnover? Market share? Share price, if it is a public company? What is their own strategic horizon? Are they interested in long-term ownership, or do they have an exit in mind? It is difficult, if not impossible, to develop an appropriate strategy unless the answers to these questions are known.

Independent directors are once again the conduit between the owners and the board. They have a responsibility to help create strategy and then monitor its implementation, in part because they have a responsibility to see that the company is well governed, and in part because they have a responsibility to the owners to see that their assets are protected. Again, it does not really matter whether the shareholders are closely engaged or not. If the company embarks on the wrong strategy, and that strategy fails, then the owners will lose their assets, just as they did at Lehman Brothers, Royal Bank of Scotland, and so many other failed companies. One of the duties of independent directors is to protect the owners and prevent this sort of disaster from happening.

Public Ownership

As I said earlier, the term public ownership can refer to a wide variety of different kinds of owners, ranging from small individuals to very large institutional investors. It is important to know what each type of investor wants and, especially, what their time horizons are. Some pension funds and insurance companies tend to be biased in their investment portfolios towards income and look for investments with high earnings per share, which can make them less interested in investing in the company's longer-term future. Some specialist investment funds, however, are focused on long-term asset growth and the same is probably true of sovereign wealth funds. Individual investors, depending on their investment portfolio, may look for either income or growth, or both.

Publicly owned companies have been around for a long time. The first British example was the Merchant Adventurers, founded in 1553 in order to develop a trade route between England and Asia; other types of public companies had been founded in France and Italy at least a century earlier. The modern form, the limited liability public company, was established in British law in 1856 and the model quickly spread to the USA and elsewhere. It is generally assumed under this model that the shareholders are the owners of the company, though some analysts have questioned whether ownership of share capital amounts to ownership of the company and its assets.

Right from the beginning, it was clear that this business model contained the potential for conflict. Both the merchants and sea captains of the sixteenth century and the owners and executives of today have different views of what the business should do. What strategy should be pursued, and at what speed? What risks should be taken? How should the rewards be divided?

Berle and Means attempted to resolve this conflict by taking owners out of the equation, but this creates other problems. Assuming owners do step back and let the managers take over, who monitors the managers to ensure they are doing their jobs properly, and not either squandering or embezzling the company's assets? The wave of corporate governance failures and ensuing bankruptcies at the beginning of the twenty-first century—Enron, WorldCom, Global Crossing, Royal Ahold, Parmalat and others—brought this issue into sharp focus. There have been a series of national and international initiatives meant to bring about better corporate governance. As a World Bank report put it, corporate governance is becoming "one of the pillars of the post-Cold War economic architecture."[18]

Corporate governance

What is corporate governance? Again, there is a wide range of literature on this subject, and I recommend Morten Huse, *Boards, Governance and Value Creation* as a starting point.[19] For our purposes here, corporate governance is essentially concerned with:

- Board structure and effectiveness
- Control and efficiency of operations
- Reliability of financial reporting

- Compliance with laws and regulations
- Safeguarding of company assets

One of the principles is that no one individual should have unfettered powers of decision-making; that is, there must be checks and balances that prevent individuals from acting in ways that could be harmful to the company. The focus of most corporate governance is on those members of the organization that are most powerful, which in practice usually means the CEO and senior executive directors.

Approaches to corporate governance vary from country to country, but there are two basic approaches. One focuses primarily on financial reporting and emphasizes strict compliance. The other approach is both softer and broader, emphasizing internal control and allowing some latitude for exceptions, but also looking at the whole span of the relationship between boards and shareholders, not just financial controls.

The first model is prevalent in the USA, especially since the passage of the Sarbanes–Oxley Act in 2002. This lays down strict standards for reporting, which all companies must follow. Any deviation is likely to lead to investigation by a regulator and/or public prosecutor, which can lead to fines, court cases, or both. In some cases, directors can be found guilty of criminal charges and sent to prison.

However, the US approach is relatively narrow and neglects other aspects of governance. For example, it is still possible for the same person to hold simultaneously the posts of chairman and chief executive. This combined role has caused problems in the USA before—Kenneth Lay was both chairman and CEO of Enron—and in my view, it may again. Despite this, a study published in *Sloan Management Review* in 2005 concluded that "no compelling argument exists for splitting the chairman and CEO jobs, particularly in light of the fact that US senior executives strongly believe that the two positions should remain combined."[20]

Since its passage in 2010, though, the Dodd–Frank Act has had a strong impact on corporate governance in US public companies, and one consequence has been the beginnings of a separation of the roles of chairman and CEO. The Dodd–Frank Act has also led to remuneration committees being strengthened, the extension of clawback provisions and the disclosure of the CEO's salary as a multiple of that of the average employee. Shareholders are also becoming more engaged. All of these trends are adding to the pressure on independent directors in particular and public companies more generally, and some observers believe that this will lead to more companies going, or remaining, private.

In the UK and most of Europe, the softer and broader approach is adopted and companies are allowed to deviate from the standards, provided they can offer a reasonable explanation of why they have done so. The UK Corporate Governance Code is typical of this approach and adopts a more holistic view of corporate governance. It is accepted that the chairman and CEO roles should never be combined; there are exceptions to this rule—Sir Stuart Rose briefly held both posts at Marks & Spencer—but they are rare. Shareholders generally have more of a say in the appointment of directors, unlike the situation in the USA where, in the words of Dutch academic Jaap Winter, "shareholders can still do relatively little about the positions of directors on boards."[21]

Around the world, these two models of corporate governance are being adapted and interpreted in different ways. Sometimes the result is not a particularly happy one. The Japanese model of corporate governance has been criticized for favoring Japanese companies over foreign competitors. In the words of Alan Macdougall of Pensions & Investments Research Consultants (PIRC): "The governance of Japan's listed companies was not working in the interests of either shareholders or other stakeholders … the managements of Japanese companies too often appeared to act as if they, rather than share-holders, were the owners of the business."[22] In China and India, on the other hand, owners of businesses tend to remain very closely involved with day-to-day management, and this too can have negative consequences for corporate governance.

There has been discussion about creating an international code of corporate governance, and bodies such as the International Corporate Governance Network (ICGN) exist with the purpose of supporting moves towards more compatible international systems. Evidence suggests, however, that there is still a long way to go. Even some large and quite developed economies, such as Russia and Thailand, are still in their infancy when it comes to developing corporate governance frameworks and structures. There is a tendency too to pay lip service to the rules of corporate governance but, in actuality, carry on very much as before. International variations in corporate governance are very much a reality, and are likely to remain so for quite some time.

The Sarbanes–Oxley Act, the UK Code of Corporate Governance, and other such codes give boards a framework to follow, but no more than that. The board then has to put in place the governance systems and behaviors that support it. "Codes provide a system for reporting to shareholders on a comply or explain basis, but it is down to companies themselves to decide how they want to govern themselves."[23] Here we come back to those key questions. What do owners want? How close will they be to the company? How often will they engage with the board?

Institutional investors

Codes and regulations are necessary in publicly owned companies in large part because investors, especially big institutional investors, have subscribed to the idea of the separation of ownership and control, either as a matter of deliberate policy or, more likely, by default. Over the past several decades, large financial institutions such as insurance companies, pension funds, investment funds, and others have come to dominate ownership of global equity. In the UK, these institutions now own more than 80 percent of equity market capitalization. The figure is lower in other countries—in the USA, which has a stronger tradition of small individual shareholders, the figure is nearer 60 percent—but even so the institutions are in a dominant position.

Large financial institutions also do not, on the whole, have a very good record of engagement with the companies in which they invest. If we ask those three questions given just now, the answers in many cases will be "they don't know," "not very close" and "seldom, if ever." They do not appear to be very interested in long-term stewardship and, with the advent of electronic trading, they are more likely than ever to buy and sell their holdings quickly; the average hold period for shares traded on the London Stock Exchange is nine months, while on the New York Stock Exchange it is just six months.

The main reason why fund managers don't get involved with the companies is lack of time and capacity. An individual fund manager may be responsible for investments in as many as one hundred companies, and one director of a major global fund estimated that it is not possible to engage with more than 5 percent of these. As a result, fund managers focus on one or two key metrics, the most important of which is quarterly financial performance. If they find that the invested firm is not performing up to expectations, there is no time to investigate and find out what is going wrong; it is easier to simply sell the shares and move on. Even where there is engagement, institutional shareholders are usually only interested in meeting the CEO and the finance director to get an idea of where those financial metrics are going.

This in turn has had a deleterious effect on corporate governance. According to Colin Melvin, head of Hermes Equity Ownership Services, "the lack of dialogue between long-term shareholders and companies has meant that directors have been hearing only a lot of short-term noise from financial markets. The priority has been next quarter's earnings, not longer-term strategy and risk management."[24] One of the reasons why Dennis Gillings took Quintiles private was that the market was not properly valuing the company and was not giving credit for the work it had done in corporate venturing, for example. If anything, since then the position has worsened. In one recent survey in the USA, a majority of directors maintained that they would cut investment in R&D or marketing in order to boost quarterly financial figures, even though they knew this was not in the long-term interests of the company. Martin Wolf comments in the *Financial Times* that many managers see their primary duty as rewarding shareholders, not looking after the long-term interests of the company.[25]

Some institutional investors, notably some hedge funds, classify themselves as "activist investors." Carl Icahn and Daniel Loeb, two of the best known of these, have become famous for their stinging attacks on boards and management. Activist investors don't just sit back and wait for dividends, they demand that CEOs and boards create value, and hold them to account publicly if they fail to do so. As a recent *Financial Times* article described, activist hedge funds are demanding action in the form of share buy-backs, divestments of subsidiaries and strategic and operational changes.[26]

This might seem like a good thing, but it must be remembered that activist investors are not necessarily motivated by a desire to do the right thing by the company; often their aim is to create value, and wealth, for themselves. Another *Financial Times* article warned that there is a danger that boards will begin listening only to activist investors, simply because they shout the loudest, and thus will not necessarily manage the company to the benefit of *all* shareholders.[27] Aware of this, some American companies are trying to change voting rules in an attempt to dilute the power of the activist investors, and these changes are now the subject of long-running legal battles in US courts. This kind of hostile relationship with shareholders will always be damaging; but directors, and independent directors, do have to remember that they are responsible for the company as a whole.

At Forth Ports, we had a generally good relationship with shareholders, and some investment funds were long-term investors, willing to give views on the company's strategic direction, dividend policy and so on. The situation at Keller was similar. At Biocompatibles plc, we had a small number of main investors, which made communication with investors and understanding their individual agendas easier. But if the shareholders of Datrontech had exercised their responsibilities more closely and held the CEO and the board to account, could the collapse of that company have been averted?

What, and how much, independent directors can do depends on the individual shareholders. Certainly it is up to the independent directors, especially the chairman, to be proactive and reach out to shareholders in order, at least, to attempt to open dialogue and establish relationships. Shareholder relations are an important part of the duties of the chairman of a publicly owned company, but I would argue that all independent directors have a role to play in ensuring good relations with shareholders. Especially when things go wrong—an economic downturn, or problems in the company itself—chairmen and independents need to keep shareholders informed and answer their questions. But, as we saw, there will always be limits to the ability of the board to have impact on shareholders. The duty of the independent director is then to be truly independent, to look after the governance of the company and ensure that its assets are used wisely, in effect stepping into the shoes of the absentee institutional owners.

Private Ownership

Some companies prefer private ownership, and there is no doubt that there are benefits. After it went private, Quintiles was able to move away from quarterly reporting and focus much more on growing the business and investing in the company. Forth Ports, which is now in private ownership, has seen similar benefits.

As I noted earlier, there are many kinds of private ownership. For reasons of space, and also because of the fit with my own experience, I will concentrate on the oldest and the newest: private individual or family ownership and private equity.

Private individual/family ownership

Private companies have existed since the time of the Roman Emperor Justinian, and are mentioned in the early sixth-century law code compiled at his request. Private ownership in the hands of individuals or families are the most common type of business in the world today. We tend to think of family businesses as being small firms, but in fact some of the world's largest companies, including Wal-Mart, Motorola and Ford Motors, have a strong element of family ownership.

Most small individually owned firms do not have independent directors, but increasingly the larger ones are recognizing the value of independent directors. CH Jones was one of these. Peter Vallance, the primary owner, wanted to strengthen his top team and brought an independent (myself) onto the board to support his executives and managers. Entrepreneurs are often prone to "tunnel vision," and need outsiders to provide fresh thinking and scrutinize strategic and operational plans.

John Wood and Thames Fulton of Heidrick and Struggles comment that: "When starting a business, founders of companies often rely on a group of external advisors—usually peers or close friends—who provide guidance on everything from the running of the business to how to transfer control to the next generation. Once the business has matured and the advisory process is more formalized, adding independent directors to the board is a natural extension of this 'kitchen cabinet'."[28] The founders of businesses can prove to be problematic if they remain on the scene for too long. The problem is that they often fail to grow with the business. Dennis Gillings of Quintiles is an exception, in that his vision and the conception of his own role have expanded dramatically as the company has grown. At both Datrontech and Michael Gerson, the founders sold the company but remained on the board; at Datrontech, they continued to act as if they owned the company, and at Michael Gerson everyone else continued to act as if Michael still owned the company. In both cases, this hampered the business.

Independent directors of privately owned firms, say Wood and Fulton, require a combination of diplomacy and "deft candour." They need to be truly independent and offer an impartial view of the company; that is after all one of the reasons why they are there. But they need to be diplomats too, aware of relationships between board members and able to operate in a more informal, shirt-sleeves environment. Being an independent director at a small firm such as CH Jones also often requires a much more hands-on approach, and the line between what an independent director should and should not do tends to shift; it is much more likely that independent directors will be required to advise on operational matters, at least at a high level. Even so, the principle that independents do not get involved in day-to-day management should still be observed.

Private equity ownership

Private equity is very different from individual or family ownership. The latter will look at the very long term and may even consider handing the firm on to children or other family members when the founder retires. Private equity, on the other hand, is almost always focused on the future exit. The reason for buying a company is so that at some later date it can be sold for a profit. Much of private equity ownership and management is built around this principle.

The modern private equity industry has its origins in the USA with the foundation of the venture capital firms, Research and Development Corporation and JH Whitney & Co. Today there more than three thousand private equity houses, and in 2013 the total of global private equity assets under management was believed to be more than $3.2 trillion.[29] Most private equity houses (excepting those in Asia) are structured as partnerships in which various investors take a stake in that house's investments. Figures 4.1 and 4.2 show the growth of the industry over recent years.

Private equity houses make investments on two levels, the fund level and the company level. In the case of the latter, they invest directly in individual companies (this is also sometimes known as direct investment). We saw examples of direct investment earlier in this book, at Vantec, Quintiles, U-POL and NFT, for example; here, a private equity house purchased a majority stake in the company and became in effect the company's owner.

Fund investment sits one level above company investment. Private equity houses set up a fund with a view to investing, usually in a particular class or type of company. Fund investment in turn is divided into primary and secondary investment. A primary investment is a commitment to invest in a new fund, while a secondary investment involves the purchase and transfer of an interest in an existing fund. Private equity houses will usually develop more

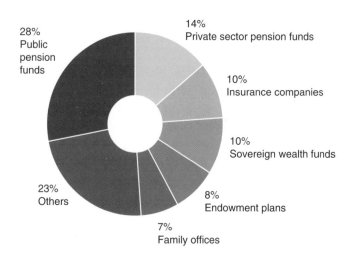

Share of capital by investor type (%)

FIG 4.1 / **Who invests in private equity?**

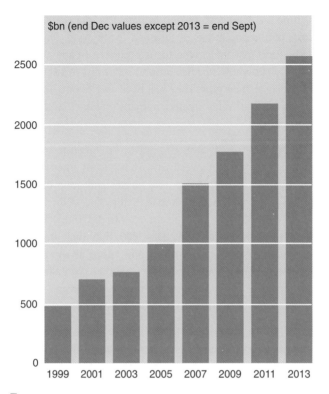

$bn (end Dec values except 2013 = end Sept)

FIG 4.2 **Growth of private equity assets under management**

than one fund; some choose to concentrate their funds in the same area, but at GOH Capital we are set on developing a "family of funds" each focusing on different investment opportunities in life sciences.

Private equity investments also fall into several different categories depending on the maturity of the funds or companies being invested in. Traditional venture capital concerns itself with start-up or very young companies. Buy-out transactions, including spin outs, typically include debt, and also involve "growth equity" in established and usually profitable companies where the private equity firm sees opportunities to establish additional value. Growth and development transactions are also made in mature companies but do not typically include debt. Finally there are very specialist funds that invest in niche areas. NovaQuest is one of these.

Private equity investors measure return on investment over the whole period of the investment, not just on an annual basis. The early stages of a private equity investment fund are often loss-making as there is a "drag effect" produced by fees and costs before any money is returned to the fund. This is known and understood by fund managers, who focus on the end game. What value will the investment yield when it comes time to sell it on? Private equity managers regard the exit as their goal. They will have an exit date in mind, coupled with a target in terms of value created, perhaps measured as a multiple of the original investment.

It follows that private equity houses tend to be longer-term investors; five years is a common term for an investment. That said, as anyone in the industry will tell you, there are bad private equity houses and good ones. The former tend to be less interested in the companies they invest in; having acquired a company, they do not give it sufficient attention. Quite a few of these PE houses found to their surprise in 2008–2009 that their investments were underwater, and they would see little if any return at the end of the day. Increasingly private equity houses, and I have worked with a few, get involved with their companies. They invest where they see potential value, and they work with the company to create that value. They adopt a strategy known as "buy and build."

NFT's relationship with Phoenix is a good example of this. Phoenix got involved with NFT, says Richard Daw, for three reasons. First, NFT was the market leader in a niche market. Second, that market had the potential for steady, recession-proof growth. Third, NFT's David Frankish was a "hugely exciting" CEO whom Richard believed had a passion for the business and was committed to it. This was, he says, "a pretty powerful cocktail of attributes."

Once involved, Phoenix set about working with David and the company to add value. The executive team was strengthened and the company was given more capacity to support necessary cultural change and growth, in part by bringing in an experienced independent Chairman (myself) who could back up David and his executive team. Phoenix also worked with the board to create a robust strategic plan. Throughout all of this work, Phoenix kept its eye on the ultimate goal, which was to create shareholder value. Everything, says Richard, strengthening the management team, investing in new systems and warehouses and supporting cultural change, was aligned with that goal. At Quintiles, Vantec and U-POL there has a been a similar alignment between the goals of the company and its private equity owners, with equally successful results for both.

There is no recipe for a successful relationship between a company and its private equity owners, in large part because PE houses themselves are so diverse in terms of philosophy and attitude. Alan MacKay, a veteran of private equity for more than twenty years who has invested in more than three hundred companies, reckons that private equity houses have a responsibility to ensure that the relationship "is what both parties intend it to be." Both sides need to sit down and talk, regularly. Alan does not believe in the separation of ownership and control; instead, he wants to see a partnership between owners and executives with both working together for the common good. Failures, he says, are usually down to personal issues and poor relationships rather than any underlying problem with the business.

What makes for a good exit? In my experience, private equity houses want boards to do the following:

1. Build an excellent company with a focused strategy and business plan that demonstrates a lot of potential for buyers;
2. Build a company that is fit for purpose in terms of organization and capabilities;
3. Develop a very strong management team with plenty of depth and breadth to develop the company further;
4. Create a track record of delivering growth and profitability;
5. Develop a portfolio of strong customers;
6. Identify the major risks and develop action plans to deal with them;
7. Create a data room that will satisfy any due diligence;
8. Develop a strong second tier of management that can run the company day-to-day while senior management is involved in selling the company;
9. Use marketing and PR to make the market aware of the company as an attractive investment, so that when it comes time to sell there is a very strong market waiting;
10. Jointly choose advisors to assist in the sale process.

Independent directors have a role to play in all of these things, either directly by working with their executive board colleagues, or indirectly by providing monitoring and oversight that ensures things get done. At NFT, U-POL, Quintiles and Vantec, we worked with the executives to develop strategy, we checked on the progress of the strategic plan, we helped to develop the top team, we assisted in the choice of advisors and we worked together as a team to get the best deal for investors, employees and everyone else. Independents play a vital role in the exit process, and it is their guidance and support that helps to keep the process going and make sure it stays on the right track.

One of the more tricky areas for private equity is management buy-outs. I experienced several of these, notably Vantec and NFT, and in both cases we faced some similar problems concerning the necessary change of culture. Both went from being rather quiet, solid subsidiaries of other companies to being standalone businesses. It was a real challenge to get staff and management to think like an independent business—and to do it quickly. The board is responsible for ensuring that the transition is both swift and smooth.

Criticisms of private equity

The private equity industry has been criticized for being secretive and lacking in transparency. Unlike public companies, PE houses are not required to disclose the performance of their funds and investments, or the remuneration of partners. Private equity firms also benefited from tax breaks, as partners are subject to capital gains tax rather than income tax for their carry (their share of the benefits from exits). However, the industry is becoming more regulated. In the USA the Dodds-Frank Act now regulates some of the activities of private equity houses, and the European Commission is implementing the AIFM Regulation.

From 2007 onward, the financial crisis affected every kind of financial institution, and private equity houses were no exception. Valuations fell, meaning expected prices at exit could not be achieved, and funds struggled to maintain earning levels. Holding periods lengthened as partners waited for a better price, and this reduced returns. Some PE houses began dabbling in emerging markets but, unless they had specialist expertise in this area, they too were affected. The later downturn of India caught several private equity investors off guard and they incurred further losses.

The question was asked, fairly, as to whether private equity houses were really as good as they claimed to be. They had generated large returns in the first few years of the twenty-first century by buying companies and then selling them on, but as several commentators have pointed out, it takes no great skill to make money by buying and selling in a rising market. The poor returns from private equity investment after 2008 showed how little value many private equity firms were really adding. Questions were asked as to what investors were doing to justify the high fees they charged (in response to which, many investors have reduced their fees).

However, it would seem that at least some private equity companies have learned from the past. There is much more of an interest now in "buy and build" models of investment, again like Phoenix and NFT. Alan MacKay detects an "underlying humility" in private equity and reckons that most private equity houses now realize that there are limits to their own knowledge and abilities.

"In mainstream private equity, you will not meet anyone who claims that they know more than the executives who run the company," he says. And, as more careful investment begins to see better payoffs, investors are being tempted back into the market. A report from Bain & Company's Private Equity Group in March 2014 suggested that the prospects for private equity were better than at any time in the past four years.[30] PE houses are also more realistic in their expectations. "Raising venture capital is the Darwinian filter screening out the entrepreneurs who are clearly unfit to survive," commented one writer in the *Daily Telegraph*. "There is little point in whinging that it is difficult to raise backing. It is meant to be hard." Most PE houses would agree with that.

Private equity and the independent director

One consequence of this change is that the role of the independent director has become more important than ever. Independents are the vital link between the owner, the private equity house, and management, and they need to be aware of that position. The relationships they have going in both directions are absolutely important. Forward-thinking private equity houses want to get involved in strategy and want to invest in the companies they own (think, for example, of Phoenix's £20 million investment at NFT). This means that independent directors have to know the company and be prepared to work with the executive team to shape strategy and create a vision for the company.

However, not all of the effects are positive. For those thinking of building NED portfolios, there is a practice among private equity houses to bring in industry specialists as independents, rather than generalists who can provide a broader background. My own appointment at Vantec was part of this developing trend, even though it happened some time ago. This narrow-mindedness on the part of PE houses means that boards don't always get the diversity of experience and knowledge that they need.

Another issue, which independent directors may come across, is a divergence of interests between the executive team and the private equity owner. For example, management might not wish to sell the company and prefer to continue the relationship with the private equity investor. It is important to manage relationships and remind the board that the exit is the main reason why the private equity firm invested in the first place. Again, keeping the strategic interests of both parties aligned is a key part of the independent director's role.

Shareholder relations are not as complex in private equity owned firms as they are in public companies, but they still need attention. The chairman's role is particularly important, as he or she acts a bridge between company and investor, keeping each informed about the other and ensuring that the ship stays on course. But, again, all independents have a role to play in investor relations. To make the point once more, they are there in part to look after the interests of the shareholder, and they have to be sure that they know what those interests are.

Globalization and private equity

Globalization is affecting private equity just like everyone else. PE houses are increasingly involved in buying and selling businesses with global reach, and this means that they too need to start adopting a global perspective (again, this is one of the purposes of the family of funds that we are developing at GOH Capital). They need to learn to adapt to cultural differences, and they need to learn about local regulatory and legal regimes, and how these affect businesses, especially when making an investment or an exit. When private equity-owned companies make acquisitions overseas, these need to be integrated skillfully into the company so as to avoid damaging or losing value. Above all, they need to be clear that any long-term strategy is in the best interests of the investors, who of course have their eyes on the exit and the price that can be obtained there. Private equity houses can also lend support through their own networks of contacts, helping with due diligence of overseas acquisitions and generally assisting deals to be done more speedily.

Independent directors contribute through their own knowledge and experience of global markets, something that may be in short supply at the PE house itself. In effect, they can end up advising both parties, the investor and the company, on the best course of action. And once again, they need to be involved in strategy and to satisfy themselves that the company is going in the right direction and creating value. Smart private equity houses will seek to appoint directors with international experience and networks of contacts that can help their companies to expand globally, as happened at U-POL.

Summary

The nature of ownership affects the structure and composition of boards, and this in turn impacts on the work of independent directors. Different kinds of owners want independent directors on the board for different reasons, and look for different traits and different backgrounds and experience. Changes in ownership involve cultural changes and independent directors must be able to master these.

One point in particular stands out, which is that independent directors need to be engaged with the company's strategy, helping to shape it and to ensure that it is effectively carried out. If they do not do so, then they cannot be said to be representing the owner's interests to the full. It is, therefore, to strategy that we turn our attention next.

Strategy

> One day Alice came to a fork in the road and saw a Cheshire Cat in a tree. 'Which road do I take?' she asked. 'Where do you want to go?' was his response. 'I don't know,' Alice answered. 'Then,' said the cat, 'it doesn't matter.'
>
> — Lewis Carroll

Strategy-making is one of the most important issues facing any board. Every business—indeed, every organization—needs a strategy that plots a clear course and focuses and guides the efforts of everyone in the organization. Without a clear strategy, a business is like a rudderless ship; it will simply drift this way and that, battered by the elements and never actually making port.

"Where were the non-executive directors?" asks Lawrence Christensen, consultant and experienced non-executive director. "Why weren't they doing their job?" He was speaking of the corporate failures after the banking crisis, and indeed the story of RBS is an excellent cautionary tale in this regard. RBS adopted a strategic course that drove the company into the ground; it was rescued only by a government bailout costing billions of pounds. This doomed strategy was approved by the RBS board. What *should* have happened was that RBS's independent directors should have asserted their independence and vociferously questioned this strategy and prevented its adoption. It is clear that independent directors need both—they need to understand strategy and they need independence of spirit—if we are to prevent such disasters from happening again.

At a much smaller level, a single strategic issue can threaten a company—even, in the case of Datrontech, destroy it. Datrontech's failure to adopt a coherent strategy led to chaotic expansion into unprofitable ventures coupled with crippling levels of debt. Despite our best efforts as a board to plug the leaks, the company sank. Forth Ports—an example of excellence in strategy-making—nonetheless faces a dangerous strategic challenge that results in part from decisions made long ago. Despite board-level strategic discussions, the firm did not develop a fully coherent logistics strategy, one that would have differentiated it from other port operators. Now, its chief asset, London Tilbury, is being challenged by the newly opened London Gateway. Had that logistics strategy been comprehensively developed, Tilbury might now have a strong competitive advantage over Gateway.

Scores of books and hundreds of articles on strategy have been written, and there are also plenty of training courses and programs. There are a variety of approaches, from the formal planned strategy approach espoused by Kenneth Andrews and others to the more ad hoc "emergent" strategy proposed by Henry Mintzberg. Academics have identified something like eleven different schools of thought on strategy, and doubtless more will pop up in the future.[31]

Here, I don't propose to get deeply into what strategy *is*. Instead, I want to emphasize how important it is for independent directors to be involved in strategy. Examples from the case studies of my involvement are shown in Table 4.7.

Who Is Responsible for Strategy?

It is the task of the directors to set out what the company's strategy should be, and independent directors have a particularly important role in this regard. It should be noted that there are variations on this theme, depending on where a company is domiciled. In countries such as Germany that have dual boards, the independent director's role in strategy-making is often more limited. The USA has a unitary board system but there is an expectation in some companies, at least, that strategy should be made by the executives and the board should confine itself to scrutinizing and approving that strategy.

However, not all US companies follow this, and others do expect independents to play a role. John Harvey, former chairman of Tibbett & Britten, is one of those who believes that independent directors should play a direct role in strategy-making. "The first task is to challenge," he says, "to ask if there is a strategy, and if so, is it the right one. The second task is to stress-test the strategy, which as an independent director you can do without the emotional involvement of the guys who have written it."

The ownership of the company can also make a difference. In companies owned by private equity, there is generally an expectation that directors will get involved in strategy. In public companies, on the other hand, there is less shareholder pressure for this to happen, and until recently it has been possible for independents to let others do the thinking about strategy. Increasingly,

TABLE 4.7 Contributions to strategy by independent directors

Biocompatibles:	developed strategy to turn the company into a profitable business; brought in expert advisors to assist with strategy; independent review of acquisitions and takeover proposals.
CH Jones:	developed a very focussed strategy for the company; advised on exit strategy and valuation.
Datrontech:	enforced a more focussed strategy; advised on disposals; assisted with the logistics strategy; took decision that the business should be liquidated.
Forth Ports:	contributed to annual strategic reviews and frequent discussions on strategy; took a view on strategic locations (for example, Tilbury, St Petersburg); involvement in discussions on property management strategy and on diversification; independent review of acquisitions; independent review of the bid for the company and subsequent sale for the best price.
Keller:	urged the need for an independent global strategic review; took part in strategic reviews by geography involving visits all over the world; independent review of ten major acquisitions; independent review of investments and disposals; independent review of major contracts.
Michael Gerson:	managed the strategic review process; helped the board recognise the need to adapt to a changing market.
NFT:	development of a highly focussed strategy for a new, stand-alone business; assisted the transition from in-house subsidiary to private equity-owned company; reviewed start-up plans for major projects; reviewed investment proposals; oversaw the exit plan including the selection of Rothschilds as merchant banker.
NovaQuest:	worked on strategy for a new fund; reviewed investments; chaired joint discussions with Quintiles on partnering; met with other partnering opportunities (e.g. AstraZeneca); met with specific investment opportunities.
Quintiles:	independent review of investments and disposals; geographic performance review visits; challenged the centralisation of the business in the USA; sat on special committee which oversaw the taking of the company private in 2003.
U-POL:	helped the company adjust from being a family business to a private equity investment; led the strategic review which pushed for geographic expansion; oversaw the successful exit.
Vantec:	helped the business adjust from being a Nissan subsidiary to being a European private equity investment; led the strategic review which recommended focussing on sectors other than automotive; introduces potential business partners (Exel); participated in business development (e.g. Mazda proposals); independent assessment of the exit to Mizhuo.

however, there is pressure on independent directors in public companies to get more involved in strategy-making. In my opinion, that is exactly what should be happening. Directors make strategy, and that includes independent directors. Directors who choose not to get involved in strategy look rather like passengers on the board.

Executive directors are usually close to the company and its day-to-day operations; sometimes, too close. They can find it difficult to keep the larger picture in mind, to separate the wood from the trees. Independent directors bring a broader, more long-term perspective to the table. Part of their job is to look out for the kinds of "big picture" issues that executives might, thanks to the pressures of their jobs, overlook.

Independent directors also bring a broader range of experience to bear on strategic problems. Their own past experiences—including experience of strategic issues and dilemmas in different business sectors—can help to introduce fresh ideas and thinking. Independents also have a duty to examine and, if necessary, question and critique the strategic assumptions that executives make. Is this really the way the world works? Is this sector necessarily growing (or contracting) at the rate we think it is? Does the acquisition of a rival company really make strategic sense? Do we really have the capabilities to grow as fast as we think we want to? These and many others are the kinds of questions that independent directors must be prepared to ask—even if it makes them unpopular with their colleagues.

Once a strategy has been decided and put into place, the independent directors step back a little. They are not responsible for implementing the strategy; that is the task of their executive colleagues. However, the process of implementation must be monitored, and here independents have a further role to play. They need to satisfy themselves that the strategy is rolling out as it should. Are we meeting our performance targets? Are there areas where we are in danger of falling behind? Do changing circumstances mean that the strategy needs to be revisited? These again are questions that must be asked, and answered.

In my experience, it is vitally important that all of the board are fully involved in the strategic process. I learned that lesson at a number of companies over the years. One recent example comes from Keller. Initially, the procedure at Keller was that the executives would make a presentation on strategy and the board would then review it, sometimes not very deeply. Then came the downturn, and we all realized that an in-depth strategic review was necessary. The culture changed, and all the board became very deeply involved in that strategic review.

At Forth Ports, on the other hand, every director was part of the strategy-making process, usually during away-days every year, and everyone had their say. We did not always agree on key strategic ideas—recall the debate over how to manage the property arm of the business—but that made it all the more important that we talk things through and reach a consensus. This meant that, when a strategy had been agreed, everyone was committed to making it work. Charles Hammond, CEO of Forth Ports when I was on the board, agrees that board support and commitment was vital in developing a workable strategy.

We followed this same principle at Biocompatibles, U-POL and NFT, where as chairman I endeavored to ensure that every director was fully committed to the strategy and prepared to get behind it. We also had strategy away-days, sometimes in the USA or Europe. Earlier in this book I cited research from McKinsey suggesting that 60 percent of directors simply "nod strategy through," taking no deep interest in the strategy either at the time of its development or during its implication. That is dangerously wrong. If only a few people control the strategy, then the risks of picking the wrong strategy or the wrong course increase dramatically. I saw the consequences of this at Datrontech and Michael Gerson.

Beyond the board, it is essential that the entire business buys into and supports the strategy too. If people are truly committed to the strategy, then it stands a much better chance of succeeding. Independent directors, especially chairmen, can play a further role in helping to explain the strategy and communicate it to investors and others further down the organization.

Reading the literature on strategy, one will come across discussions of whether strategy should be "top down" or "bottom up." That is, should strategy be planned and worked out at board level and then disseminated downward through the organization? Or should strategy "emerge" as a response to what is happening on the ground? Should lower levels of the organization set out their own strategic priorities first, while the board's task is to synthesize these into a coherent overall strategy? In fact, my experience suggests that strategy should be simultaneously both top down and bottom up. There should be wide-ranging consultation to provide inputs into strategy, but ultimately it is the board, including the independent directors, that takes responsibility and decides what the overall strategy will be. At Quintiles and Keller, both very large multinational companies, we looked at the situation locally in different markets and took inputs from our business units around the world, but when it came to deciding on the right strategic course of action, the buck stopped with the board. The decisions, and the responsibilities, were theirs.

When it comes to the question of who makes strategy, it is important to have as many inputs as possible. That often means bringing in outside experts to give advice and views. Here again independent directors can get involved by using their own networks of contacts to identify appropriate experts and reach out to them. At Biocompatibles we took advice from scientific experts when making strategy, and at NFT we brought in logistics experts such as Lawrence Christensen to make presentations to the board. This meant that the board could make better-informed decisions with a broader and deeper range of knowledge available. It is important to remember that the experts don't make the strategic decisions, nor should they be asked to do so; they provide advice, and the board then decides whether or not to take that advice.

The same is true of strategy consultants, who can be of considerable value. At Keller, for example, we used consultants to conduct an independent global strategic review, which resulted in important and very positive changes for the company. Once again, though, consultants don't run the company. It is up to the independent directors and the executives working together to monitor the work of consultants and ensure that they are delivering value for money.

Finally, investors should also be encouraged be fully involved. This is particularly the case when the company only has a few owners, for example a private equity house. At U-POL and NFT, we found that when private equity investors understood and bought into the strategy, they became more supportive and were more likely to invest in the firm to help it meet its strategic objectives.

Dimensions and Criteria

Strategy should always begin with defining the overall strategic objectives. What is the vision? Where does the company want to go? These objectives should first of all be realistic. Royal Bank of Scotland's ambition to the biggest bank in the world led directly to its over-expansion and demise. A decade earlier, Dutch supermarket group Royal Ahold and Canadian telecoms company Nortel followed the same trajectory of boom-and-bust. Second, it is important for the board to agree fully on what the main strategic objectives are, and to be united in their determination to pursue these. Only once the objectives are fully understood and shared can the process of making strategy begin (see Table 4.8).

No two companies are the same, and no two strategies will ever be the same either. That is as it should be. Companies need to differentiate themselves; otherwise, like Forth Ports, they will come under attack from rivals who do

TABLE 4.8   Ten criteria for a successful strategy

To be successful, a strategy should be the following:

1   **Challenging**
    Biocompatibles' strategic plan required the company to re-imagine itself, turning from an R&D operation into a profit-making company. NovaQuest set itself a challenging target of raising private equity funds in the toughest market for many years. Both companies believed in themselves, and challenged themselves to succeed.

2   **Comprehensive**
    NFT's transition from subsidiary to stand-alone was backed up by a comprehensive strategy which showed the way forward.

3   **Collaborative**
    At Forth Ports, the whole board participated in strategy-making and regular strategic reviews. We developed strategy as a team.

4   **Clear**
    CH Jones' strategy was simple and clear, and left managers and staff in no doubt as to the direction the company intended to take.

5   **Complementary to shareholder objectives**
    NFT's strategy was designed to meet the objectives of the owner, Phoenix Equity. The fit between strategy and goals was so close that Phoenix was willing to invest further in the firm.

6   **Customer-centric**
    Quintiles' strategy is based on relationships and partnerships with pharmaceuticals firms. It exists to service customers, and its strategy reflects this.

7   **Competitive advantage**
    Keller is the world leader in its field, thanks to its expertise. Its strategy aims to cement that top position by continuing to provide the best quality of service.

8   **Convincing** (investors will believe in it)
    U-POL developed a strategy so convincing that its owner, Graphite Capital, described it as 'a British gem'. Biocompatibles, in a high-risk market, convinced investors to give it time to develop its product offering. CEO Crispin Simon described investors as 'remarkably patient'.

9   **Capable of being communicated**
    NFT's strategy, developed by the boardroom team, was communicated clearly to the rest of the organisation. Once again, everyone knew what they were there to do.

10   **Creative in adding value**
    Vantec added value by expanding and growing into other sectors and other geographies, meaning that the company was sold on to Mizhuo for a very attractive multiple, and then floated for a still higher price.

the same things as they do (and perhaps better). Let me take private equity for an example. I mentioned that NovaQuest has been successful in raising funds during the toughest market in private equity history. One reason for this success is that NovaQuest is a specialist fund. Its focus is on structured finance offerings with biopharmaceuticals products. There are some PE houses that invest in particular sectors—leisure and hotels, for example—but many simply look for the best business opportunities they can find anywhere, and thus are in strong competition with each other.

Even for businesses like NovaQuest, though, the strategic picture will always be constantly changing and require new and different responses. In order to devise a sound business strategy, we need to ask certain questions. Many of the questions will be the same ones, over and over again. It is the answers that will differ.

What questions are asked depends on the level one is at. Large corporations like Keller and Quintiles have semi-independent business units with their own boards which set their own strategies within the framework of the larger corporate strategy. For those business units, strategy is much more a matter of focusing on customers and operational matters. Here, the questions that need to be asked include the following:

What business are we in? Who are our customers and what do they want from us? What value do we give them? It is important to dig deeply for answers and really understand what it is that you do. For example, are train companies in the train business? Or are they in the transportation business? Are oil companies in the oil business, or the energy business?

Where do we make our money? Which customer segments are most profitable? Which products and services? Where is the potential for future growth?

How good are our competitive positions? What are our real sources of competitive advantage? Is our business model easily replicable by competitors, or is it secure? How vulnerable are we to disruptive technologies, or new entrants into the market?

What skills and capabilities underpin our success? What are our human resources needs, now and in the future?

What do our customers think of us? What is our reputation? How strong is our brand? Are we sufficiently differentiated from our competitors in the minds of customers?

What about our competitors? What are they doing? What moves are they making, or have planned? What strategic options exist for them?

How can we increase profits quickly? Again, where are the opportunities for growth, especially in the short term?

How can we build long-term value? Having captured a market position, how can we make it secure and establish long-term competitive advantage?

These are also the sorts of questions that a small- or medium-size company board would be asking. At the level of large corporates, though, strategy is much more about the big picture. There are, in my view, five dimensions to corporate strategy, and I will go through them briefly. Once again, the independent director must be comfortable with these issues and able to think them through.

The first dimension is to *evolve the firm's genetic code*, or in other words, create and develop the characteristics that make it unique. This idea has its roots in Peter Johnson's ecological theory, and ultimately in Darwinian theories of evolution. Every firm is unique: even companies of the same size operating in the same sector will differ, and therefore every strategy has to be different too. Here is an example of the genetic code in action.

In the 1990s, Exel was able to develop a highly successful automotive logistics business, in large part because the company had a history of involvement in this sector dating back to its roots in British Road Services. A few years later, however, Tibbett & Britten tried likewise to get into automotive logistics and experienced major problems. Why? Because, initially, Tibbett & Britten did not understand the unique characteristics of this sector. There were strong labor unions, which did not know Tibbett & Britten and had no relationship with the company. Car transporters are specific types of equipment with a different utilization: they do not make round trips; they only carry cargo from the factory to dealers. The demand for cars is highly cyclical, and companies need contracts that protect them from the effects of cyclical demand. Tibbett & Britten initially did not fully understand much of this. Exel did. That is why it succeeded, and the other company initially failed.

The second dimension is to *back winners and cull losers*. This is not as easy as it sounds. It can be very difficult to determine who or what are the real long-term winners. At Forth Ports we looked at a variety of options and finally settled on waste management as a possible winner, but the latter never quite delivered what we hoped it would; the waste management business was sold off. It is equally important to recognize which businesses and business units are not contributing all that they should, and sell them. We adopted that strategy at Datrontech, although in the end it was not enough to save the company.

The third dimension is to *become the best possible parent*. This is extremely important. Companies spend enormous amounts of time, effort and money making acquisitions; and then, having made them, forget about them. The board's attention moves on to the next acquisition or the next project. This is one reason why acquisitions so often fail to yield expected value. What companies should be doing is looking after their new children, caring for them, and investing in them, in hopes that they will turn into high-performance swans rather than under-performing ugly ducklings.

The fourth is to *place astute bets on growth*. "Astute" means being astute about the kind of growth you are going for. It is easy to be persuaded to go for simple top-line growth, but companies need to search for deeper sources of value. For example, what geographical markets should the company expand into? This was a question we often asked at Keller and U-POL. In both cases, there were plenty of opportunities, all of them promising, but which ones would really deliver that growth? We had to pick the best opportunities, and agree to set the others to one side.

And finally, the fifth dimension is to *create a new ecosystem*. For example, Quintiles largely created the marketplace for outsourced clinical trials. Getting away from the competition and redesigning the competitive field in a way that suits the company is a goal to which many companies aspire but few actually achieve.

Richard Koch, in *The Financial Times Guide to Strategy*, describes a number of characteristics of a good strategy.[32] First, he says, a good strategy needs a very clear sense of direction that everyone understands. In my view, this is perhaps the most important characteristic of all. As noted above, everyone on the board of a business has to buy into the strategy, accept it and be prepared to support it. Without that support, the strategy will stall.

Koch also believes that a strategy must be selective and focused. Again, this is vitally important. No company can do everything; most cannot even do everything that they want. It is necessary to focus on the possible, the achievable, and the necessary. Many companies come to grief by overreaching themselves strategically; in my own experience, that was one of the problems at Datrontech. At Forth Ports, NFT, U-POL and Keller, by contrast, we stuck to our knitting and did what we were best at doing to proficient at. Expansion outside our core competencies was to be undertaken only slowly and after mature consideration of the options.

Third, says Koch, strategy is always risky. This is true, and any consideration of strategy needs a consideration of risks. Risk management is discussed elsewhere in this book, but it is worth reinforcing the point that independent directors need to be able to assess and understand different kinds of risk. Following on from this, a strategy must also be flexible. Times and circumstances change, and strategies must change with them. There are few things more harmful to a company than sticking with a strategic course even though that course is no longer valid because the market has changed. Michael Gerson's decline owed something to that lack of flexibility. Markets, Koch reminds us, are nearly always disrupted and changed fundamentally by forces outside the company's control, by new entrants or new technologies that change the rules of the game.

Koch has a few other useful observations too. More top-line revenue, he says, is not necessarily good. Growth is not in itself a good thing; it needs to be *profitable* growth, and too often rising costs associated with growth swallow up the increase in revenue. It is important to analyze growth opportunities and look at the underlying costs and profits. And finally, Koch reminds us that leaders are flawed decision-makers. Strategy is too important to entrust to any one person, or even to a few people. Individuals are blinkered by their circumstances; they lack experience in vital areas; they make mistakes. Leaders need strong and capable advisors to monitor what they do and provide checks and balances. That is where independent directors come in.

What Do Directors Need to Know about Strategy?

Strategy is, as I said, a complex subject to which reams of print have been devoted. There are many different views on what strategy is and how it should be done, ranging from the formal "planned strategy" approach advocated by people like Andrews, to the more ad hoc "emergent strategy" championed by Mintzberg and James Brian Quinn. I find the ecological theory of strategy as described by Peter Johnson to be particularly interesting.[33] As usual, all of these theories have something interesting to offer, but none offers a complete picture.

There are certain strategic decision-making tools that all directors need to understand and be able to use. They include techniques like the SWOT analysis first developed by Andrews, and Michael Porter's five competitive forces. These are, admittedly, rather basic in nature, but they are effective in that they allow us to make a "quick and dirty" appraisal of most situations. Some of the other basic tools that independent directors need to know about include the balanced scorecard, business process re-engineering, just-in-time management and lean engineering, segmentation, leverage, and the ability to classify products and businesses into categories, such as cash cows, stars, dogs and so on. Important strategic concepts that they should master include competitive advantage, barriers to entry, outsourcing, continuous improvement, diversification, economies of scale, globalization, learning organizations, shareholder value, strategic alliances, the value chain, and mergers and acquisitions. That is by no means the complete list, but it is a start.

Why are these basic tools and concepts important? These are the sorts of topics taught to MBA students, even to undergraduate commerce students, and yet surprisingly, boards often do not discuss them sufficiently. Take outsourcing as an example. In my experience, the pharmaceuticals industry could, and should, outsource much more clinical research than it currently does, yet few boards of these companies sufficiently consider strategic partnering in this area. Why not? Independent directors need to be sure that all relevant issues are covered and discussed—even if sometimes this means thinking the unthinkable.

After that, it gets more complicated. The nature of strategic decision-making varies, depending on the size of the company and the sector or sectors in which it operates. Some sectors like oil are long-term in focus. Others such as high-tech are much more vulnerable to short-term fluctuations. Some such as shipping and steel—or construction—are very vulnerable to economic down-turns, while others are more able to ride out shocks.

There is some debate as to how often and how far into the future firms should plan. Certainly one must beware of over-planning, for people in the firm will get fed up with a constant stream of new plans and initiatives. It is better by far to have a simple plan, which is well thought through and evaluated before putting in to practice. The key determinants of when to plan and for how long are the level of forward investment required and over what period—oil companies, again, plan far into the future because the investment in new projects tends to be very large—and the dynamics of the market—how swiftly or slowly market trends emerge and change.

From a risk perspective, there is also the need to have at least basic contingency plans for disasters and economic downturns. This was one of the problems at Keller: even though we knew we were in a cyclical market, we did not have a fully comprehensive contingency plan for how to deal with a downturn. However, these plans need not be detailed. There is much to be said too for having a strong board that can think flexibly and react quickly to unexpected circumstances. Again, there are some interesting cultural differences. In my experience, Spanish companies are very good at this kind of reaction; the Spanish business unit of Keller, for example, was very quick to respond to the 2008 downturn. On the other hand, Japanese companies tend to take their time and evaluate a situation, consulting widely before making a decision. When they do move forward, they have buy-in from everyone involved, and that kind of commitment usually means that they get the job done; though of course, it often takes longer.

Sector knowledge is very important, and if directors move into a sector in which they have no previous experience—as I did when I joined Quintiles—it is important to get that experience and learn one's way around the sector as quickly as possible. It is very difficult to appreciate the wisdom of a particular strategy without knowing the dynamics of the industry and competition. However, sector knowledge is not *all*-important, and as I have said elsewhere in this book, it is good to have directors with diverse backgrounds too.

In strategy-making, there is no substitute for experience. I draw on my own experience very heavily when thinking about strategy. What worked well when we confronted similar situations in the past? What did not work? What did we do, and what should we have done? What is possible, and what is perhaps desirable but too risky to undertake? Experience helps me to find the answers to these questions. And of course, it is not just my own experience that matters. I am part of a team of executive and independent directors, and if that team is working well, all the others are drawing on *their* experiences too, each thinking about problems and issues from different angles. That is true strength in strategic decision-making. As important as the textbooks and theories are, in the end good strategy-making depends on the collective wisdom of the board and the advisors they call upon to help them.

And finally, the independent directors in particular have to get to know the company. John Harvey makes this point strongly: "You have to understand the business you have joined. Any non-exec worth his salt spends the first six months listening, getting out, and walking around the company. Once you've done that you can start challenging, asking what the strategy is." B.K. (Robbie) Burns, former managing director of Exel, agrees. He thinks independent directors have to "understand the tempo of a business" on an emotional, almost intuitive level, as well as being financial and strategic guardians. "And you can't do that sitting in the boardroom," he says. "You have to get out, and get to know the business."

Mergers and acquisitions

That wisdom should guide directors towards good decisions and away from bad ones. Let us take as an example a common strategic issue: whether to merge with or acquire another company. I have seen many mergers and acquisitions: Keller and Quintiles both grew rapidly by acquisition, and Datrontech attempted to do so with, in the end, fatal results. Mergers and acquisitions are very good ways of expanding *provided* they are done for the right reasons. A combination of reading other people's research and personal experience suggests that there are good and bad reasons for doing an M&A. Good reasons include:

- Improving the product offering in some way, either by moving into a new sector or new country (how Keller did it), creating value through vertical integration, building up networks, or acquiring new technical and managerial skills that complement what already exists.
- Increasing market share, for example moving into new markets or increasing reputation by acquiring well-known brands (as Tata Motors did when buying Jaguar and Land Rover).
- Gaining better access to customers, for example by moving from primary into secondary distribution.
- Diversifying into new products and services, as Quintiles and Biocompatibles did and Datrontech tried to do.

These are all valid reasons for making an acquisition, but it does not follow that companies *must* make acquisitions. Indeed, three of the companies I worked with—NFT, U-POL and CH Jones—relied almost entirely on organic growth. Yet there are plenty of companies, and boards, that will still plunge into acquisitions in the belief that they are a good thing, whereas in reality they are making acquisitions for the wrong reasons. Those wrong reasons can include:

- Because it's for sale. There are shopaholic companies that cannot resist making acquisitions even when they clearly are not suitable and there is no fit with the company's strategy. Datrontech is a good example of this.
- Kleptomania. This is another form of obsessive-compulsive disorder by boards and CEOs, which sees them want to grab prizes out from under the noses of other companies. Kleptomaniac companies acquire other companies endlessly, even though they have no need of them.
- The ego of the CEO or chairman gets in the way. Big acquisitions are big news, and so is rapid growth. Successful dealmakers are lauded as heroes and have profiles written about them in the financial press. Few stop to examine whether the deals they make are good ones.
- Career opportunity for the promoter of the M&A. Similarly, other executives will push for acquisitions in order to make themselves look good and boost their career chances, hoping to gain a reputation as "the guy behind that famous merger."
- Market rationalization, or buying companies in order to close them down so as to eliminate competition.

It may seem strange that any rational-thinking chief executive would consider an acquisition for these reasons, or that a board would sanction it, but in fact these kinds of bad acquisitions happen all the time. Research suggests that at least 70 percent of acquisitions fail to achieve their targets in terms of generating greater shareholder value or other benefits. Some are actively toxic; they destroy value.

What goes wrong? One common problem is that the synergy that the company hoped to create through the M&A was never there in the first place. The acquiring company was mistaken about the value in the target company, its own needs, or both. Inadequate due diligence may have missed financial or other problems that meant that the acquired company had problems or was simply not worth the sum paid for it. The acquired company may not have a realistic business plan. Companies sometimes rely on financial advisors who are have conflicts of interest or simply give the wrong advice. Poor handling of management contracts might allow managers of the acquired company to walk away and start a new, rival business—taking their old customers with them—unless they are prevented from doing so by non-compete clauses, for example. Customers who were loyal to the old brand of the acquired company may drift away if they perceive that brand to have been devalued, unless they too are bound by contracts.

Poor management might mean that the integration of the two companies was not properly carried through, and this is quite common. There are many kinds of post-acquisition failure. I noted above how some companies, having gone to all the effort to acquire another company, then forget about the acquisition and do nothing, leaving the acquisition to wither on the vine. Sometimes they fail to invest in the right areas to support the acquisition. And then there are issues of cultural fit; do the culture and management systems of the acquired company mesh with those of the new owner? When they do not, the results can be spectacular failures. Few are quite as catastrophic as the merger of AOL and Time Warner, which resulted in losses of $100 billion in the first year after the merger was concluded, but there have been many other failures and setbacks.

Why do these problems happen? Because boards make bad strategic decisions. Whatever the source of the advice they might receive, it is down to the boards themselves to make the best decision for the company and shareholders. Independent directors have a particular duty to scrutinize possible acquisitions. They need the skills and experience to conduct a truly independent scrutiny, to lift the lid, and look underneath the presentations and PowerPoints and analyze the investment itself. Then, they need to be prepared to ask tough questions. Is this the best move? Will this acquisition be good for the company? Will it contribute to achieving strategic goals? If they believe that the CEO is wrong and that this acquisition will be a bad move, they have a duty to say so.

Success and failure are determined not just by trends in the environment but also by the nature of companies themselves, the genetic code that I mentioned earlier. Some companies can make acquisitions quite casually, while others need to make sure that there is a strong cultural fit. Quintiles, for example, experienced integration problems after acquiring a Spanish firm, set up by an entrepreneur some years earlier. There was very little in the way of cultural fit between them. They had incompatible information systems and there was no match between their human resource systems and policies.

In some companies, this might have been okay. Keller is highly decentralized, and when it acquired companies it basically left them alone. The existing management stayed in place, sometimes the existing brand was retained too, and acquired companies continued to do local business in their local markets. Only over time did they gradually take on Keller culture. But Quintiles is highly centralized, and its customers are global businesses who ask—demand— common systems around the globe. When Quintiles makes an acquisition in its core business area, it has to spend time and money to integrate it fully into the Quintiles family. The important point is this: is there fit? Will the acquisition really add value for the acquiring firm and its customers and shareholders?

From mergers and acquisitions, let us turn in the opposite direction to consider disposals. Companies sell off subsidiaries for a variety of reasons, but we can group these roughly into two categories: defensive and proactive. Defensive disposals could include the sale of subsidiaries to raise badly needed cash (for example, if the rest of the company has run into trouble), or if the original acquisition or start-up does not fit with the company's strategy. At Datrontech, the advent of a more focused strategy showed that a number of the company's subsidiaries, which had been acquired in a rather random way, no longer fitted with the strategy and indeed were holding it back. Disposing of these was one way of attempting to concentrate the company more closely on its goals. Quintiles, too, had invested substantially on acquisitions in the 1990s and not all of these had a good fit with the company's strategic goals as they developed. Disposing of them streamlined the company and made it more focused.

Proactive disposals are more considered affairs where a subsidiary or business unit, which had once been part of the main business, is now surplus to requirements, in part because the business itself has moved on. Keller's disposal of its housing company, Makers, is an example of this. As Keller globalized and became a world leader in ground engineering, Makers no longer had a place in its portfolio. Northern Foods' decision to sell NFT was made for similar reasons (though ironically, Northern Foods has now disappeared, while NFT has gone from strength to strength). There was perhaps a fire-sale element to Nissan's disposal of Vantec, but in fact that disposal would have made sense even if Nissan had been in better financial shape.

But, just as with acquisitions, disposals can be made for the wrong reasons if companies don't think carefully about their own strategies and ensure that disposals fit with them. Forth Ports had been selling parcels of land piecemeal. Once the property strategy was reassessed, Forth Ports stopped selling land in this way and began considering how to use it more profitably. Once again, independent directors have a role to play in all these strategic considerations.

Long-Term Trends to Watch

Finally, independent directors should be aware of long-term trends in the business environment, which could affect their companies. There are many, many trends and their number and nature will vary from sector to sector, but I will highlight four that are important to every independent director, everywhere: the increasing public scrutiny of business; the changing nature of customer demand (driven in part by new technology); the transformation of management from an art to a science; and globalization.

We have already established that independent directors are responsible for their companies, and in many jurisdictions are legally liable if something goes wrong and the company is judged to have done harm, for example, injury to people or damage to the environment. Today there is much more transparency in business, thanks in part to social media and communications technology, which push mainstream media to get on top of stories very quickly, often while they are still happening. It is much harder to hide mistakes, and even trivial incidents can be picked up by the press or politicians looking for a soundbite, and greatly magnified.

I think that on balance this greater transparency is a good thing, as it enables businesses to be held to account. But, this has consequences for independents. They need to play their part in ensuring good corporate governance, excellent health and safety standards, and high standards of quality. If they fail, the company fails; and if the company fails, the world will know about it by dinnertime. At Quintiles and Biocompatibles, we are acutely aware that our work is under intense scrutiny by regulators, but it is not only big pharma that needs to be transparent. Every company could potentially come under the microscope (British readers will recall the intense scrutiny of the Co-operative after the problems at its banking division in early 2014).

Secondly, customer demand changes all the time. Change in demand is driven by technology, by fashion, by economic forces and many other factors, but it is important to stay on top of it. At U-POL, products were as popular as ever but changes in the structure of the European car repair industry had an impact on market position. At NFT, increasing demand for salads and cook-chill meals had a positive effect on demand for our products and we were able to move to meet it. At Michael Gerson, by contrast, demand for the core service eroded and there was no alternative strategy in place.

And finally, there is no doubt that management is becoming more scientific. Fifty years ago, even thirty years ago, management was almost entirely a matter of relationships. Computers were rare, there was no internet, and no big data. If you wanted information about a client, you talked to their managers and executives and they told you their story. Today is a million miles away from that. Today, directors who do not use technology are a dying breed. Customers expect you to be familiar with their businesses, to have analyzed them and their markets, and to understand where they are and where they are going. The most extreme example is Quintiles, which has to manage a vast amount of data on client research products and clinical trials. This does not mean that the human element is no longer present in management; it is, as strong as ever. But we are using more data and more science in our management methods than ever before.

Globalization and internationalization are powerful and unstoppable forces, which affect every business, large and small. The changing nature of the world economy is a challenge that we all have to face, and one that is going to become stronger and stronger with the passage of time. Independent directors have to take this into account in their thinking. I will move on to a full discussion of globalization in the next section.

Summary

As an independent director, you are responsible for the direction the company takes. Your job, in the words of Peter Waine of Hanson Green, is "to help the CEO dream dreams, but in a proper, thought-out way." You have a duty to be involved in strategy, to help influence strategic direction and plans, not just approve what others put in front of you. It is up to you to step up and play your part in making strategy.

This section has looked at some of the general issues involved in making strategy. Let us turn now to look at one of the most important strategic issues of all: globalization.

Globalization

> No culture can live if it attempts to be exclusive.
>
> — Mahatma Gandhi

Two of the toughest and most complex of all strategic issues faced by boards today are internationalization and globalization.[34] Internationalization affects almost every company, everywhere, and even companies that trade in very tightly defined national markets are increasingly vulnerable to international competition. Every board, and every independent director, must understand the international business environment, the forces of internationalization and globalization, and how these impact on their business.

Every board with which I have been involved has had internationalization on its agenda at some point. At Datrontech, the failure to develop a coherent international strategy led to badly planned and unprofitable expansion, which in turn led to the downfall of the company. Fortunately most of the companies in my portfolio were very successful in their international development. They looked at international growth in different ways, and came to various conclusions depending on the size and nature of the companies, and the sectors in which they operated. But all had to consider the international marketplace and competition—whether they wanted to or not.

We saw in the last chapter how CEOs cannot, and should not, make strategy on their own. They need the wisdom and experience of independent directors to help them find the right way forward. Especially they need chairmen and independent directors who have experience of international business and can help guide their thinking. The experience of these directors and chairmen is valuable in a number of ways. Firstly, their knowledge of other countries and markets can help the board as a whole decide what countries it wants to be in—or not be in—and the best strategy for effecting market entry. Secondly, they can help the board decide which areas are best suited for international expansion. Thirdly, they can help the board understand market developments and customer behavior.

Their experience of international competition can also be invaluable in helping the board understand what competitors will do next and what threats they might pose. International competition is no longer something that only happens to companies that go overseas. Increasingly, Chinese and Indian companies are coming to us and competing on our own home soil. An Indian business group, Tata, is now the largest manufacturing employer in the UK. Times have changed, and there are few, if any, companies in the world that are not vulnerable to international competition. This challenges the independent director to develop his or her own expertise in international business, in order to play a full part in developing good, clear, and successful strategies (see Table 4.9).

Globalization Is here to Stay

Globalization is sometimes spoken of as a "new" force that is changing the business landscape. In fact, people have been trading internationally and even globally for a long time, pretty much since the beginning of civilization. For example, the East India Company in the eighteenth century had trading operations in Europe, Asia and the Americas. What happened in the second half of the last century was that the scale of international trade increased enormously. We saw the emergence of trading blocs such as the European Economic Community (EEC, now the European Union, EU), North American Free Trade Agreement (NAFTA) and Association of Southeast Asian Nations (ASEAN). Then there was the move towards global free trade through the creation of the General Agreement on Tariffs and Trade (GATT). Political events such as the fall of the Berlin Wall and economic reform in China and India brought more countries into the international trading networks. And finally, advances in communications technology have increased the speed of global trading interactions, and allowed even very small companies to compete internationally.

The McKinsey Global Institute estimates that over the last twenty years the value of cross-border economic flows has risen more than fivefold, from $5 trillion to $26 trillion.[35] These flows are no longer a matter of cross-border investment (which has actually declined) or low-cost production and offshoring. The new growth has come largely from services, especially knowledge-intensive services, with India and China now formidable competitors to the West.

The old economic dominance of Europe, North America and Japan is being challenged as never before. China is now the world's second-largest economy,

TABLE 4.9 The global environment affects everyone

Biocompatibles:	It was essential that Biocompatibles, as part of its commercialisation strategy, break into the American market, in part because of its size and in part because getting FDA approval is helpful in reaching out to other markets. Europe and Japan were also important markets.The company also used international acquisitions in the USA and Europe to obtain additional medical technologies.
CH Jones:	Based entirely in the UK, CH Jones was vulnerable to competition from rivals that could offer a single European-wide service. CH Jones never managed to counter that threat. In the end the company was purchased by an American firm that saw an opportunity to use CH Jones and its position in the British market as the foundation for a move into mainland Europe.
Datrontech:	Expansion without a well-founded business plan was one of the causes of Datrontech's failure. At one point the company had operations in ten countries, but some of these were loss-making or barely profitable, and the company had gone heavily into debt in order to fund acquisitions.
Forth Ports:	Seaports are terminals for the international maritime trade, and what happened in world shipping had a direct impact on Forth Ports' business. The board considered international expansion on several occasions, but was hesitant about committing; the single toe-in-the-water venture in Russia was sold a few years later. Time will tell whether this was the right position to take. The company was purchased by an Australian infrastructure fund.
Keller:	Already an international company when it bought itself out of GKN, Keller continued to expand through acquisition. After a period of exploration of alternatives, Keller adopted a strategy of sticking to its core business in ground engineering and expanding geographically, rather than diversifying into other business areas. It made acquisitions in the USA, Europe and Asia, but one of the issues it faced was how to grow organically and quickly in those countries where there were no acquisitions. Because markets are quite local and business came in the form of individual, site-specific projects, Keller chose a decentralised model which gave local business units plenty of freedom to operate. This may have come at the expense of central control.
Michael Gerson:	The core business, moving business executives from one country to another, meant that Michael Gerson operated in an international environment and was affected by fluctuations in the global economy. For example, the company was affected by 9/11 and the slowdown in corporate moves in the months and years immediately following. Over the long term, Gerson failed to read the changes in the environment and did not realise that its core international market was shrinking.
NFT:	Of all the eleven companies, NFT was least directly affected by global competition, but even then we had to take account of international trends in food production and consumption. And, if we were to grow the company further, expansion into Europe was an option that would need careful consideration. When we came to the exit, we saw an international round of bidding with an Asian investor succeeding and buying the company.

(Continued)

TABLE 4.9 Continued

NovaQuest:	Like Quintiles, NovaQuest is part of the global pharmaceuticals industry. Its first fund was raised in the USA. It raises money and invests in very specific opportunities wherever on the planet these are to be found. NovaQuest has to watch simultaneously the trends in global life sciences and those in the global private equity market. One of the questions we face at the moment is: are we 'global enough' in our thinking whether in raising money, finding co-investors, or finding investment opportunities? A second issue is the development of a family of funds focussed on a range of mandates in life sciences, again with a worldwide remit.
Quintiles:	The globalisation of the pharmaceuticals industry compelled Quintiles to follow suit as it kept pace with its clients. Quintiles adopted a centralised model in order to control key processes and research quality. For more on Quintiles, see below.
U-POL:	With manufacturing facilities in the UK, U-POL sells into markets around the world; the USA, continental Europe and Africa are particularly important and the company is watching developments in India and China. The key issue revolves around how to create the most effective marketing system. A pragmatic mixture of on-the-ground sales offices and direct export from the UK has been adopted.
Vantec:	Spun off from Renault-Nissan, Vantec set itself the goal of becoming an international logistics company. The most obvious move was to expand in the USA and Europe, but Vantec also spotted an opportunity in China's growing automotive industry, where its core expertise in automotives logistics could be leveraged. Vantec looked for opportunities that suited the company, rather than simply engaging in random expansion for its own sake.

set to overtake the USA by mid-century. The BRICS countries are established economic players; now eyes are turning to the MINT countries and other nations are rising fast behind them. "If we look at the next ten years," says Professor Anil Gupta of the University of Maryland, "the rise of emerging countries will cause a bigger structural change in the world economy than any decade in the last 200 years."[36] In other words, the changes of the last twenty years are nothing compared with the changes still to come.

The question for boards is: how do we choose the right strategy to navigate through this area of constant and increasing change? As in the previous chapter, the first and most important point is to be very clear about the overall strategic goal. It is relatively easy to expand into international operations; it is much harder to do so profitably. Companies that succeed in this area are ones that have a clear strategic goal in mind, identify opportunities, and stick to them, ignoring distractions. The ones that fail are the ones that have no clear goal and grab at each opportunity as it appears, or simply refuse to engage with the issues of internationalization and globalization at all.

The Challenges of Globalization

As with strategy, I do not intend to go too deeply into the subject of globalization here. Once again, there are many books on the subject. Japanese management guru Kenichi Ohmae, who is credited with introducing the term "globalization" into management, has written several well-known books including *The Borderless World* and *The Next Global Stage*. Janet Morrison's *The Global Business Environment* is an excellent introduction, and *Managing Across Borders: The Transnational Solution* by professors Sumantra Ghoshal and Christopher Bartlett offers a good academic perspective. There are also plenty of country-specific or market-specific books and guides, such as Ravi Venkatesan's *Conquering the Chaos: Win in India, Win Everywhere*, which is a good introduction to business in India.[37] Readers will doubtless have plenty of other titles in mind.

What do independent directors specifically need to know about internationalization and globalization? First of course, there is the simple awareness of difference. Recipes for success in one market will not necessarily work in another. Transferring a brand from a home market, where it is well known, to another market where there are incumbents in place and where your own brand is unfamiliar is not an easy thing to do. Cultural differences mean that managing people can be a very different experience. Culture itself is a huge subject, as studies like those of Geert Hofstede and the later Global Leadership and Organizational Behavior Effectiveness (GLOBE) Research *Project* found: national cultural differences can have a profound impact on everything from market demand to management and leadership styles see Figure 4.3 and Table 4.10.[38]

These and other studies confirm that, as strong as the force of globalization is, the differences between countries can be stronger still. Comparing the management cultures and business models of, say, Japan and Britain (see the earlier case study of Vantec, for example) show that localism is alive and well. There are many, many local issues that will confront directors as they seek to expand.

Does the country you wish to enter have a strong or weak economy? If the former, there may be a strong middle class with lots of spending power; in the latter, personal spending power may be weak. Less strong economies may also be more subject to exchange-rate fluctuations, or have legal barriers impeding the inflow and outflow of capital. Political systems differ too. Does the country have

TABLE 4.10   Two nations divided—Anglo-Dutch translation

What the British say	What the British mean	What the Dutch understand
I hear what you say...	I disagree and do not want to discuss it any further	He accepts my point of view
With the greatest respect...	I think you are wrong (or a fool)	He is listening to me
That's not bad...	That's good or very good	That's poor or mediocre
Quite good...	A bit disappointing	Quite good
Perhaps you would like to think about it... I would suggest...	This is an order. Do it or be prepared to justify yourself	Think about the idea, but do what you like
When appropriate locally...	Do what you like	Do it if you can
Oh, by the way.../ Incidentally...	The primary purpose of our discussion is	This is not very important
It was a bit disappointing that.. It is a pity you...	I was most upset and cross	It doesn't really matter
Very interesting	I don't agree / I don't believe you	They are impressed
Could we consider some other options	I don't like your idea	They have not yet decided
I'll bear it in mind...	I will do nothing about it	They will probably do it
Please think about that some more	It's a bad idea; don't do it	It's a good idea; keep developing it
I'm sure it's my fault	It is your fault	It was their fault
That's an original point of view	You must be crazy	They like my idea!
You must come for dinner sometime	Not an invitation, just being polite	I will get an invitation soon
You'll get there eventually	You don't stand a chance in hell	Keep on trying for they agree I'm going in the right direction
I almost agree...	I don't agree at all	They're not far from agreement

a business-friendly government, or one that sees business as potentially a threat to its own sovereignty? Different regulatory regimes—or their absence—may pose challenges for corporate governance. Issues such as bribery and corruption, unknown in one market, may suddenly rear their head in another where the rule of law is less strong and regulations are not enforced. Independents need to bear all of these things in mind when looking at any proposed international

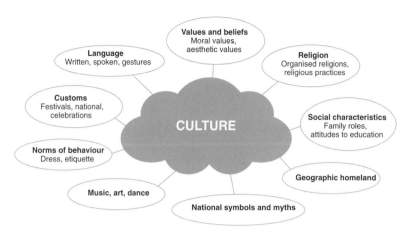

FIG 4.3 / Aspects of culture

Source: Janet Morrison, *The Global Business Environment*, Basingstoke: Palgrave Macmillan, 2011, p. 269

expansion, and run their eye carefully over the strategic plan. If they see anything in the plan that looks like it will not work, or is based on an over-optimistic assessment of the situation, then they must speak up see Figure 4.4.

What business the company is in also affects how it manages international expansion. For example, at GOH Capital we are facing up to global issues as we build our family of funds. One of the questions we are facing is: do we need to have people on the ground in various geographies, or would it be better to work through partnering? We have a wide range of skills sets that need to be covered; we need people who can do fundraising, who can make investments, who can administer the funds themselves, and so on. How do we configure the family of funds? How do we organize people? Getting these decisions right is not easy; many other private equity funds have tried to go global and failed, 3i being a classic example. The same problems affect the retail business, where no one seems to have found the right organizational recipe for international expansion. WalMart has probably come closest, but giants such as Tesco and Marks & Spencer have failed badly, particularly when attempting to enter North America.

All of these obstacles have implications for the board and, of course, for the independent director. One of the common causes of failure in this field is for boards to decide on a strategy and then plough steadily on, regardless of the mounting evidence that the strategy is not working. Independents, from their independent perspective, can take a longer view, see the signs of success or

FIG 4.4 / Global legal risk

Source: Janet Morrison, *The Global Business Environment*, Basingstoke: Palgrave Macmillan, 2011, p. 197

failure, and let the board know when they think a change of course might be called for.

For boards, all this means that careful attention must be paid to the composition of the board itself. The board needs directors with international experience, and especially with experience of the areas they have targeted for expansion and growth. These directors can offer advice based on experience. They can provide teach-ins for other board members, passing on knowledge about the local economy and culture. They can travel to these geographies and get a view of conditions on the ground. All of this, of course, adds to the work of the independent director. A certain amount of international contact can be maintained through video-conferencing, but there are times when there is no substitute for getting boots on the ground.

Referring back to our discussion of strategy, we find that independents need to know several things. Firstly, they need to know what is going on in the broader world environment, not just their home country. What is happening in the wider economic context? Which economies are rising, which are stagnating, or failing? What are the current economic trends; what countries will be the stars of the next decade, and which are ones best avoided? What political or environmental risk factors are present? What are regulatory regimes like, how easy is it to actually do business in other countries? What is the best mode of entry into a particular market? Reading books like those listed above will provide some help in finding answers to these questions, but there is no substitute for personal experience. One of the most valuable things an independent director can bring to a board is the personal experience of working in a particular country and market, and the advice he or she can give to the rest of the board can make the difference between a successful strategy and a failed one. For example, when Biocompatibles was contemplating entering the Korean market, it relied on the advice of independent director Sir Tom Harris, who had been the British ambassador there.

Secondly, independent directors need to know "how to do it," how to achieve successful entry into new markets. Again, it is important to remember the role of independents who are there to advise, guide thinking by contributing their own ideas, suggest solutions when problems occur—as they inevitably will—and then monitor progress towards agreed goals.

As an example, let us use modes of entry. There are a number of different modes of entry into new markets, any one of which can be useful, depending on the circumstances. I shall run through these quickly:

1. *Exporting*. Perhaps the oldest form of internationalization, this is a relatively low-risk option in terms of financial commitment and may have less impact on the organizational activities of the firm. On the other hand, exporting firms have little control over the supply chain and are forced to rely on distributors and shipping companies; this can be problematic. Exporting firms are also heavily exposed to exchange-rate risk. U-POL, for example, profits when the pound is weak against the dollar, but is likely to see its profits fall when the dollar weakens in turn, unless a good currency hedging strategy is in place.

2. *Licensing*. Licensing allows other firms to use the licensor's intellectual property, such as patents and trademarks, in their own business in exchange for a fee. For example, rather than trying to enter the Japanese market directly, Biocompatibles entered into a licensing arrangement with its partner Eisai. This again is a low-cost option, but does carry the risk of losing control of intellectual property.

3. *Distribution agreements*. Companies can also enter into agreements with local partners to distribute products and services. Biocompatibles has adopted this mode of entry with good effect in the USA and continental Europe. A distribution arrangement is particularly useful in small markets where it may not be worth investing in a direct presence, or for smaller companies that lack the resources to commit to foreign direct investment; or, of course, for both.

4. *Franchises.* These allow use of the company brand in exchange for a share of the profits, and are good ways to minimize financial risk and have a low impact on the franchising organization. Of course, the brand has to be well known already in the market, otherwise the franchisee might struggle to gain traction. Restaurants and hotel chains often use the franchise model to expand both domestically and internationally.

5. *Joint ventures.* These are the most popular mode of entry into the markets. Partnering with a local firm gives foreign companies quick access to markets, supply chains and resources, and local partners can also help with regulation and provide access to key people such as regulators or politicians. Volkswagen famously used joint ventures with local firms to establish itself early in the Chinese car market, and went on to dominate that market for many years.

   In some emerging markets, foreign companies are required to engage in joint ventures as a condition of market entry. In other cases, the foreign company uses joint ventures to give it experience of the market before proceeding to a wholly owned venture. Joint ventures are not a trouble-free option, however. Mismatches between partners can lead to misunderstandings, cultural clashes and problems with ethics and governance (especially if the partners come from countries where ethical standards and understanding of good governance are quite different).

6. *Greenfield investments.* Sometimes also known as wholly owned investments or ventures, these involve the company replicating its domestic operations in some form in another country, setting up its own production and/or distribution and marketing operations. Although Quintiles has relied heavily on acquisitions, it has also used greenfield expansion strategies with good effect, especially in Europe, Africa and South America. In these places, where Quintiles could not find suitable companies to buy, it set up its own operations.

   Greenfield investments give the company complete control, and in some countries local governments will welcome greenfield investments and make the path smooth for their establishment, perhaps even providing subsidies or tax breaks. However, greenfield investments are expensive, and can be very slow to show a return on investment. This option is best for companies that are prepared to invest and take risks over the long term.

7. *Acquisitions.* This is another popular way to establish a physical presence in overseas markets. Acquisitions are quicker than greenfield investments and, if handled properly, will yield a faster return on investment. Sometimes, particularly in mature markets, an acquisition is the only way to create a market presence. However, as we saw in the earlier discussion on strategy,

acquisitions can be problematic and many fail to deliver value. Making the right acquisition in the right place is important, as is good due diligence. Keller is an excellent example of a business that has expanded successfully, largely through acquisitions, especially in the USA, Asia and Australia; although, as with Quintiles, a shortage of available businesses to buy in Europe meant that Keller had to adopt more of a greenfield model there.

8. *Brownfield investments*. This is a variant on the acquisition, in which a firm is acquired and heavily restructured and reformed to make it "fit" into the acquiring company. New staff, new systems and new technology mean that acquired company is now in effect a new firm. Brownfield investments are common in emerging markets, where outside firms "buy into" the market by picking up a local company and integrating it fully into their own operations.

When considering which mode of entry to adopt in a particular country or geography, what questions should the independent director ask the rest of the board? To some extent, the questions will depend on the nature and size of the company and the proposed market, but there are some questions that almost always need to be asked. For example:

1. What experience does the company have of the different modes of entry, for example, overseas acquisitions?
2. What analysis has been carried on the costs and benefits of the different options?
3. What are the implications of the recommended approach, for example, of a joint venture rather than a wholly owned venture?

And again, once the decision has been made and entry is underway, here are some of the questions that the independent director should continue to ask, to ensure that the strategy is executed successfully:

1. What are the results compared to the project proposal?
2. Is the recommended strategy still the best course of action?
3. What lessons have been learned, which are transferrable to other geographies?

Quintiles: Globalization in Practice

Of the companies with which I have worked, Quintiles offers perhaps the best example of a globalization strategy and the issues that confront all directors — executive and independent alike. The strategy was described in the Quintiles case study earlier in this book. Here I want to talk about the strategy-making process.

In the case studies earlier in the book, I noted how the pharmaceuticals industry changed at the end of the 1990s. There was a significant restructuring of the entire sector, with some players merging or disappearing entirely. Those that remained were, increasingly, very large global companies. The biotechnology industry, with which pharmaceuticals are strongly linked, had also become much more globalized. Quintiles needed to adapt and grow too in order to keep pace with its clients and continue to provide the things the latter demanded. These included:

• Common service standards in clinical trials no matter where in the world the company operated;
• Common systems to enable integrated global communications with clients and management and enable the spread of best practice;
• Common technology platforms to enable these systems;
• The ability to conduct trials in the most cost-effective locations; and
• High standards of corporate governance throughout worldwide operations.

At the same time, Quintiles was under pressure to become more efficient and, as it was then a quoted company, to maximize investment returns. Quintiles was operating in a world where people, goods, technology, and capital were becoming more mobile, and at a time when there was a marked shift in economic power towards Asia with the rise of India and, especially, China.

Up to that point, Quintiles' growth had been mainly—though not entirely—concentrated in North America. Asia and EMEA accounted for relatively small percentages of group revenue. To survive and grow in the new world order, Quintiles faced a number of challenges. These were some of the questions that confronted the board:

• How do we develop common systems and service standards that can be applied across all countries and cultures? How do we communicate between and across cultures?
• How do we develop the expertise required to work in emerging markets, given that most of our experience so far has concentrated on the developed world?
• We are a highly centralized group; can we continue to operate this way, or do we need to decentralize and give the regions more responsibility? What happens to our common systems if we do so? How would we align regional business objectives with our global objective?
• Some of our customers are organized globally, some are not. How do we distinguish between them?
• How do we implement and maintain a matrix structure based on geographies and functions? How do we implement a team-working culture?

• How do we persuade employees to buy into our new strategy? What sorts of investment will be needed, in people and in systems, especially information systems?

To deal with these issues successfully, we needed to build a number of things into the firm. These included (1) a range of new management skills and capabilities, including multi-lingual capacity, multi-cultural awareness, matrix management, change management, team-working, and project management; (2) the ability to match people and jobs, so that we had the right people in the right places doing the right things; (3) the creation of a knowledge culture so that good practice could be shared quickly and easily within the group; (4) the linking of all jobs to profit and growth maximization so that everyone would find their personal goals aligned with the strategic goals; and (5) giving everyone the courage to challenge and speak their mind so that if things started to go wrong at any point, top management would be aware of this and able to move quickly to rectify matters. (This last was difficult in some of the cultures we worked in, such as Japan where deference and respect for superiors is strong and people do not openly criticize those in high places.)

Quintiles shows the range of issues that boards have to confront when dealing with international and global strategy. Independent directors, as part of the strategy-making process, must be able to engage with all of these issues—and more. They can learn a great deal about international and global business by studying, and they can learn much more from networking experience, drawing on the countries and companies with which they have worked in the past. Ultimately, though, there will still be gaps in their knowledge. In that case, they need to get to know the company, market and culture in which they operate. That can be very challenging, particularly in emerging markets.

Emerging Markets

I cited above Professor Anil Gupta's view that emerging markets are about to effect a revolution in the world economy. The late C.K. Prahalad offered a similar view in his book, *The Fortune at the Bottom of the Pyramid* and, more recently, Vijay Mahajan's studies of African and Middle Eastern consumers, *Africa Rising* and *The Arab World Unbound*, suggest that the revolution is already beginning.[39] Increasing private consumption, urbanization, and infrastructure development in these countries present both challenges and opportunities.

But are Western businesses ready for this? Not according to Aidan Manktelow of *The Economist*, who commented in 2014: "Despite the opportunities that growth markets offer global firms, they are often unable to find the capital, talent and other resources that they need, and are constrained by the still cautious outlook that overshadows decision-making emanating from the post-crisis 'rich world'." He goes on to say: "Part of the reason for the failure of many companies to fully exploit the opportunities in emerging markets is that senior management teams back in European or US headquarters are too distant."[40]

All of these authors are of the view that the emerging markets hold one of the keys to future growth and prosperity, and furthermore, that Western companies need to get moving quickly in order to seize the opportunities being held out to them. But many companies still have a Western outlook, and regard the home market as the most important. Often strategy is still formulated at head office, not on the ground. Most resources are still committed to producing and selling into the mature markets of Europe, Japan, and North America.

The reason is partly psychological. These are the markets that these companies and their executives know best. They are comfortable here. Working in emerging markets requires them to confront and rethink their approach to a whole variety of issues. These include government policies, especially in countries where "government" is a rather shaky concept; local regulations; local workforces and their expectations; sources of local managerial talent and skills necessary for innovation; cultural issues; infrastructure and property issues; supply chains and distribution (or the lack of them) and marketing channels; differing standards of ethics and governance; the list goes on and on.

Part of the answer, in my view, is for senior executives and independents to get out of their head offices and look at the situation locally. They need to see for themselves what is happening. And they need to start devolving more authority to the local regions, where people who are close to the market can make key strategic decisions. As I said, I understand why Quintiles adopted a centralized approach, but in my view they went too far in that direction. What is ultimately required is a change in mindset as well as a change in organization. Ultimately, at Quintiles, Dennis Gillings established a series of regional boards.

Some companies have gone so far as to create two separate management teams, one to run operations in the developed world, another to look after emerging markets. But, unless these two teams are carefully controlled, then there is a real danger that the company could end up with two cultures, perhaps even effectively two firms in one and that the two could clash. Boards

Quintiles In India

Quintiles India was founded in 1997. The business has since grown to a turnover of over $140 million, covering clinical development, commercialization, and data management. It employs over 3,000 people.

The Indian company was originally structured as a 50–50 joint venture between Quintiles Transnational and an Indian vehicle, which brought in local management and expertise. Global clinical research organizations had not established themselves in India at the time, although they had begun to evince interest. Dr Dennis Gillings, founder of Quintiles Transnational, had an early vision of how the industry he had helped to create would globalize. He realized that the Asian markets, already formidable in volume terms, would grow. Powerful market forces driving demand included large populations, rising income levels, growing aspirations of doctors and patients for the latest medicine, and an ever-increasing burden of disease.

Quintiles India had several differentiating features from inception. Local management had the freedom to run and grow the business within the ambit of global governance parameters. Managers needed to be empowered, nimble, and innovative. There was a need to work effectively with regulatory authorities and to encourage the adoption of new rules and guidelines for clinical research. The global corporation provided necessary resources and training for growth and the Indian subsidiary expanded to different cities, building strong teams with a focus on leadership development. Young talent was mentored and there was a strong sense of ownership and corporate responsibility within the organization.

However, sharing work between countries, each with its own profit and loss statement, was a perpetual challenge. Business development therefore became an important initiative, with senior leadership selling the India story aggressively to internal stakeholders and external customers. The story met with significant resistance from a conservative industry.

Fortuitously, the biopharmaceuticals industry was under pressure to transform its processes at around the same time. Long fed by a steady diet of blockbuster drugs, the industry had failed to embrace technology and efficiency paradigms that had permeated other industries. A cozy camaraderie between executives in the industrially developed countries worked against the globalization of drug research and the induction of talent from other industries. All this changed as traditional drug pipelines started drying up and societal scrutiny on drug pricing and disease outcomes increased dramatically.

Drug companies facing increasing pressure on their earnings were compelled by multiple stakeholders to change rapidly. Asian geographies suddenly became important, both as markets and offshore destinations for developing new drugs more efficiently.

Quintiles India was able to ride this wave, thanks to having already established a local presence, a strong management team, and a growing reputation in the market. The company's local management team had also initiated various technology businesses in India. These businesses established outposts in Western markets and globalized rapidly. The impetus and leadership for these ventures came from the local subsidiary in India. At a later date, large global verticals within Quintiles, such as data management, were also led from India.

Although Quintiles was the most international of all Contract Research Organizations (CROs), it continued to have the legacy of its parent industry and had to therefore cede market share to IT companies such as Cognizant, Accenture, and Tata Consultancy Services. The battle for market dominance continues today with IT companies buying domain knowledge and consulting capabilities. CROs are responding by strengthening their ability to deliver technology services in a scalable manner at a global level. The top CROs, such as Quintiles, are also trying to gain an edge by partnering with pharmaceuticals companies across the value chain and focusing on customer outcomes. One can argue that competition has strengthened the industry and has better enabled it to serve its customers and its ultimate consumers, the patients. The India venture, with its humble beginnings in 1997, has played a catalytic role in transforming the CRO industry.

Note: This is an abridged version of a case study originally developed by Farzaan Engineer. Many thanks to Farzaan for giving permission to reproduce this.

will need to look at their own management structures and their own composition and culture if they are to manage this process effectively.

How Should Independent Directors Respond to Globalization?

First and foremost, they need to develop expertise. It is too much to expect an individual to be familiar with every culture, and no one should try. My advice is to specialize in a particular area or areas that interest you. Learn about the culture, the language, the politics, and governments, the ethical frameworks, and the market mechanisms such as property, infrastructure, supply chains, markets, competition and so on. That way, you will have the necessary expertise to convey to your board colleagues in order to help them and advise them.

That means reading, studying and working networks of contacts to get access to the experience of others, but it also means travelling. Independents need to get out of head office to travel and visit operations. Only then can they get the true local perspective that will tell them whether the overall international or global strategy really makes sense.

Biocompatibles, when I joined the board, had no experience of commercializing its products. It was a research organization trying to make the transition to being a full-blown commercial business. We had a product in which we had confidence, the drug-eluting beads. The board had to consider its options. We could establish a global sales force, but that would take a long time and cost a lot of money. We then considered whether to work with a distributor, but upon looking around found that there were no distributors with global reach. So, we began to consider which markets to try to reach.

Emerging markets, sadly, had to be ruled out as the product is expensive. In the USA and Japan, on the other hand, there are affluent people who can and will pay for this kind of treatment. There were distributors of the kind we needed in the USA and Europe, and we entered into agreements with them. In Japan, on the other hand, we discovered that a licensing agreement with Eisai was more likely to give us traction in the market, and accordingly went down that road. We chose, in the end, quite traditional methods of market entry that were also low-risk. That was what was necessary for that company at that time and place.

Vantec: Changing to a Global Mindset

Although the car-maker Nissan had a global presence, its logistics subsidiary Vantec had never worked with major clients outside of Japan. Its ethos was not just Japanese, but Nissan, and its staff and managers from top to bottom of the company were "Nissan men."

Upon becoming independent, Vantec faced two challenges. First, if it was going to grow its customer base and therefore its business, Vantec would have to look for customers outside of Japan. The Japanese economy was moribund, with very low or nil growth rates, and there was plenty of domestic competition. And, that competition was about to intensify with international players like TNT and Exel also poised to enter the market. These big companies with their global reach could offer services that Vantec could not. Finally, the private equity owners of Vantec had set growth targets that had to be met.

In order to grow, Vantec had to become more international and that required a change of mindset. Things really began to move when we brought in an outsider, Yamada Toshi, to take over as CEO. Unlike some of the Japanese board members and senior executives, Toshi had a great deal of international experience. He also had the character and personality required to ensure that the others listened to his views. Despite skepticism, with the support of the independent directors Toshi led the way in working out and then implementing an international strategy. Vantec expanded in Europe but, as already recounted, made a major breakthrough when it established a position in China, developing clients in that country's fast-growing automotive industry.

Vantec was a success story, but it would not have been so without the teamwork between Toshi and the independent directors who persuaded a skeptical executive team that internationalization was not only inevitable, it was the only way the company could grow.

Summary

Internationalization and globalization are not going away. And the old way of trying to run everything from head office is looking increasingly obsolete. Writing in the *Financial Times*, Andrew Hill suggested that local responsiveness will increasingly be part of the winning formula in international competition. If he is right, then independent directors have a powerful role to play in helping boards find that responsiveness. Of course, international expansion is not without its risks; and it is now to the subject of risk, and the role of independent directors in managing risk, that we turn next.

Risk

> Truth is a gem that is found at a great depth; whilst on the surface of this world, all things are weighted by the false scale of custom.
>
> — Lord Byron

The past decade has seen an increasing incidence of corporate governance failures arising from risks that were either not understood, or were badly managed, or both. We have all seen the headlines: banks mis-selling insurance and hedging products, and investing in highly risky derivatives; international retailers and on-line companies avoiding tax; mining, oil, and pharmaceuticals companies involved in corruption; energy companies engaging in anti-competitive behavior; companies of all sorts ranging from newspapers to banks engaging in unethical practices.

Each time one of these scandals erupts, it causes damage. Sometimes, entire companies are brought down, or have to be bailed out by the taxpayer. Sometimes the companies survive but their reputations are forever tarnished. That too has costs, in terms of reputation, goodwill, and trust on the part of customers and employees, and loss of these things has a knock-on financial effect. And, each time I read an account of one of these events, I ask myself the question again: where were the independent directors? How and why did they allow this situation to develop in the first place?

What is the role of the independent director in risk management? Some, like Paul Hopkin (whose *Fundamentals of Risk Management* is widely read by managers and directors) appear to believe that the role of the independent director should be limited to "audit, assurance and compliance activities."[41]

I do not think that Hopkin is trying to downplay the importance of the independent director in risk management; he just seems to believe that it should be very limited. But why? By the time audits and compliance exercises expose risk, it is very often too late; the risk is already present, and the consequences are already present too. Ensuring compliance with health and safety policies, for example, only ensures that present policies are being followed; it does not ensure that those policies are the right ones.

In my view, independent directors must be much more than just auditors. They need to be proactive in their approach to risk. Understanding the risk position of any venture, says Steve Edge of Slaughter & May, is one of the key duties of any director, independents included. For example, they should be totally involved in the development of a comprehensive risk management strategy, including identifying and assessing risks from the very beginning of any new project, and their expertise and experience should always be brought to bear.

Only then can the board be sure that a full range of views on risk have been considered and that directors have a realistic picture of the risks the company faces, and that the procedures the board puts in place to avoid or mitigate these risks are also realistic. And let us be quite clear: it is the responsibility of the board to ensure that risk is managed effectively. The buck stops at the boardroom table. That is not just a responsible and ethical way of looking at the issue; increasingly also, this principle is becoming enshrined in law.

Hopkin's approach is an example of what has been the view of many independent directors in the USA. In the UK, there is already much more of an emphasis on risk assessment as a key function of independent directors. But the picture is changing in the USA too, and boards and independent directors are appreciating that they must become more directly involved. Television news programs showing directors being dragged away to jail have probably helped to concentrate the mind, but recent laws such as the Dodd–Frank Act are also putting more pressure on directors of all types, independents included, to be more proactive about risk.

Why Does Risk Matter?

Risk is omnipresent. Every company faces risks of some sort. Some of these risks are relatively minor and can be easily managed. Others are more complex, and failure to manage them can have widespread ramifications, including

TABLE 4.11　Risks in the 11 case studies

Biocompatibles:	issues with distributors; manufacturing problems
CH Jones:	fluctuations in fuel prices; information systems problems
Datrontech:	prices of imported products; technological innovation; financial risk due to over-gearing
Forth Ports:	significant marine incident; pension scheme funding
Keller:	health and safety; cyclical nature of market; ground conditions associated with specific projects
Michael Gerson:	shrinking core market due to the banking crisis; breakages or losses of high value items
NFT:	changes in volume of the shared user network; temperature control issues affecting food safety
NovaQuest:	inadequate due diligence of specific investments; financial climate affecting the raising of capital
Quintiles:	quality control issues leading to the failure of clinical trials; regulation and compliance
U-POL:	prices of raw materials; credit control issues with overseas purchasers
Vantec:	start-ups of new operations; customer issues (over-dependence on Nissan)

financial loss to the firm and/or its employees and customers, damage to communities in which the firm operates, and possible harm to employees and customers. Table 4.11 shows some of the key risks that faced each of the eleven companies profiled earlier. This is not a complete list, of course, but it gives an idea of the range of risks that companies face.

A More Detailed Example of Risk

Pharmaceuticals research in development is inherently risky for a wide variety of reasons. Here are some of the risks faced by Quintiles on an on-going basis;

Business risks

- Loss or reduction in contracts. If pharma companies cut back on spending or choose other service providers, Quintiles needs to react.
- Wrong pricing. Getting the pricing of services right is both difficult and imperative.
- Failure of information systems. These are a key part of Quintiles' competitive edge, and if they go down, the damage to the company would be considerable.

- Quality-control issues in carrying out clinical trials. The reputational risk of a quality failure is immense.
- Difficulties in patient recruitment for specific therapeutic areas. If this occurs, then the possibility of carrying out a successful clinical trial could be compromised.
- Loss of key personnel. Experienced and skilled staff are essential to the business.
- Company restructuring and organization changes. These are always risky, as they can cause problems with communication and staff morale.
- Specific customer issues. Can Quintiles meet customer expectations?

Industry risks

- International economic, political and social changes. Which markets are rising and which falling?
- Foreign exchange rates. Even a small rate change can affect income figures drastically.
- Competitor activity. Quintiles is the industry leader, but for how long?
- Outsourcing trends by customers. What sorts of services do pharma companies outsource, and will they continue to do so?
- Healthcare reforms. What does Obamacare mean for the drugs market in the USA?
- Regulatory approach to specific clinical trials. Regulation is tightening all the time; how much will Quintiles have to invest to remain compliant?
- Technological change. Will new technologies upset the market and render some classes of drug obsolete? Or will they offer new ways of conducting clinical trials?

From the director's point of view, it is important to recognize that it is not just companies, employees and customers who may suffer harm. If there is a problem, the directors themselves will come under scrutiny, and if they are found to have failed in their duty then their reputations will be damaged. In serious cases, there could be civil or criminal prosecutions of directors, and it is not unknown for directors to be extradited to face trial in other countries.

Historically, the biggest risk for directors was large-scale financial or accounting fraud of the sort that we have seen at Enron and WorldCom or Société Générale. These risks are still present, but effective internal controls and external auditors can keep them to a minimum. Much more common, and equally potentially damaging, are failures in legal and operational compliance.

These kinds of failure are harder to prevent, as it is more difficult to establish effective controls and monitor compliance with either the law or internally established standards.

Some laws that regulate companies, like anti-competition regulation, have been around for a long time. Laws on bribery have a long history too; the USA passed the Foreign Corrupt Practices Act back in 1977, and the UK has recently updated its own legislation in the form of the Bribery Act. In the UK too, the director of the Serious Fraud Office has made it clear that he regards the task of his organization as prosecuting those who break the law, not helping companies and individuals to interpret the law and avoid prosecution. A similar ethos prevails in the USA (though other countries are more lax in this respect). In other words, ignorance of the law is no excuse; it is down to directors to understand the law and comply with it.

The increased scrutiny of business by regulators, employees, and the public has created an atmosphere where corporate and individual wrongdoing is much more likely to be uncovered than was the case, say, twenty-five years ago. Whistleblowing is becoming more prevalent, and whistleblowers are beginning to use new routes to disclose what they believe to be illegal or unethical behavior, such as blogs, social media, and activist websites. The Serious Fraud Office and the US Department of Justice, as well as regulators in several European countries, have official channels through which whistleblowers can report companies, and in the USA the Dodd–Frank Act now offers a bounty to whistleblowers whose exposures of companies lead to successful prosecutions. These payouts can be substantial (although at time of writing is not yet known if they have led to any overall increase in whistleblowing).

The point I make here is not that directors need to be ethical and honest in their own behavior, although that is very important. They also need to be alert to the possibility of dishonesty, ethical failures and just plain bad management elsewhere in the organization. They are responsible for the failures of others, not just themselves.

Are directors aware that they are both responsible for risk and can be prosecuted if they are seen to have failed in their duty? A survey conducted in 2013 by London-based legal firm Allen & Overy and international insurance broker and risk advisor Willis suggested that 30 percent of directors did not realize that they faced personal exposure to penalties or to anti-trust enforcement; and this despite the likelihood that financial and other regulators will go after directors who are perceived to have been derelict in their duty.[42] There have been high-profile arrests and convictions that have made the front pages, but there have been many more less publicized but still expensive fines and sanctions meted out to others. The number of fines handed out by the Financial Service Authority in the UK rose by 45 percent between 2008 and 2012. And it needs to be emphasized again that the law applies to independent as well as executive directors. Independent status confers no immunity.

Clearly, independent directors need to understand not only the principles of risk management but also best practice: not only so that they can fulfill their statutory duty and ensure that companies are managed in the best interests of all stakeholders, but also to protect themselves.

Types of Risk

Risk is inevitable in business, and companies will always face risks whatever they do. (I will come to the question of "how much risk is appropriate?" in a moment.) There are some types of risk which it is not really possible to eliminate, such as lightning strikes or earthquakes. One can take reasonable precautions and try to mitigate the effects of these things—reinforcing buildings in known earthquake zones, for example—but one cannot prevent them from happening.

However, there are many other kinds of risks that can either be prevented or else hedged against to an extent as to render their effects less dangerous and damaging. The problem is that people *don't* prepare for these risks, either because they do not know how to manage risk or because they are not sufficiently aware that the risks exist in the first place. Take for example the banking crisis, which we know happened because banks failed to assess the financial risks accurately and lent very large sums of money in a very risky way. Why did they do so? Some of the reports into the crisis have highlighted the fact that many banks had directors—including independent directors— who were insufficiently familiar with the business, either their own company or the sector as a whole. They did not understand the complicated derivatives that were being traded. They also acquiesced in bonus schemes that rewarded executives for top-line growth, without waiting to see what the consequences of that growth would be. Today, at least one lesson has been learned and remuneration committees are delaying the payment of bonuses for three years, until the full impact of decisions can be assessed. There are also clawback provisions requiring bonuses to be repaid if they are subsequently deemed to be undeserved.

Risk management is a complex subject, and once again I don't intend to go into too much detail here. There are excellent books available on the subject, including Paul Hopkin's *Fundamentals of Risk Management* and also Thomas Coleman's *A Practical Guide to Risk Management* and Michel Crouhy, Dan Galai and Robert Mark's *The Essentials of Risk Management*.[43] Here, the main point is to make it clear how important it is that independent directors understand risk and risk management. Ideally they should have prior executive experience of assessing and managing risk, as well as a sound base of theoretical knowledge.

Paul Hopkin categorizes risk into four different types: *hazard risk, control risk, opportunity risk,* and *compliance risk.* Hazard risk, or pure risk, is what most people think of when they think of risk. It is concerned with issues such as health and safety, fire prevention, the consequences of defective products and services, and the avoidance of theft and fraud. It is very much centered around operational risk issues, though of course these can have financial and reputational consequences.

Hopkin describes hazard risk as being risk to any or all of the following: *people, premises, processes,* or *products.* Table 4.12 gives examples of each.

Hopkin goes on to describe what he calls the "bow-tie" model of risk impact which is shown in Figure 4.5. On the left side of the bow-tie are the sources of risk: strategic, operational, tactical or compliance-related. The centre of the tie shows the impact on the firm, and the right side shows the consequences. Although he talks here primarily of hazard risk, it seems that the same kind of approach—source-impact-consequences—can be used to understand other kinds of risk.

Of the other main categories, control risk, also known as uncertainty risk, is the risk that we face when we can no longer entirely control operations or events. Entering into a joint venture with another company represents a control risk as some part of control must be surrendered to the partner. In this example, control risk can be mitigated by carefully vetting partners and getting to know them before signing any deal.

Opportunity risk, or speculative risk, is the risk we take when embarking on any new venture. Moving into a new product market or geographical market represents an opportunity risk, the level of risk being determined by things such as levels of competition, regulation, the existence of functioning supply chains, the regulatory environment and so on. These risks can be mitigated by either using prior knowledge fully or gaining new knowledge so that the market and environment are fully understood. Opportunity costs can be assessed, and the best and most profitable opportunities identified. With more knowledge comes better decision-making and so less risk. Finally,

TABLE 4.12   Categories of risk

Category	Examples of disruption
People	Lack of people skills and/or resources
	Inappropriate behaviour by a senior manager
	Unexpected absence of key personnel
	Ill-health, accident or injury of people
Premises	Inadequate, insufficient or denial of access to premises
	Damage to or contamination of premises
	Damage to and breakdown of physical assets
	Theft or loss of physical assets
Processes	Failure of IT hardware or software systems
	Disruption by hacker or computer virus
	Inadequate management of information
	Failure of communication or transport systems
Products	Poor product or service quality
	Disruption caused by failure of supplier
	Delivery of defective goods or components
	Failure of outsourced services and facilities

Source: Paul Hopkin, *Fundamentals of Risk Management*, London: Kogan Page, 2010, p. 32

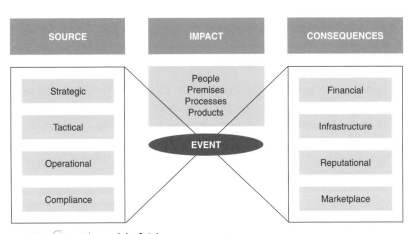

FIG 4.5   Bow-tie model of risk management

Source: Paul Hopkin, *Fundamentals of Risk Management*, London: Kogan Page, 2010, p. 152

compliance risk is the risk of not fully complying with laws and regulations. Some industries such as financial services and energy are particularly exposed to compliance risk due to the large body of regulations by which they must abide, but every company has some level of compliance risk (see Figure 4.6).

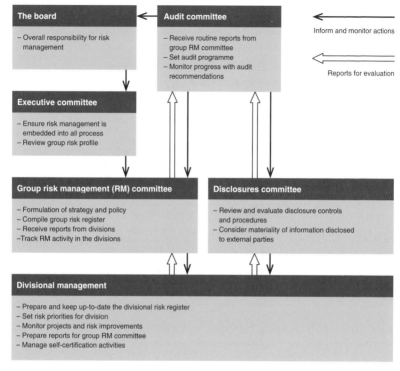

FIG 4.6 / Risk management architecture

Source: Paul Hopkin, *Fundamentals of Risk Management*, London: Kogan Page, 2010, p. 103

As noted, when many people think of risk they think of hazard risk. It is important that independent directors open up their thinking and consider risk on all four levels across a broad spectrum. Executives, who have to concentrate on day-to-day management, are sometimes preoccupied with hazard risks. It is up to the independents to remind them of other kinds of risk and ensure that the best possible decisions are made.

How Much Risk?

Andrew Marshall, audit partner at KPMG, comments that different boards have different appetites for risk, depending in part on the nature of the business and in part on the culture of the company and the board itself. All firms face some sort of risk, but the right balance will vary from firm to firm. However, that balance must be found. Too much risk is definitely dangerous, but too little can be harmful too. Unless firms are willing to take at least some risks, they will never progress; there will be no diversification, no innovation. I have worked, and still work with, companies that I consider to be too risk-averse. Forth Ports was very cautious in some areas, such as international expansion.

NovaQuest is very risk-averse; the executive team have seen too many things go wrong in investments, and are determined to avoid mistakes. Yet the pharmaceuticals research business is terribly risky. The probability that a research team will find a molecule that will be a cure for a particular disease is less than 1 percent. Entrepreneurs trying to set up such teams need money to fund their activities, but they struggle to get it because banks and other investors are at the moment very unwilling to take risks.

What, therefore, is the acceptable level of risk? Every firm will have a different level, depending on the market it is in and the attitudes of the chairman, CEO and individual board members. Oil exploration is a very risky business, and boards need to have a fairly strong appetite for risk. Banking, by contrast, was once a very risk-averse sector; until boards decided that they were willing to take more risks in the pursuit of higher profits. That brings up another point, which is that the appetite for risk varies over time; at the top of the economic cycle firms are willing to take more risks, but when the downturn comes they grow more risk-averse. This is not always logical, but it is understandable.

Boards, and independent directors, have a very important part to play in making sure that not too many risks are taken, but also that *enough* risks are taken. There are no guides to tell you how much risk is enough; it is largely a matter of judgment and experience. This is an area where independent directors have an important role to play, stepping back and looking at the larger picture and taking a considered view on what the risk appetite should be, which risks are acceptable, and which are not.

How Risk Should be Managed

I say "how risk *should* be managed," because all too often risk is managed very badly.

First and foremost, the board should take responsibility for assessing the major risks facing the business and challenging the assumptions underlying all risk assessments. There should be a top-level risk-management strategy that sets out the overall approach to risk and then feeds into strategy, projects, and

TABLE 4.13   Board responsibilities for risk management

Risk management responsibility
1   Board is responsible for governance of risk.
2   Board is responsible for determining the level of risk tolerance and risks it is willing to take (risk appetite).
3   Board should be assisted in carrying out its risk responsibilities by the risk committee or audit committee.
4   Board should delegate to management the responsibility to design, implement and monitor the risk management plan.
5   Board should ensure that risk assessments are performed on a continual basis.
6   Board should ensure that frameworks and methodologies are implemented to increase the probability of anticipating unpredictable risks.
7   Board should ensure that management considers and implements appropriate risk responses.
8   Board should ensure continuous risk monitoring by management.
9   Board should receive assurance regarding the effectiveness of the risk management process.
10   Board should ensure that there are processes in place to ensure complete, timely, relevant, accurate and accessible risk disclosure to stakeholders.

Source: Paul Hopkin, *Fundamentals of Risk Management*, London: Kogan Page, 2010, p. 67

operations. Paul Hopkin lists the following board responsibilities with relation to risk (see Table 4.13):

In the USA, when a company is put up for sale or listed on the stock market, it is required to produce a list of risk factors. At Quintiles, this list ran to fifteen pages! However, these reports should not just be one-off affairs. There should be regular reports of key metrics over all major risk areas, and thorough investigation of all incidents, and these should also be summarized in the annual report. At NFT, we reviewed the main risks every month at the board, and considered the actions being taken to deal with them. Keller and Forth Ports also reported regularly on risks and included a risk summary in its annual report. Here too, specific risks were detailed along with the actions taken to prevent or mitigate them.

The quality of risk disclosures in annual reports has come in for some criticism and there are complaints that the descriptions of risk are too vague or too technically complex for most people to understand. The Institute of International Finance reported in 2008 that "the lack of a comprehensive firm-wide approach to risk management often meant that key risks were not identified or effectively managed."[44] There is as yet no broadly accepted framework for risk accounting or the presentation of risk management in annual reports. PWC have suggested a number of practical tips for risk reporting:

- Present a balanced image;
- Be specific instead of generic;
- Focus on the principle risks;
- Articulate the risk appetite of the company;
- Link the risks to strategic and operational objectives;
- Show the potential impact of each risk on results;
- Quantify the impact of specific risks;
- Articulate the company's risk response;
- Seek alignment with disclosures in financial statements;
- Be up-to-date;
- Be transparent about internal control issues; and
- Use plain language to aid understanding.

One important tool of risk management is the development of a risk-aware culture, in which everyone in the company knows what the risks are and what their role in prevention or mitigation is. Engineering and steel companies adopting a "zero harm" approach to health and safety, for example, work to build awareness of risk into the corporate culture. Regulation and enforcement are part of the picture, but only part; in order to achieve zero harm, everyone in the company has to want to do so. Table 4.14 shows the key aspects of a risk aware culture.

Keller is in a business where the health and safety risks are very high. Preventing employees from being killed or injured is very expensive. Yet, apart from human considerations, there is also the question of opportunity costs. What does it cost the company in terms of money and reputation when there is an accident? This issue was brought into sharp relief after several accidents in which four people died. This was the catalyst for action. It will be recalled that Keller was a very decentralized business, and up to that point health and safety had been the responsibility of the individual business units. It was now decided to have a group health and safety policy, and a board-level health and safety committee to design that policy, oversee its implementation, and monitor it. The chairman of the health and safety committee was an industry expert who knew the issues very well. We, the board, then took the lead in developing this culture. Every time we vested a country, such as India, we insisted on

TABLE 4.14　Risk-aware culture

Leadership	Strong leadership within the organisation in relation to strategy, projects and operations
Involvement	Involvement of all stakeholders in all stages of the risk management process
Learning	Emphasis on training in risk management procedures and learning from events
Accountability	Absence of an automatic blame culture, but appropriate accountability for actions
Communication	Communication and openness on all risk management issues and the lessons learnt

Source: Paul Hopkin, *Fundamentals of Risk Management*, London: Kogan Page, 2010, p. 110

visiting a building site so that we could see what was being done in terms of health and safety. Gradually, this attitude began to permeate through the rest of the company.

Part of a good risk culture is the insistence on prevention rather than cure. That is why I take issue with the audit and compliance approach to risk. Identifying a problem after it has happened is like shutting the stable door after the horse has bolted. Curing a problem once it has happened takes a lot of time and resource. At NFT, for example, if something had gone wrong with the distribution chain we would have had to buy in agency labor and vehicles, bring in consultants to see what had gone wrong with the systems, send people to talk to our customers to explain the situation and keep them happy, and so on. We preferred to identify the risk early on, and then take steps to ensure that the problems never happened. That approach was cheaper, safer, and in the long run, easier.

Independent Directors and Risk

What role do independent directors play in risk management? At the outset, I made it clear that I do not agree with limiting the independent director's role to audit and compliance. To me, it is self-evident that independent directors play a vital role in overall risk assessment and risk management.

Let us take the four kinds of risk identified by Hopkin: hazard risk, control risk, opportunity risk and compliance risk. Turning first to hazard risk, it is clear that independent directors can influence hazard risk management in several ways. At Keller, we created a health and safety committee, and then the independents got behind the policy and made it work. At Biocompatibles we created a quality committee to ensure a structured approach to our main risk issues, failures of clinical trials and manufacturing problems. Independent directors chaired and/or formed much of the membership of these committees. In both cases, the independents had specific expertise and experience, which other members of the board lacked, and they could bring their knowledge to bear on decision-making and problem-solving. Without their input, the board would have been much less effective.

In terms of control risk, at Biocompatibles the quality committee aimed to reduce uncertainty by giving us more control over operations. At NFT, as chairman I would insist that before a new operation started, we as a board had sight of the operation plan. The whole of the board had to be satisfied that risks had been identified and plans were in place. That kind of oversight means a much greater probability that issues will be spotted. At Datrontech, on the other hand, control was never fully established and strategic drift set in, unstoppable until it was too late.

Independent directors also have a role to play in terms of opportunity risk. For example, take the issue of entering new markets. Entering a new country market is risky, but if there is an independent director on the board who has worked in this country before, or knows how these markets function, then his or her advice can help the board decide whether and how to enter that market; in other words, whether the risk is worth taking. This was important at Quintiles, Keller, Biocompatibles, and U-POL, and made for better decision-making in every case. Unfortunately, many companies are like Datrontech, expanding at random into countries where they have no background and little knowledge, and then paying the price for it. And finally, independent directors play an important role in dealing with compliance risk, particularly through the operations of the audit and remunerations committees, but also in helping to establish a culture where compliance with the law is part of the core business model, not a grudging duty added on top.

A Proactive Approach to Risk

A purely audit-based approach to risk is itself risky. Audit is of course vitally important (and a legal requirement), but directors should be taking a more proactive approach, attempting to identify future risks. Otherwise, there is a danger that too much time will be spent looking backwards, and that by the time the risk has been spotted it is too late; the stable door will be barred, but the horse will already be long gone.

Whenever any new venture or project is considered, directors must consider and discuss the risks. What are the things that can go wrong? How will we attempt to prevent them from going wrong? If they do go wrong, what will we do to mitigate the effects? All of these questions should be asked, and the answers should be embedded in a well-thought-out project plan.

Take for example a company switching its logistics and distribution from one provider to another. Such a transfer always holds the potential for disruption; the company may have to make changes to its own internal procedures, staff have to get used to working with the new provider and build new relationships, and so on. How do we manage the risks? By identifying the risks in advance, and planning for them. Or take the introduction of a new IT system. Unless the system is carefully planned for and sufficient run-throughs conducted before the system goes live, then the company is running a risk: the system may not work properly at first, and this could cause confusion for employees or customers.

Independent directors should be fully involved in this sort of planning at board level. Once again, they have a set of skills and experiences that can be valuable to the entire board. They may have past experience of similar situations; they may also have seen systems or operational failures in the past and be able to draw lessons on how to prevent them in future. Either way, independent directors represent a resource that can help boards and companies reduce future risk.

Once again, though, planning for risk does not mean that no risk is involved. Chris Welsh, former CEO of CH Jones, warns that independent directors can sometimes adopt a "safety first" mentality. "They need to remember that their job, and the company's, is to take a balanced view of risk," he says. "Independents must accept their share of that risk." Independents are part of the team, and they share the consequences of risk-taking; but they also share the consequences of *not* taking risks.

Summary

All business is risky, and risk can never be avoided entirely; nor should it be. Growth and expansion are not possible without risks, and without growth and expansion companies will wither and die. However, there are risks and there are risks. Smart boards know how to take calculated risks, but steer clear of those that are too dangerous. They also know how to plan ahead, taking a proactive approach to risk management and mitigation.

One way to reduce risks is, of course, to call upon external advice. Consultants, auditors, lawyers, bankers and other advisors can render valuable service to companies, thanks to their specialized knowledge and expertise. We move on, then, to discuss these advisors and their roles.

Advisors

> Learning and innovation go hand in hand. The arrogance of success is to think that what you did yesterday will be sufficient for tomorrow
>
> — William Pollard

I have mentioned previously that boards need a requisite level of diversity, a range of background experiences and skills that will enable them to see problems from different perspectives and enable better decision-making. No matter how diverse the board is, however, there will always be times when people need to be brought in from the outside to give advice and counsel. Independent directors, like all board members, need to know how and when to appoint such advisors and how to manage them, to ensure that their advice is useful and that they provide sufficient value for money to the company.

In nearly all of the eleven companies profiled earlier, external advisors played an important role at some point. We used accountants, lawyers, investment bankers, headhunters, and a wide variety of consultants, including strategy consultants, remuneration consultants, operational improvement consultants, and market analysts. That did not mean that we always employed advisors continuously. We retained lawyers and auditors, but we were not in constant communication with them. We used strategy consultants to conduct strategic reviews, but we did not rely on them to make decisions for us. It is important to remember that advisors do just that: they advise. They do not run the company, and they do not make key decisions. Good advisors lay out the options, explain the consequences of each, and then ask the board to make a choice Table 4.15 shows examples of the use of advisors by the companies in the case studies.

I say "good" advisors, and it is also important to remember that there "bad" advisors and "ugly" advisors as well. Bad advisors give bad advice, and ugly ones give advice that is largely in their own best interest, and not that of the client. I have seen all three over the course of my career as both a senior executive and an independent director. I have seen investment banks get the valuation of companies wrong, as happened at Quintiles when Dennis Gillings moved to take the company private. I have seen accountants in southern Europe keeping two sets of books, and I have encountered corporate lawyers in Spain who were obviously in collusion with lawyers representing other parties in disputes. I have encountered consultants whose primary motivation appeared to be to generate more consultancy fee income, and at National Freight Corporation I experienced an executive team that became increasingly paralyzed, almost

TABLE 4.15   Advisors and how we used them

Biocompatibles:	headhunters to strengthen the board
CH Jones:	investment Bankers to develop an exit strategy
Datrontech:	accountants to assess the viability of the company
Forth Ports:	remuneration consultants to advise the remuneration committee; investment bankers to advise on takeover bids received
Keller:	consultants to assist with the strategy review
Michael Gerson:	accountants to carry out the external audit
NFT:	lawyers to assist in the exit process
NovaQuest:	lawyers to assist in formation of the fund
Quintiles:	investment bankers to advise on the flotation on the NYSE
U-POL:	consultants to advise on the market opportunities
Vantec:	headhunter to advise on the CEO search

afraid to move without first checking with a consultant. In that case, there was a serious question as to who was actually running the company.

On the other side of the coin, boards don't always make the best use of advisors. Firstly, they are expensive. Secondly, executives sometimes resist bringing in advisors who might give advice that is contrary to their own point of view, or that they simply don't want to hear. At Keller, some of the executives had their own ideas about the future strategy of the company: wait, and let the market bounce back. When the rest of the board wanted to bring in consultants to conduct a strategic review, there was initial resistance. What could consultants tell us that we don't already know? As it turned out, they made a significant contribution to the strategic review process.

A good advisor is expensive, but good advisors also provide value far greater than the fees they earn. A good advisor is worth his or her weight in gold.

Independent directors can help boards work more effectively with advisors in several ways. Firstly, they can help identify cases when advisors need to be called in. To cite the Keller example again, the strategic review might not have been conducted without pressure from the chairman and independent directors persuading the executive team to change their minds. Secondly, they can assist the process of choosing advisors by contributing their own experience, identifying good advisors and issuing warnings about the bad and ugly ones. Finally, they can help to ensure that the advisors are well managed and provide value for money.

The relationship goes both ways; independents also gain benefit from working with advisors. Andrew Marshall, partner in the audit practice of KPMG in London, reckons that "there is a tripartite relationship between auditors, executives, and independents." The executives run the business, while part of the task of the independent director is to ensure that the company is being well run and properly governed. To do so, independent directors need auditors. "The auditor is the non-executive director's 'eyes and ears' in the company," says Andrew. "We go into areas of the business in more detail than they are able to. At the same time, our role is driven by the independent directors. To some extent, we focus on what they want us to focus on." With other types of advisors, the relationships are different, but there is no doubt that independents both influence and are influenced by external advisors.

Why Use Advisors?

As noted, some advisors are retained continuously, while others are brought in on an as-needed basis. Generally speaking, however, advisors are brought in for a particular reason, to look at a particular issue. "For the most part, people come to us when they have a problem," says Steve Edge, partner at the legal firm Slaughter & May. "Sometimes people come to us when they want to check that what they are doing is right and consistent. In times of crisis they will seek our help and, similarly, if there are major regulatory changes." On the other hand, says Steve, the firm will sometimes make first contact with clients if they learn something that might be useful to that client.

Simon Massey, tax advisor with Menzies, says the same. "If you know the business, you might go to them and say, here is something that has changed, or this is on the horizon." Both make the point that whether and how often advisors contact their clients depends on the relationship they have with that client. There is a wide range of relationships, ranging from close ones where both parties will not hesitate to get in contact with the other, to more distant ones where contact might occur once a year, if that, and then only to deal with any necessary formalities. The range depends on the type of advisor and the culture of the client.

Generally speaking, boards call upon advisors for the following reasons (among others):

- Legal requirements. For example, public companies are obliged by law to use external auditors.
- Specialist expertise is required which the board does not possess. Strategy consultants can conduct a thorough strategic review because they are specialists in this sort of work. The board could try to conduct its own review, but it might take longer and be less thorough.

- It is necessary to demonstrate transparency. The appointment of a head-hunter to find candidates for a senior post demonstrates to all that the selection process will include external candidates and that the search has been professionally carried out.
- It is necessary to demonstrate fairness. Bringing in an outside remuneration consultant helps to demonstrate that a fair remuneration policy has been adopted.
- To get a second opinion on an important subject. For example, when devising a health and safety policy it might be wise to bring in specialist consultants who can advise on issues such as legal compliance.
- A privately owned company is about to be floated on the stock market. Corporate finance specialists and underwriters will be needed to assist the flotation process.
- A company is seeking to acquire another company. A variety of advisors will be needed, including lawyers and others to undertake due diligence and handle the legal requirements of the takeover.
- The company is up for sale. Again, a variety of advisors will be needed, including lawyers and investment bankers.

It is very important from the outset to be clear about *why* one is bringing in an advisor. The point has already been made that advisors are not cheap, and using them wrongly can be a very expensive process. It is also important to remember that advisors—even the good ones—have their own self-interest to consider. They are not charities; they run businesses of their own and need to make a profit. Before engaging an advisor, it is a good idea to look closely at their fee scales and structures, and understand the implications of these. For example, investment bankers' fees are often on a ratchet. The higher the value of the company when it is sold, the more they earn. It is in their interest, then, to sell the company at the highest possible value, and that might not necessarily be good for the company. (Curiously, this does not stop some investment bankers from consistently undervaluing companies up for sale.) "A good investment banker," says Stuart Vincent, managing director of corporate finance advisory at Rothschild, "will put their hand on the shoulders of the chairman and advise them not to sell, if the offer is not right." Not all investment bankers are so scrupulous.

How to Choose Advisors

Finding advisors is both easy and difficult. If you want to hire auditors, for example, there are trade directories with long lists of firms willing to conduct audits. But which of them are any good? How do you know you are hiring the right advisors? Which of them has the right level of international experience?

Firstly, personal experience is very important, and independent directors can contribute a great deal by exploiting their own networks. If a firm wishes to hire strategy consultants, directors can ask around among their own networks and hear the experiences of companies who have previously worked with consultants. Which ones really delivered, and which ones have big reputations but don't necessarily follow through? Discussions and informal contacts can bring in information to help the board compile a shortlist of possibles.

It is essential to take references when appointing new advisors. One useful practice is to ask for references, not from the advisor's best clients, but from its most difficult ones. Learn the worst about your potential advisors, not just the best, and learn how they handle problems.

Finally, have a "beauty" parade and ask potential advisors to pitch to you. However, beware: the person who makes the pitch may seem entirely plausible and look like the kind of advisor with whom you want to work. But some firms employ partners or directors whose main responsibility is to pitch for new business. Once the contract is signed, they hand over to someone else and move on to the next prospect. Make sure that the person making the pitch is the person with whom you will be working.

The key criteria for selecting advisors include the following:

- Capability. Does the advisor have the skills and experience that are needed? Do consultants know the sector? Do investment bankers have the right contacts?
- Chemistry. Is there a fit between the advisor and the board? Does the board trust the advisor to do what they say they will do? Will accountants be diligent in their scrutiny and work closely with the audit committee?
- Commitment. Is the advisor whole-heartedly committed to the company and ready to put its interests first? Will headhunters find the best candidates who will add value to the board, or will they simply fill the job and take their fee?
- Strength and independence. Will the advisors give impartial advice? Or will they collude with either independent directors or the executive team and become a partisan voice?
- Performance rewards. As noted above, what is their fee scale and how will they be rewarded?

Figure 4.7 shows the criteria used by NFT to select a financial advisor.

Scoring matrix for potential financial advisors (out of 10)

1. Positioning the business

> Understands and can sell NFT's market + growth story
> Key selling messages for trade
> Key selling messages for PE
> Likely buyer concerns regarding the business and strategies for mitigation
> Likely trade and PE reaction (positive and negative) to acquiring St Albans freehold as part of transaction
> Key issues and opportunities to be addressed prior to selling the business in order to maximise value

2. Buyers

> Key trade and PE buyers and contacts (balanced capability)
> Recommendations regarding debt strategy to support buyers

3. Valuation

> Valuation ranges, trade and PE buyers and contracts
> Assumptions: business trades in line with attached briefing document

4. Process

> Recommendations regarding sale process, including strategies to ensure maintenance of confidentiality
  of IP and existence of process
> Timetable options to achieve full valuation, with completion Q3 2013 to Q4 2014 (calendar)
> Will limit downside distraction to NFT Management

5. Engagement

> Team composition and credentials. Who will be our point person?
> Why should we appoint your firm?
> Relationship (with management team)
> Strength in depth

6. Track Record

> Completed deals
> Recent history

7. Fee Structure

> Quantum
> Incentivisation

8. Stability of Firm

TOTAL SCORE

FIG 4.7 **Selecting an advisor at NFT**

At all costs, be sure to distinguish between the person and the firm. When you appoint an advisor, your contract will be with a firm: KPMG, Rothschild, Hanson Green, LEK and so on. But you will be working with a person, or at the very least a small team. The firm may have a great reputation for service, but that means nothing if there is no chemistry between the board and the advisor it sends to you. The advisor may not be competent, may lack experience, may be too self-interested, or unable to work with whatever culture is prevalent in the boardroom and the company. When choosing an advisor, do not just look at the firm and its brand. Assess and choose the person and get the commitment from him or her.

What are some of the traits that should characterize a good advisor?

1. The advisor should understand the board and its members, and what their needs are. "If you know what makes the client tick," says Simon Massey, "how they operate, and who the key stakeholders are, you can give them better advice."

2. The advisor should seek to bring a fresh perspective to the board. As David Maistor points out in his book *The Trusted Advisor*, advisors will come into a company and see things that the board cannot see, because they interface with the company at different levels. Auditors will find flaws that are invisible to the board, for example. Stuart Vincent at Rothschild notes that when big, transformational decisions are being made, such as selling the company, boards can find themselves outside of their comfort zone. In these cases and others, the advisor should be genuinely committed to helping the board reach a greater level of understanding, not just telling them what they already know.

3. The advisor should help the board think through issues, challenging assumptions but without forcing their own opinions on the client. "We are there to encourage the thought process," says Simon Massey. "We ask the questions that they should probably be asking themselves anyway." Steve Edge talks about "balanced advice," which lays out options and explains consequences.

4. Advisors should not substitute their own judgment for that of the board. William Underhill, partner at Slaughter & May, argues that "the client must feel responsible for the decision. If they have understood the advice and take a business decision that is not the one I would have taken, that is fine." He gives as an example a client who was in dispute with one of its own customers, and was advised to settle the matter in the court. The client chose instead to settle out of court, on the grounds that it wanted to protect its long-term relationship with that customer. "Once I understood the grounds

for their decision, I was entirely satisfied," says William Underhill. Simon Massey agrees that "for entirely rational reasons," boards might not agree with the advice he gives, and has no problem with this.

5. The advisor should be calm and professional in manner. Many of the companies that call in advisors are suffering from some kind of stress— flotation and exit can be highly stressful exercises—and the temperature in the boardroom may be running high. The advisor needs to be the sort of person who can keep his or her head when all about are losing theirs, and help people to reach decisions calmly and clearly rather than in the heat of the moment. A sense of humor to help defuse difficult situations is certainly an asset. He or she should be someone with whom the board feels comfortable.

6. The advisor does not pull punches, but tells it like it is. Candor and honesty are absolutely essential. Trying to conceal or play down unpleasant truths is highly dangerous and will probably come back to haunt both the client and the advisor. Transparency about working methods is also very important.

7. The advisor is in it for the long haul, and is committed to the company rather than wanting to get in, collect fees, and get out. He or she should be committed to the whole company and not take the part of any party, executives, or shareholders.

8. The advisor should provide clear explanations backed up with reasoning and evidence. Advisors who cannot communicate clearly may be of little value.

9. Above all, the advisor should be honorable. He or she must be the sort of person whom the board can trust. No satisfactory long-term relationship will be possible if the advisor cannot be trusted.

If you can find an advisor who is all of these things, then you stand a good chance of making the relationship work and getting the advice that you need.

How to Manage Advisors

Advisors don't simply turn up, do their job, and go away again without the board needing to get involved. Advisors need to be managed, and as well as helping to choose them in the first place, independent directors also need to ensure that advisors are well managed. Even in cases where the advisor reports to the chief executive, rather than the audit or remuneration committees or the board as a whole, the independents should be prepared to play a role by checking that the advisors are delivering on what they promised and giving value for money.

The relationship between boards and advisors has changed over time, and will continue to change. Andrew Marshall of KPMG remarks that twenty years ago, the relationship between boards and advisors tended to be very formal. Today there is more informality, which means that people on both sides speak more freely and are less afraid to challenge each other. Andrew also makes the point that the relationship has changed from the advisor's side as well. Auditors, for example, are far more heavily regulated than before and this has an impact on their relationships with boards and audit committees.

Others notice differences too. William Underhill of Slaughter & May notes that boards and companies have many more internal capabilities than before. Big companies now have very strong internal legal teams, for example, and these may want to exercise control over the relationship between externally appointed lawyers and the board. In investment banking, Stuart Vincent comments that, whereas investment banks once built very long-term relationships with clients, in recent years a more transactional approach has developed with banks sometimes being brought in just for particular pieces of work. He emphasizes that the long-term approach is still preferred.

Independent advisors who serve for any length of time need to be aware of these changes, both cultural and regulatory, and be prepared to move with them. On the other hand, there are some things that have *not* changed, and there are some rules that always need to be followed when dealing with external advisors, no matter who they are.

The first rule is: be very clear about what you want the advisors to do, and make it equally clear to the advisors what is wanted from them. Unless you control this aspect of the relationship very tightly, advisor services tend to snowball. To make the point again, the advisors themselves come from profit-making firms. With the best will in the world, there is a tendency for the advisor offering to snowball, so that a year later the board is still employing them for a variety of purposes that were never intended in the first place.

Of course, if in the course of performing their duties the advisor notices something outside their original remit, then the advisor has a duty to speak out, and the board equally has a duty to listen and take note. The point made above about the auditor being the "eyes and ears" of the board is very well taken. However, this does not mean that advisors should be given *carte blanche*. The board, not the advisor, decides when and where to employ further advisors. This is partly a matter of control, and partly a matter of expense. Good advisors are not cheap, and should be used wisely.

Again, there is a responsibility for independent directors to get involved in this process. Andrew Marshall points out that while it is the duty of the auditor to challenge what they find in companies, "it is also quite important for the independent directors to be challenging us, to make sure that we in turn are challenging management and coming to the right conclusions, and that those conclusions are clear and objective." In other words, the auditor may be the independent director's "eyes and ears"; what the auditor looks for is in some respects guided by what the independents desire. The same is true of other advisor relationships.

Secondly, it is important that the details of the relationships are managed. Advisor contracts should be checked carefully, and in particular the details of expenses that advisors may claim should be checked; these have a tendency to mount up even faster than fees. There should also be a very clear timetable for delivery; consultancy contracts in particular have a tendency to stretch as the consultants "discover" more and more things that need their attention.

Thirdly, there is the issue of trust. "Trust is the key word," says Stuart Vincent. "Confidentiality is essential. Companies need to have people on whom they can rely." When boards hire an advisor, to some extent they are putting themselves in the advisor's hands. Advisors have access to many parts of the company. In order to do their jobs properly, they see information that normally no one outside the company—even outside the board—would see. They are privy to the company's secrets. It is therefore imperative that advisors be trusted. David Maistor calls his book *The Trusted Advisor*, and really, there can be no other kind.

Trust goes both ways, and advisors also need to be able to trust boards. An adversarial advisor relationship simply will not work; both sides need to trust each other to the extent that they are willing to work closely together for what should be the common goal, the good of the client's firm. Independent directors can play an important role in this trust-building process. They can help earn trust in the first place and build on those newly established relationships. And to repeat Andrew Marshall's point above, as well as giving advice, advisors also need information from the board.

The trust-building process is well known, and readers will have doubtless encountered it during their careers as executives. The basic steps are as follows: (1) engage with the other party and choose language that shows you are genuinely interested in them, (2) listen to what they are saying and understand them as people, (3) share and understand their perspective, and (4) demonstrate a willingness to work together to achieve a common objective. Trustworthy people are credible and reliable, able to build relationships on a personal as well as a professional basis, and put other people before themselves. These are all useful traits in an advisor; but as an independent director, one might equally try to cultivate these traits in oneself.

Lessons Learned

Here are a few of the lessons I have learned over the years when working with and employing advisors. In no particular order:

- A good search consultant does not just accept an assignment to recruit a new director. He or she also offers advice on options for board composition.
- When engaging an advisor, insist on commitment from the individuals with whom you want to work, not just from their firm. It is the individual relationship that matters.
- Investment banks can be conflicted. Beware of their advice on what price to sell a business, and consider options.
- When choosing an investment bank to advise on a sell mandate, take into account their skill in selling businesses, not just their process capability.
- Consultants, when giving recommendations normally, recommend further the need for more consultancy, with associated additional fees.
- Expect external auditors not just to prepare the audit but to also be the "eyes and ears" of the audit committee in identifying risks, assessing the strength of the finance team and generally adding value.
- Remuneration consultants *MUST* understand that they report to the remuneration committee, not the CEO.
- Beware of advisors who sell quick-fix solutions rather than first understanding the board, the company and its needs.
- Advisors need to be managed. Independent directors need to check that advice is being delivered and gives good value for money.
- Property valuations can change very dramatically in a short period of time.
- Remuneration consultants seldom conclude that executives are overpaid.

Summary

A good advisor can indeed be worth his or her weight in gold. A bad advisor can do a great deal of damage. Advisors need to be carefully chosen and managed. In both cases, the independent director can render a great deal of service to the rest of the board, and the company. By ensuring that advisors give value for money, the independent director supports the executive team and ensures that the latter have the information they need to do their jobs, while at the same time protecting the interests of the shareholders by ensuring good corporate governance. It is to the executive teams, and their relationships with independents, that we turn our attention next.

Executive Teams

> If I have seen further than others, it is by standing on the shoulders of giants.
>
> — Sir Isaac Newton

In order to be successful, any business must have a strong and capable executive team. Members of the team must have the requisite talent and experience to help the business execute its strategy and reach its goals. That is axiomatic.

However, that strong and talented top team cannot do everything on its own. Its members require counseling and advice and guidance, and this is where the independent directors come into the picture. Good independent directors don't just review and monitor performance and then hold the executives to account when targets are missed. They are also active partners who help the executive team do their jobs more effectively.

This is particularly true of the chairman. The relationship between the CEO and the independent chairman is probably the most important relationship in the entire business. A good working partnership between the two can be a source of great strength to the business; a bad relationship can have a drag effect on the company and even lead to organizational paralysis. The fit between chairman and CEO is all-important.

Many people reading this book will have had executive experience themselves and thus have first-hand knowledge of what CEOs and other senior managers do. In this chapter, our purpose is to look specifically at the relationship between the executives and independent directors and show how they should ideally work together. The relationship between the two groups can be fraught with difficulties, and in some companies it breaks down altogether. Good independent directors will work hard to maintain that relationship and ensure that their own contribution to the board and the company is a positive one.

Smart CEOs are also aware of this, and harness the knowledge and skills of independent directors and get them involved in high-level decision-making.

This can happen through a variety of channels, including formal board participation, the setting up of expert panels to advise executives, or informal one-to-one discussions of issues in which the independent has particular expertise. Especially for smaller companies, independent directors offer a very cost-effective pool of wisdom and guidance, and can be both more useful and cheaper than external consultants.

"If you just have executives talking to each other all the time, you get a declining quality of debate," says Biocompatibles CEO Crispin Simon. Crispin likes the stretch he gets from talking to independents. Answering their questions forces him to think about issues, sometimes in ways that have not occurred to him before. "Even if the questions you were asked were not always right on the button in terms of relevance, that didn't matter. It still felt like you were being tested." Other CEOs such as Chris Welsh of CH Jones and Justin Atkinson of Keller agree. Ron Wooten of NovaQuest thinks diversity is the key element that independents bring to the board. "If you populate your board with people of like experience, you don't get the diversity of thinking," he says. "If no one is challenging you, this can lead to bad decisions. It is very important to have people of diverse backgrounds."

The CEO should ensure that there is an open dialogue between executives and independents on all matters of importance to the board. In practice this means two things: provision of information in an easily digestible form—especially if there are non-specialists on the board—and open access to all employees. CEOs should also work to develop relationships with independent directors so as to get their constructive input at board level. An atmosphere of transparency, openness, and trust between the CEO, executives, chairman, and independents is absolutely essential.

How Independent Directors Contribute

Alvarez & Marsal, the turnaround and performance management specialists, recently carried out a survey of CEOs in which they identified three key situations where executive teams are likely to turn to their independents for help, and where the latter can make strong contributions. These were (1) market disruption, where there is a need to deal with a fundamental shift in market conditions (the financial crisis being an example); (2) major transformations of the company, for example, following a takeover or change of ownership; and (3) situations where the company's reputation is at risk, or potentially at risk.

Keller endured a classic example of market disruption, when the 2008 financial crisis precipitated a downturn in the construction industry. When the crisis came, the board was reassured that the company was in a strong competitive position and had robust margins that could withstand the downturn to a large extent. However, it soon became very clear that this was not the case, and profits fell from around $100 million to around $20 million.

What should we do next? The executive team, especially in North America, the worst-affected region, took the position that this was primarily a matter of economic cycles and the market would bounce back. The independents argued that while the market undoubtedly would recover, the process might take four or five years. In the meantime, the company needed to start taking steps to recover its own position. We started by looking at the cost base with a view to becoming efficient, but realized fairly quickly that this would not be enough. The next step was an in-depth strategic review, bringing in outside consultants. Some in the executive team initially resisted this, arguing that they themselves knew what was best for the company. We felt that it was imperative to get an impartial review. After a long process of discussion, the independent directors and the chairman persuaded their executive colleagues to go along with this and the consultants were called in.

Justin Atkinson, CEO of Keller, acknowledges that some executives are so close to the company that they find it hard to see the larger picture, and this can also make them resistant to change. That was the case at Michael Gerson, where the independents argued that the executive team had to take steps to change strategic direction when their core market of international removals began to dry up. Unwillingness to admit to the need for sufficient change, and our failure as independent directors to persuade them, led to Michael Gerson's sale at a fraction of its former value.

In terms of the second area, company transformation, there are several examples in the case studies of independent directors helping an executive team to find its feet in a new environment. At Vantec we worked with the executives of a company making the transition from the in-house logistics arm of an automotive giant to a stand-alone company. Only a few members of the executive team had experience of operating in the global logistics market; we independent directors did. They relied on us to help them plot a new strategic course. Much the same happened at NFT, another corporate spin-off, and the formerly family owned U-POL when it was sold to a private equity house. Jean-Charles Julien, CEO of U-POL had no previous experience of private equity and did not know what to expect of the firm's new owners. It was up to the independents who did have experience of private equity to help him make sense of it all. Unfortunately, at Datrontech the story did not have a happy ending. We attempted a corporate transformation, bringing in a turnaround specialist, but nothing could stop the chronic cash-flow problems we faced and finally the bank pulled the plug; a salutary reminder that while independent directors can advise and assist, there are limits to what they can actually achieve.

Finally, the survey says, independent directors can make important contributions in situations where there is a reputational risk. In my experience, this consists largely in reducing that risk. Health and safety issues at Keller were a serious potential risk to reputation—had industrial accidents continued, our reputation would have suffered with employees and clients and alike—while at Quintiles a single significant quality failure during clinical trials could have had very damaging implications. Board-level committees on health and safety at the former and quality at the latter monitored the key issues and helped to reduce the risk. Independent directors played a key role on both committees, bringing in outside expertise. Table 4.16 shows some examples of the contribution made by Independent Directors concerning executives in the case studies.

What If There Were No Independents?

Supposing a company did not have independent directors, what would the executive team miss? Ask some executives, especially after a long and bruising board meeting, and they would probably mutter, "not very much." In fact, though, the CEOs I know and have met regard independent directors as indispensable.

TABLE 4.16   **Contribution of independent directors**

Some of the ways in which independent directors supported the executive team:	
Biocompatibles:	finding commercial management
CH Jones:	finding a CEO
Datrontech:	finding a CEO with turnaround expertise in the sector
Forth Ports:	property management
Keller:	succession for the senior management team
Michael Gerson:	finding management with the skills to diversify the service offering
NFT:	building a comprehensive strong team following the MBO
NovaQuest:	building an international team with private equity skills and life sciences
Quintiles:	succession for the founder
U-POL:	commercial management succession
Vantec:	finding Japanese management with international experience

As we saw earlier, some privately owned companies do not have independent directors, and some private equity houses prefer to dispense with independent directors and bring in consultants to advise the board instead. But the relationship between an executive team and a consultant, and the relationship between an executive team and a non-executive director, will always be different. The former will often be more distant; the latter should be more dedicated to the good of the company and have more of an interest in ensuring that it is well run.

Without independent directors, the executive team would lack the range of experience that is necessary for good due diligence. Again, consultants can be hired, but they will not always scrutinize investments as intensely or evaluate them as carefully as an independent director might. Without independent directors, too, the company would lack an effective governance structure. As Chris Collins says: "Today's executives are mercenaries, giving their all to their current employer but prepared to move to greener pastures at the drop of a hat. This requires the independent directors to act as guardians of the firm."

Independent directors offer guidance and counseling to the chief executive, and this affects the team as a whole. They offer expertise in specific fields, such as geographies and markets, or issues such as audit and remuneration. If there is no external involvement in remuneration, then how can anyone be sure that remuneration policies are fair and transparent, and that the executives are not favoring themselves at the expense of shareholders or employees? Finally, independent directors give the company access to best practice in other companies, geographies, and sectors. Their experience of the broader business world feeds into the firm's overall stock of knowledge. CEOs who have spent thirty years in one sector know that sector very well, but they probably know little about the rest of the business environment. Independent directors can fill that gap.

Chris Welsh, CEO of CH Jones, has thought about the relationships between independent and executive directors very deeply, and he offers three further dimensions. First, says Chris, independent directors "have to have the wisdom to ask the right questions, and not let the executives distract them or put them off. That can be a challenge, especially where the managerial teams are strong." Chris says he has seen cases in other firms where independents did not have the courage to ask questions in the face of a very powerful and dominant CEO.

Second, according to Chris, they need the "wisdom to know when to intervene and begin questioning, rather than just accepting that the executives are doing the best that they can." This can be a problem too if the management team is dominant—or, conversely, if the independents are too close to the executives and feel sympathy for them; the former may be inclined to "go easy" on their colleagues and not ask overly difficult questions. For this reason Crispin Simon, CEO of Biocompatibles, feels that "a certain distance between executives and independents is very helpful."

Finally, Chris Welsh argues that "it is very easy to identify a poorly performing senior executive, but it is very difficult to identify one who is just not performing very well." The first can be spotted and either given support to improve their performance, or removed from their position. The difficulty with the second group is that standard performance metrics will pick up people who are underperforming, and those who are outperforming the norm, but not necessarily people who are simply dawdling along in the middle. While not really doing anything wrong, the latter can act as a brake on growth and innovation. Shrewd and experienced independent directors, however, can pick up the signs and alert the CEO or chairman before a problem develops.

For all of these reasons and more, CEOs and their executive teams should and must work closely with independent directors. However, they don't always do so.

Relationships between Executives and Independent Directors

The independence of independent directors, and especially their responsibility for corporate governance, can sometimes drive a wedge between the CEO and the executive team on the one hand, and the independent directors on the other. Executives can feel that independents are meddling in their work, that they are asking unfair questions, even that they are persecuting the executives. If there is a clash between owners and managers, the latter might perceive independent directors as "stooges" or spies. On the other side of the divide, independents might suspect that executives are trying to freeze them out, withholding information and keeping them out of vital decisions.

If relations between executive teams and independent directors sink to this level, then the company is in real trouble. Corporate governance will be unimportant, and secrecy and conflict will become the order of the day. I count myself fortunate that I have never been involved in such a dire situation, but I know of people who have. The experience for them was highly unpleasant; the experience for the companies was catastrophic.

More common is a kind of general unease, in which executives are not really sure what the independent directors are for and are uncomfortable with them becoming too closely involved in the firm. When I joined Keller, the chairman,

Mike West, the man who had led the buy-out of Keller from GKN, had set the boundary between independents and executives in what I would call an American fashion; that is, independent directors were there primarily to handle governance and should let the executives get on with running the business. Shortly after I joined the board, I mentioned that I wanted to visit some of our North American subsidiaries. Eyebrows were raised; this was not the sort of thing that independent directors did. To be fair, as time went on Mike changed his mind and overseas board visits became the norm.

Some executive teams see the board as a process to be worked through. At Datrontech, the executive team operated on a philosophy of "we're going to carry on doing what we have always done." Lip service was paid to corporate governance and board requests; there was bare compliance, but little active cooperation. One chairman, Ian Kirkpatrick, resigned in protest at the behavior of the executives. We did manage to bring in a new management team and change the culture, but it took time; and at Datrontech, time was one of the things we did not have.

If a gap opens between the executives and the rest of the board, what is the best solution? In my view, heavy-handed measures by shareholders or the board itself seldom work. Here is where companies require a chairman with excellent diplomatic skills. It is up to the chairman to bridge the gap, and then help both parties find ways of closing it. He or she needs to counsel and guide both the CEO and the other independents and help them to develop better relationships with each other.

A breakdown in the relationship between CEO and chairman is particularly critical. As I said earlier, the relationship between them is one of the most important in the business, absolutely fundamental to success. If this relationship does not work, as I know from experience, it makes life very difficult for everyone. For the most part I have been fortunate in my relationships with CEOs such as David Frankish, Crispin Simon and Jean-Charles Julien, but I have also experienced some very difficult relationships and have seen the impact on the business as a whole.

Things can go both ways, of course. Over the years I have met CEOs who have complained to me about their difficult chairmen and how hard they make life for them. The problem is not an easy one to solve. Chairmen can fire CEOs, and CEOs can enlist support from the rest of the board to fire the chairman, but the process is never easy and is often bloody. It is much better to try to work things out, but that is not always possible. Sometimes, the personal chemistry between the parties is wrong from the start.

Usually, though, even the most difficult relationships can be managed. Unofficial, informal get-togethers can be a very useful tool. At Keller we often arranged directors' dinners, not before every board meeting but a few times a year, so that we could get to know each other as people. In my experience, this kind of relationship-building is extremely important. If, as an independent director, all you do is show up at board meetings, you will not get to know your colleagues and will not be able to work with them effectively. Get to know the CEO and understand the business, go to site visits or country visits with him or her, get the other executives to open up to you and tell you about their professional issues and problems. I worked out a good many problems at Vantec by playing golf with Okuno-san and later with Toshi Yamada. I take Justin Atkinson's point about preserving a certain distance in order to remain independent, but too much distance can lead to remoteness and lack of contact. The executives are a team, but they are also part of a greater team: the board.

Getting the balance right, between independence and team spirit, can be tricky. Over-enthusiastic independent directors who try to get too involved can be a problem. "The independent director has to be there to guide and help the executives, not to make extra work," says Chris Welsh. And there are times when the independents do have to step back and let the executives get on with it. Chris recalls when CH Jones, like the rest of the British haulage industry, was affected by the fuel blockades. Although a potentially serious situation had arisen, this was not an issue that independent directors could do much about. "We reassured them that we were dealing with it," says Chris. "For their part, the independent directors realized there were no sensible questions they could ask that would help the situation." I think Chris is quite right. Part of the skill of being an independent director lies in knowing when to let the executives just get on with running the business.

And, of course, relationships will change depending on the characters of the individuals involved but also on the owners and the tone that they set. Jean-Charles Julien, CEO of U-POL, noticed a difference in style and culture when Graphite Capital, the private equity house, sold the company to ABN AMRO. At Graphite, he recalls, the board and the chairman (myself) were "very hands-off, and that suited me to a tee." The two independent directors appointed by Graphite were bright, friendly young people who did not know much about the business but did have a large store of best practice from other firms in their portfolio that they were willing to share. They were casual in their approach and dress, sometimes coming to meetings in jeans and T-shirts. When ABN AMRO took over, the atmosphere in the boardroom became much more correct and austere. Relationships were good, but strictly professional. Jean-Charles points out that both types of relationship worked well and were very effective. What is important is that he and his team had the skill to adapt.

Working with the Executive Team

Earlier in this chapter we identified the kinds of situations where the executives are likely to turn to the independent directors for help. Beyond these, however, the independent directors have a duty both to work with and monitor the executive team over time. This duty comes in several forms, and I will now touch on some of the most important of these: getting the right management team in place; ensuring that the business is well-led; ensuring the CEO is close to the business; and ensuring that the business has the right strategy.

Getting the right team in place

In order to execute a strategy, a company has first to have the right executive team in place. The constitution of that team depends on the balance of skills and capabilities needed, and this in turn depends on where the company is now, and where it wants to be.

For example, at the time of the spin-off from Northern Foods, NFT had a very small management team, a legacy of its original status as a subsidiary. In order to transform itself into a stand-alone company, NFT had to develop its management team substantially. Among other things, a business development director, finance director, human resources director, and senior operational management had to be added to the team. At U-POL, on the other hand, a good management team already existed and there was no need for the new owners to make wholesale changes (although we did appoint a very good finance director, Andrew Ayres).

Independent directors play an important role in ensuring that the right top team is in place. Some authorities hold that the independent directors should only be concerned with the appointment of the CEO, but I disagree; I think they should be involved in top-level appointments, recommending potential candidates for posts and getting involved in the selection process by scrutinizing candidates or sitting on interview panels; for example the chair of the audit committee should be involved in selecting the finance director. Again, we come back to the need for a plurality of views, of ensuring that the right person is selected, not just the person whom the CEO likes most.

At both NFT and Vantec, the independent directors played an important role in recruiting and building the management team. At Biocompatibles, the independents helped to choose the new commercial director, a vitally important post if the company was to become fully commercial. At Datrontech, we changed the people at the top in an effort to turn the company around. In all three cases, the selection of the right people for the executive team was vitally important if the company was to succeed.

But, of course, Datrontech failed because we were not able to get the right team in place in time to make a difference, and there is a lesson to be learned there: if the executive team is not performing, then the sooner changes are made, the better. That said, one has also to be careful about making changes for change's sake. Newly appointed CEOs often want to make wholesale changes to the management team for reasons not necessarily related to the strategy of the company. They may not like the culture or attitudes of the managers, or they may simply want to bring in their own people, with whom they have worked before and whom they trust.

Who serves on the management team in turn has a powerful impact on the strategy and culture of the company. At Quintiles, with a new CEO there has been a marked change of direction concerning strategic partnering, which has in turn had an impact on the company's partners such as NovaQuest. Earlier, I described how the change in top management at National Freight Corporation following Christopher Bland's appointment as chairman led to a massive cultural change and the end of employee ownership. Independent directors need to be involved in the appointment of senior managers. If they do not, there is a risk that the wrong people could be appointed, with harmful or even fatal results for the company. Table 4.17 shows some of the executive team characteristics that one has to deal with.

Ensuring good leadership

The key to a winning team is having a good leader. Identifying the right leader is another difficult task. Leadership is not something you can put in a bottle, so that when you don't have enough of it you can simply open the bottle and take a dose. Everyone's definition of leadership is different, and everyone's style of leadership is different too. People who might appear to be good leaders can fail, for no immediately obvious reason.

Take for example the now famous case of Manchester United. Sir Alex Ferguson was manager of the team for 16 years; his successor, David Moyes, lasted for eight months. Moyes is presumably a very good leader, or else the owners and board of Manchester United would not have hired him. So, why

TABLE 4.17   Executive team characteristics

The **bulldog** – aggressive, inclined to argue, but often knowledgeable. Try not to sit directly opposite the bulldog but have them on your immediate left in a non-confrontational position.

The **horse** – willing, dependable, keen, often knowledgeable and likes to show it; too quick with answers and often no one else gets a turn. Take up their points and ask others what they think.

The **fox** – devious, determined to undermine your leadership. Likes to pick a topic they know you are weak on and display their own knowledge to your disadvantage. Be honest. Say "I'm afraid that's not one of my strong points, would someone else like to pick up this topic?"

The **monkey** – disruptive, know-it-all, often the office clown. Be careful how you handle the monkey, they are often very popular. Use this to your advantage; show you are human and enjoy the joke but bring the conversation back on course.

The **hedgehog** – prickly, unreceptive to change, unwilling to participate and not inclined to be helpful. They have ability and experience, however, so try to involve them even if they are negative.

The **giraffe** – lofty, superior and above-it-all. Observers by nature. Treat them with respect and encourage them to contribute by asking a direct question. Don't pick a fight with them or they may cease to participate.

The **hippo** – loses interest and may even doze off in meetings. Don't allow this to happen. Check that they are still with you by speaking to them by name and drawing them into the proceedings.

The **wide-mouthed frog** – talks about anything except the topic in hand. Be assertive but tactful and refocus the issue. Use time as a valid reason for ending their chit-chat.

The **gazelle** – young, new or part-time. Not necessarily shy. It is important that you involve them but don't ask them questions until you are confident they can answer correctly. Embarrassing them will scare them off.

Source: Kevin Benfield, *Create a Winning Team*, London: Hodder Education, 2011, p. 170

did he fail? The reasons may lie not so much with him, as in the interaction and relationships between him and the rest of the team.

Getting the right leader is often a matter of style as much as anything else. Some business leaders like to immerse themselves in the business. Dennis Gillings of Quintiles was like that, and this is often the case with the founders of business who can find it hard to relinquish control. Jean-Charles Julien at U-POL and David Frankish at NFT both spent many years with their companies and know them from the ground up; they too like to be in control. Other leaders are happier to delegate and let individual team members take responsibility. Justin Atkinson at Keller is in this position, though the decentralized structure of Keller means that he has only a limited ability to reach out and control what happens in the subsidiaries.

Leadership styles also vary according to national culture. In France and Spain, leaders are expected to be "the boss"; they give orders and other people obey them. Hesitation or indecision will immediately be noticed and the leader's reputation will suffer. In Japan, the leader is held in great respect, even awe, by the lower ranks, but this has a corollary; the leader is personally responsible if anything goes wrong. North American leaders tend to be more authoritarian too. In Britain, however, there is much more willingness to question the leader and take contrarian points of view, rather than simply following orders. The point is that any leader of a company operating across national boundaries— and these days, that means most companies—has to be capable of adjusting his or her leadership style to different cultures.

With the exception of the chairman, independent directors are not expected to be leaders. Instead, their role is to see that the company has the right leader for the right times, a leader who can take the company where it wants to go and help it achieve its goals. They also have an important role in ensuring that there is a succession plan in place. CEOs don't last forever; indeed, the average tenure of CEOs with any given company is falling steadily. Some have argued that the first task any CEO should undertake upon assuming office is to begin to identify his or her successor. A well-planned succession means a smooth transition between leaders with a minimum of uncertainty and disruption, and ensures too that the new CEO is the right person for the job.

In reality, most CEOs do not pay enough attention to succession planning, and therefore it falls to the independent directors to push for a succession plan and ensure that one is in place. And in my view, this applies not just to the CEO, but to all senior posts. Independent directors should have a say in the succession planning for every member of the senior executive team.

Another aspect of ensuring good leadership is appraisals. One of the tasks of the chairman is to appraise the CEO. Often this is done informally, through private conversations, but in my view this is insufficient. The process should be formal and transparent, done according to agreed rules so as to ensure that the CEO receives a fair appraisal and the rest of the board gets a full view of his or her performance. Also, in my view, the process does not stop with the CEO. As chairman of NFT, I did not get involved in the appraisal of other senior executives, but I made it my business to see their appraisals. Some would argue that this is wrong, that this only the business of the CEO, but I would counter by saying that the chairman needs to be sure that the CEO is getting the support he or she needs from the rest of the team. Further, if another member of the team is having problems, the chairman can often identify ways and means of offering support.

Of course, chairmen themselves should also be appraised and, especially in public companies, this is the role of the senior independent director. I conducted several of these appraisals of chairmen, and I began with a list of what the chairman was supposed to do, then asked all the executive and independent directors for their opinions and looked for gaps. I then summarized and anonymized their views and presented them to the chairman. This is often a very useful exercise for the chairmen themselves and tells them things they may not have realized. For example, at Keller the chairman's appraisal highlighted the fact that Roy Franklin needed to spend more time with the CEO, advising and counseling. That issue might not have been recognized without the appraisal.

Ensuring that the CEO is close to the business

"Among all the legions of lawyers, financiers, bureaucrats and masters of business administration strutting into the American economy from the nation's leading business schools," wrote George Gilder in *The Spirit of Enterprise*, "nothing has been so rare as an Ivy League graduate who has made a significant innovation in American enterprise."[45] Gilder was not criticizing business schools; rather, he was describing the arrogant attitude of some business leaders who think that they know it all and their mere presence in the boardroom will make everything the business touches turn to gold. The reality is described by Jamie Oliver and Tony Goodwin in *How They Blew It*, a painfully accurate account of what went on behind some of the major business failures of the past decade.[46] Oliver and Goodwin show how, over and over again, self-important CEOs disregarded the need to get close to the business and concentrated instead on building their own egos. Many were blissfully unaware of the impending catastrophe, and even after disaster struck they failed to realize what had happened. Other reports of the banking crisis have shown how executives were distant from the business and did not understand what was really going on.

One of the tasks of the independent director is to scrutinize the activities of the executive team and ensure that they are in touch with the business and know what is happening. If they feel that the executives are losing touch, then they need to speak out. Of course, "getting close to the business" means different things in different companies, and it is particularly difficult to stay in touch with very large companies with global reach. Think of Keller, operating on six continents and with only a small management team, or Quintiles, which has operations in a hundred countries. Yet, strenuous efforts have to be made. When I was chairman of the EMEA division of Quintiles, I made sure that I visited every country at least once every two years, and the bigger operations more often than that. Dennis Gillings goes still further; he has a private airplane and spends much of his time traveling the globe visiting his far-flung operations.

It requires immense effort, but what is the alternative? A CEO and executive team locked in an ivory tower, making decisions about the company without being aware of the reality on the ground? That is a sure recipe for repeating the disasters of 2008. Independents must make sure that the executive team members are in touch with reality. And, they need to make their own visits too. They need to see the business on the ground and understand what it does, and how, and why. They can then feed their own views and observations back into boardroom discussions, enriching them as a result.

A great deal can also be achieved through mentoring, coaching, and acting as a critical friend. "Mentoring has always been important but it has only become a much more recognized skill in recent years," says Robbie Burns, former managing director of Exel. "Mentoring from non-executive directors is relevant because senior executives need someone on whom they can rely for advice." As well as being governors of companies, independent directors need to support executives and "promote confidence and bravery." Earlier I quoted Peter Waine of Hanson Green on the need to help CEOs dream their own dreams. In my own career, I have acted as a mentor several times, not just for CEOs but other directors as well. Robbie is quite right: senior executives need someone to whom they can turn and talk openly and frankly, and independent directors are ideally placed to fill that role. Fran Moscow, a highly experienced executive coach, offers several tips for mentoring and coaching:

- The relationship between mentor and mentee, or coach and coachee, is "a relationship of trust." All conversations must be 100 percent confidential.
- Learn as much as you can beforehand about the person to be coached or mentored.
- Who are the other stakeholders in the process? It is crucial to contract with them and the mentee or coachee as to how feedback is shared and at what intervals.

Strategy

We discussed strategy earlier in this book, but let me reiterate a key point: while executive directors implement strategy, independents should be involved in making strategy—and at the very least, ensuring that there *is* an appropriate strategy. They should encourage a focus on long-term performance for the good of the business, and in my view should also conduct regular strategic updates, not just once a year as is standard practice.

The appointment of executive teams also depends crucially on what the strategy is. Recall the decision we faced at Forth Ports, as to whether to make property management a central part of the business or to hive it off. If we wanted to keep property management in-house, then we clearly needed a property director to provide professional management over this activity. If we planned to spin off the property portfolio, then perhaps no such post was needed. And, as times change and strategies change with them, the board needs to ensure that the management structure evolves to keep pace. Key people may need to be changed, posts may need to be created or may become redundant. Of course, the CEO plays a pivotal role in all of this, but the board should be involved too, supporting and advising.

Organization

The ways in which the executive team and the employees are organized is often (maybe too often) an issue for companies. Companies are not always as well organized as they might be. It is not uncommon for incoming CEOs, for example, to reorganize a company so as to put their own mark on it. Reorganizations are often carried out without sufficient planning or forethought. For example, matrix organizations are very popular but they are also very difficult to make work well. This does not stop businesses from enthusiastically converting to matrix form (or attempting to do so) without first working out what problems might be encountered or what difficulties might emerge.

Some would argue that how the company is structured is a matter for the CEO and the executive team, not the independents, and that getting involved in issues of organizational structure crosses the line between the two. I disagree. How the organization is structured is fundamental to its performance. Look back at the organizations we saw operating on a global basis, such as Quintiles and Keller. Each had quite different business models—one highly centralized, one highly decentralized—but each configured so as to best meet the needs of the company's strategy. And that is precisely the point. If we accept that independent directors should be involved in strategy, we must realize that how a company is organized impacts directly on how well it can achieve its goals. Independent directors are unlikely to get involved in implementing reorganizations, but their experience and wisdom should feed into the process of deciding what organizational form will be adopted.

Boards have several choices when thinking about structure. One is the classic functional structure where business functions—R&D, marketing, production, finance, etc—each occupy their own departments. One of the risks of this type of structure is that each department will become inward-looking, evolve its own culture and lose sight of the organizational goals. Secondly, there is the divisional structure with companies organized along product or business lines, brands, or geography. Thirdly, as mentioned, there is the matrix structure, which aims to combine coordinated product management and regional centers. In practice this is very difficult to achieve, as communication lines get crossed and line management authority is unclear.

Whatever model is chosen, the parts must function efficiently as part of a greater whole. The company needs to be able to focus on its corporate goals, while at the same time remaining agile in local markets. As the Keller and Quintiles stories show, exactly how this is done depends on the company and the nature of its business. There is no one best form of organization, no off-the-shelf model that can be bought and applied. Organizational decisions need just as much care and consideration as strategic ones.

Working with the founders

A particular issue arises when the people who founded the company, but later sold it, are still on the board. I have worked in several such situations, at Tibbett & Britten with John Harvey, at Datrontech and Michael Gerson, and also at Quintiles where Dennis Gillings remained on the board, and Keller, where Mike West, the chairman, was also the person who had taken the company public. These people occupy unusual positions. They have sold the company, but in the eyes of many around them—and often in their own eyes too—it remains "their" company. They have immense moral authority. Long-serving colleagues continue to defer to them and are often unwilling to challenge their decisions.

Psychologically, these founders are in a difficult position. All that we know about the psychology of entrepreneurs tells us that they are not really in it for the money, at least not first and foremost. They like the challenge of creating and building something. They have dreams and visions, and they sweat blood to make those dreams come true. Selling the company can be a little like a bereavement. They find it very, very hard to let go; and who can blame them?

However, their presence on the board can make things extremely difficult. Firstly, the founders often sit as chairmen—Dennis Gillings and Mike West being examples—and this can create an unintended conflict of interest. The chairman, at least in the UK, is supposed to be independent like the other independents; but how independent and unbiased can you be about a company that you have created yourself? Secondly, there is the issue of a lack of challenge, which happens even if—or perhaps, especially if—the chairman and CEO get along well. Chris Welsh, CEO of CH Jones, was so concerned about this that he asked his chairman if they could bring in an independent director just to make sure that their thinking got the challenge it needed.

Chris Welsh had a very fair point. Someone needs to provide the founders with challenge, and if the executive team members are too respectful or too frightened to raise a challenge, than that someone can be an independent director. It is their task to ensure that the boardroom is full of clear and objective thinking and that all options are explored, even if those options are unpalatable to the founders. Remember always that it is no longer their company; the interests of shareholders, employees, and customers also have to be protected. Independent directors must be prepared to be the most unpopular people in the room.

Summary

The relationship between the independent directors and the executive team is of first-water importance, and that is especially true of the relationship between chairman and CEO. If both are prepared to work together as a team, as two halves of the same whole, then their combined wisdom and experience should enable the company to prosper and grow. But if there are splits between them, if executives try to "work through" the board or if independents cross the line and dabble in organizational matters, then problems will occur. Both sides need to remember that the organization is bigger than them, and that they are its servants and not its masters.

We have now covered a number of aspects of the independent director's task: the nature of boards, the impact of ownership, the importance of strategy and globalization, the role played by risk, the selection and use of advisors, and relationships with executive teams. It is time now to draw all these concepts together and look at the vital and challenging role of the independent director, and it is to this that we turn next.

Independent Directors

Leadership and learning are indispensable to each other.
— John F. Kennedy

The *Financial Times* once described the role of the independent director as "a task for which no one is qualified."[47] This was not a comment on the quality of independent directors—though plenty of people would be happy to agree with that assessment—but rather, a comment on the expectations that regulators and others now have of independent directors. The *Financial Times* goes on to list these:

> The list of attributes required of the non-executive director is so long, precise and contradictory that there cannot be a single board member in the world that fully fits the bill. They need to be supportive, intelligent, interesting, well-rounded and funny, entrepreneurial, objective yet passionate, independent, curious, challenging and fit. They also need to have a financial background and real business experience, a strong moral compass, and be first-class all-rounders with specific industry skills.[48]

In Chapter 1 we saw some of the criticisms that people have leveled at independent directors. In truth, there is a wide spectrum of opinions about them. Critics of the independent role are numerous. On the other hand there is Steven Fine, managing partner of brokerage house Peel Hunt, who argues that "the current generation of independent directors operate(s) on the front line of the businesses they serve. They are often the passionate driving forces behind a company's most successful innovations and initiatives."[49]

Both are right to an extent. There are excellent independent directors who do their difficult job conscientiously and well, and there are others who are like nodding dogs at the board, acquiescing in whatever the CEO and chairman say, or as Patrick Wilson of Hawkpoint Partners says, "too many people who sit on each others' boards, and as a consequence don't ask enough of the right questions or demand good answers." As I argued in the introduction, the role of the independent director is much more regulated than before, and the duties associated with that role are increasing, at the same time as public scrutiny of independent directors is also on the increase.

And, of course, independent directors are liable if things go wrong, and will be held to account if they have failed in their own duties. This is even more true of the most prominent independent directors, the chairman and the senior independent director (I will have more to say about both these roles below). When disaster strikes, for the chairman in particular there is no place to hide.

The role of the independent director has changed and grown considerably over the past few decades. Jeffrey N. Gordon of Columbia Law School estimates that in the USA in 1950 the proportion of independent directors on the boards of large public companies was 20 percent. By 2005 that figure had risen to 75 percent. It is now a requirement of all companies traded on both the NYSE and NASDAQ to have a majority of independent directors on their boards. Regulatory changes have pushed that number up, but Professor Gordon believes that the primary motivating force was a greater emphasis on shareholder value. In order to maximize their own wealth, shareholders began increasingly to use independent directors to monitor the affairs of the companies they own.[50] Certainly this fits with my own experience.

In Britain, the turning point came with the Cadbury Report (officially titled "Financial Aspects of Corporate Governance") in 1992, following a series of corporate scandals, including the collapses of the Bank of Credit and Commerce International, Maxwell Communications and Polly Peck. The Cadbury Report defined the role of the independent director for the first time; thereafter, boards of public companies were required to have a majority of independent directors. A series of committees and reports, including the Greenbury Report (1996), the Hampel Report (1998), the Higgs Report (2003) and most recently the Walker Report (2009) and the Code of Corporate Governance (2012), have further defined and refined that role in the UK.

Other countries have followed similar paths. The dual board systems in place in parts of Europe already include a number of independent directors on supervisory boards, and European countries with unitary boards have tightened their own regulations. India now requires that a majority of directors of public companies be independents, this move again taken partly in response to a series of corporate scandals. Around the world, independent directors have been moved into the frontline of defense against executive malfeasance.

Not every company has independent directors. Publicly owned companies are required to have them, but many small private companies do not have independent directors. Some private equity funds do not generally appoint independent directors, preferring instead to bring in consultants to advise the board. Others say that they cannot get the same level of influence and leverage through consultants, and that independent directors give them a direct conduit to the board.

As we saw earlier in the discussion of ownership structure, the role of the independent director on private equity-owned companies is somewhat different from that in public companies. In public companies, shareholders are often rather remote. In PE-owned companies the connection is much closer and the investor (usually) takes a deeper interest in the company, particularly in its strategy and whether it is still on course for a successful exit. Independent directors, and especially the chairman, have a strong role to play in both representing the investor's interests and in acting as a bridge between owners and managers.

More small and medium-sized firms are also appointing independent directors. CH Jones was a good example of this; as a privately owned firm, there was absolutely no need for an independent director to be appointed. Nevertheless, managing director Chris Welsh felt that something was needed. "Board meetings were too comfortable," he says. "Papers weren't necessarily well focused. Major management decisions were far too cosy." Chris felt that the company was in danger of stagnating, intellectually if not financially. "I wanted someone to come in from the outside who would challenge us, and who would occasionally say no." Increasingly, small firms are realizing the benefits of independents and following the example of CH Jones.

The role of the independent director is also expanding outside of business. Charities, trusts, hospitals, schools and universities, and many other institutions now appoint independent directors to their boards. They do so for many of the same reasons as small firms do: to bring in other points of view, to provide challenge and stretch, and to increase the general stock of knowledge and experience around the boardroom table. Non-profit businesses will often invite independents from a business background, or a military background, in the belief that they have an extra dimension of experience that is lacking. Some argue that business boards could learn from this: why not appoint an independent director with a background in charitable work?

Who Becomes an Independent Director?

"Directors become independent directors to broaden their experience and develop skills, to be stimulated, and, to an extent, to give back to other companies," says *The Director*.[51] Steve Edge, partner at the legal firm Slaughter & May, emphasizes the point that executive experience is essential. A large part of the value that independent directors bring to their posts is the experience and expertise they have gathered elsewhere. Some, especially the younger ones, will also be executive directors elsewhere, thus serving two different roles in two different companies.

Independent directors used to be almost exclusively white, male, and (at least) middle-aged. There is pressure now for boards to become more diverse and include people from different ethnic and cultural backgrounds and, especially, more women. In this last area, progress has been very slow. In 2000, there were thirteen women on the boards of FT-100 companies; by 2013, the number had increased to twenty, still a fraction of the total board population of around 285. In some countries, notably the USA, the situation is a little better; in many others it is worse, and nowhere is it ideal. My own experience is that women who succeed at this level are very able: Ruth Cairnie at Keller, Marie Louise Clayton at Forth Ports and Anne Fairey at Biocompatibles are examples of this.

The headhunting firm Spencer Stuart compiled a list of ten questions that prospective independent directors should ask themselves before taking up an appointment. These are:

1. What do I have to offer?
2. How will I find the right board?
3. How much due diligence should I do? (Spencer Stuart adds: "be rigorous")
4. Do I have the time?
5. Can I contribute?
6. Will I learn?
7. Will it be fun?
8. What is the time commitment?
9. Is my current employer fully supportive?
10. Should I expect a board induction?

Independent directors and others to whom I talked while writing this book broadly concur with all of these points, especially the need to think carefully about the responsibilities of the post and the need for due diligence. "People need to be very clear about the risks and rewards," said Stuart Vincent, managing director of corporate finance advisory at Rothschild. "There was a time when the role of independent director was seen as risk-free, but that is no longer the case. The role has very significant responsibilities and affects your reputation over the whole of your working life. When things go wrong, people remember, and they remember forever." Martin Webster, partner at law firm Pinsent Masons, puts it more bluntly: "When things go wrong in a business, the independent directors are an easy target, and are frequently the ones who get it in the neck."[52]

This can of course put some people off the role entirely: why take such risks, for comparatively little reward? More worryingly, there is a danger that independent directors will become too risk-averse, more worried about their own reputations than about what the company might need. It can take a considerable act of will to sublimate one's own concerns and act in the best interests of the company. Courage is not the least of the attributes of a successful independent director.

What Do Independent Directors Do?

"The commitment and engagement required, especially in big business, is vastly greater than one might imagine," wrote Stefan Stern in the *Financial Times*. "You are not there to be a bauble, have lunch, make polite conversation and pick up a fee. There is a job to do: a vital and challenging one."[53]

There is no doubt that the job of the independent director is changing. Once, the independent director was seen as a gifted amateur, needing no knowledge directly relevant to the company's operations but, again, that day is passing. Today, industry experience and executive experience are essential.

So too is training. There are training programs for independents. Business bodies such as the Institute of Directors in the UK offer training, as do some universities, executive search firms, and audit firms. It is important to attend a training program that really gets to grips with the basic elements of the role and provides an opportunity to hear from practitioners; many focus on corporate governance and compliance, which are only part of the job. Even more important is induction into the company and the sector in which it works. You cannot simply turn up for your first board meeting ready to go to work. You need to get to know the company, its culture, its people, its purpose and values, its ways of doing things. The same applies to members of committees. Members of health and safety committees need to be familiar with the regulatory and legal regimes in which they work, with the company's own health and safety standards, and with the health and safety risks that its employees face. Member of audit committees must be financially literate to a high standard and be trained in how to analyze financial statements, and so on.

Independence is key to the role. The British use the term "non-executive director" to describe the role; Americans prefer "independent director," but as stated in Chapter 1, whatever you call the role, independence is one of its most important attributes. Investors expect any independent director to bring independence of both thought and experience to the board, to both assist and constructively review key executive team decisions. *The Director* magazine quoted Richard Wilson, a partner at Ernst & Young, as saying that the role of independent director was part coach and part referee: "You are there to coach and help enhance performance, but also to challenge the management around governance and performance."[54]

The challenge for the independent director is, on the one hand, to remain independent of the business and its day-to-day operations, while, on the other hand, to develop a level of knowledge that will allow them to ask insightful and objective questions, provide strategic advice, and be a voice for the shareholder. The independent has to get involved with the company, but not too involved; be close to the company, but not too close. Above all, there is the line between the duties of the independents and executives that must not be crossed. Crossing it could jeopardize the independence of the independent director.

That independence is especially vital given the pressures that independent directors are now under. Investors are increasingly expecting independent directors to take a leading role in preserving shareholder value. There is now an increased emphasis on independent directors having a wider set of competencies, including the ability to evaluate operational, financial, and reputational risk, meaning that they are more directly responsible for ensuring that the company is run in a prudent manner. When companies, or their strategies, fail, it is now the independent directors who are often among the first to face difficult questions. Where were they when it happened? Why did they not foresee the crisis, and do something to prevent it?

Social media and online communication mean that any mistake can be communicated around the world in an instant. Reputations take a long time to build; in the current climate, they can be obliterated almost in the blink of an eye. And, finally, with the increasing use of board appraisal and evaluation of chairmen and independent directors, there are fewer places for an under-performing director to hide. Small wonder that independent directors are being encouraged to think very seriously before taking up the role!

Appointments used to be more informal, where personal friendship with the chairman or senior independent director was often enough to secure an independent directorship. This too is changing and, especially in larger companies, nomination committees are now under pressure to use open advertising or executive search. From my experience I have drawn up a specification of the role of independent director, which sets out what is often expected from independent directors. What follows is a summary of that specification.

Chairing committees. Independent directors are often expected to chair at least one board committee. In order to do so, they need to develop expertise in the committee's area of focus. Audit committee chairmen must be qualified accountants; remuneration committee chairmen must be familiar with the issues around remuneration and so on.

Due diligence. As well as overseeing formal due diligence, independent directors are expected to scrutinize valuations, consider the strategic importance and value of any new acquisition, advise on the competencies of its management team, and consider any broader business issues.

Business strategy. Independent directors should be able to analyze the company's current strategic position, understand key strategic issues (including marketing, financial, operational and human resources issues, and the relative of merits of mergers and acquisitions and alliances or partnerships), be able to develop strategic options, assist in the choice of a strategy, and then monitor its progress.

Resourcing. The directors should be familiar with human resources management, including appraisal, recruitment, selection, training and development, and remuneration for the executive team in particular. They should also be financially literate and be able to understand cash flow and liquidity, debt-to-equity ratios, profit forecasts, capital requirements, financial controls, bank support, and insurance.

Corporate governance. They should be aware of how corporate governance has evolved and be familiar with the relevant codes. They should be directly involved in a range of issues, including directors' remuneration, shareholder relations, and in particular relations with institutional shareholders, audit, and reporting requirements.

Independent advice. Among the roles independent directors are expected to play are those of sounding board, counselor, challenger, facilitator, and coach to the CEO and other senior executives. They are there to assist the executive team, but not follow them blindly and must be prepared to stand up and be counted if they disagree fundamentally with what the executives propose to do.

Bridge between investors and management. Independent directors oversee the relationship between shareholders and management. This means understanding shareholders and building personal relationships with them. It includes monitoring investor communications and taking appropriate account of different shareholder perspectives on the company's strategy and business issues, for example executive remuneration. Supervising exit strategies and change of control of companies require special attention

Assistance to the executive team. This is a catch-all category that includes technical advice, liaison with customers, visits to operational sites, making personal introductions to advisors or partners who might be useful, and getting involved in financing and fundraising.

I have also developed a list of competencies and characteristics of independent directors, which is set out in the box below.

Characteristics and Competencies of Independent Directors

Personal
- Integrity
- Judgment
- Leadership
- Motivation
- Communications skills
- Interpersonal sensitivity
- Listening skills
- Intelligence
- Cultural flexibility
- Sense of responsibility
- Independence

Professional and managerial
- Strategy
- Technical
- Organizational
- Analytical
- Problem solving
- Chairing
- Committee membership (audit, remuneration, nomination)

Entrepreneurial
- Vision
- Judgment
- Conviction
- Decisiveness
- Commercial acumen

It will be apparent from these lists that most companies are looking for all-rounders, people who are able to analyze and understand everything about a business. Of course, not everyone is equally expert in every field, nor is it likely that any board will comprise people who are brilliant at everything. But the independent director must know enough about all of these subjects, and have enough of these traits, to be able to discharge his or her duties of analysis, scrutiny, advice and, where necessary, challenge.

A more general set of guidelines was offered by the magazine *Boardsearch*, and its "ten commandments," lists of dos and don'ts for boards seeking to recruit independent directors, is reproduced in Table 4.18.

TABLE 4.18 Ten commandments for boards

Guidelines on searching for independent, part-time or non-executive chairmen or directors

DOs	DON'Ts
1 **Involve whole board**, ideally through a nomination committee with a majority of NED's, chaired by the chairman or an NED.	1 Leave selection method, and appointment, to chairman / executive directors alone.
2 **Aim high**. The quality of NEDs measures the stature of the chairman / company. Use a professional search firm.	2 Settle for easiest or second best, or limit search to those already known to chairman / board, or already Plc main board.
3 **Be creative / imaginative,** seek agents of change.	3 Regard appointment as normal gap to be filled, faithful retainer to maintain status quo.
4 **Start with the task / role**, skills / experiences and 'chemistry' most needed to complement and strengthen existing board.	4 Start with names and then design role to suit each candidate.
5 **Consider wider than traditional sources,** eg: – Divisional Directors, not yet main board, of major companies – Public / voluntary sector / academics – International business people – Qualified / relevant women or younger (40s-50s) candidates.	5 a) Limit selection or follow fashion, unless relevant to task – e.g. existing Plc main board only, token woman, title, former politician / civil servant / diplomat / trade unionist. b) Appoint from existing professional advisers or former executives – duplicates / misses opportunity to broaden.
6 Seek individuals with **genuine independence** from chairman and fees - beholden to shareholders, employees, and local community.	6 Hire those seeking only extra fees, power, prestige, etc.
7 Seek individuals with some **spare availability** for special projects, emergencies; and pay fees reflecting time committed.	7 Appoint where already over-committed or for regular board meetings only.
8 Ensure **several** independent directors (minimum 3 for Plc) with **clear leader** (e.g. Deputy Chairman, particularly where (unusually) chairman / CEO same).	8 Appoint only one, or less than 30-40 percent of board.
9 Appoint for a **specified term** – e.g. 3 years with a formal review.	9 Make open-ended appointment, or imply automatic reappointment.
10 Have **letter of appointment**, setting out duties, committees, terms of office, fees and review procedure / timing.	10 Leave vague the role, term of office etc, or (particularly if a large Plc) permit participation in a performance pay, share option or pension schemes.

Source: boardsearch

The case studies earlier in this book show too how independent directors get involved in a wide range of issues. Here is a quick summary of the contributions made by independent directors, including myself in each case:

Biocompatibles: independent review of acquisitions; review of takeover proposals; obtained best price when business sold; use of external expert advisors to develop strategy; decision to use Medtronic royalty to pay a dividend; focus on the use of clinical trials; focus on partnering with pharma companies; setting up of quality committee; counseling and appraisal of CEO; introductions, for example to Quintiles and to Japanese contacts.

CH Jones: advice on exit strategy and valuation; development of a very focused strategy; advice on integrated fuel management approach and its value to logistics companies; corporate governance issues on board best practice; introductions to logistics companies as potential clients; counseling of CEO.

Datrontech: enforced a more focused strategy; enforced the application of corporate governance standards; divestment of loss-making businesses; assisted with the logistics strategy; took the decision that the business should be liquidated.

Forth Ports: review of acquisitions; review of major investments; review of the bid for the company and its subsequent sale for best price; operational visits; contribution to strategic reviews; review of geographic options; highlighted the need to manage property more professionally with a different strategy; board changes, especially retirement of the chairman; introductions to potential clients (for example, NFT); counseling of CEO.

Keller: review of acquisitions and back check on their performance; independent review of major investments; review of major contracts; strategic reviews by geography involving visits all over the world; use of external consultants to carry out global strategic review; decisions to expand into other geographic areas; help on growing the business organically more quickly; retirement of the chairman and of all of the independent directors over time; dealing with increasing involvement by investors; central initiatives to share best practice in a very decentralized organization.

Michael Gerson: helping the board recognize the need to adapt to a changing market; managing the strategic review process; finding a new chairman; introductions for new business.

NFT: developing a very focused strategy; divestment of property; helping the team in the transition from being an in-house subsidiary to a stand-alone company; recruitment of senior executive team; involvement in resolving a major customer issue with Sainsbury's; involvement in reviewing start-up plans for major projects; review of investment proposals; use of external expert advisors and introductions to these; appraisal of CEO and counseling; overseeing the exit plan, including the selection of Rothschild as investment banker.

NovaQuest: reviewing investments; introductions on fundraising; chairing joint discussions with Quintiles on partnering; meeting with specific partnering opportunities and investment opportunities; counseling managing partner; working on the strategy for a new fund; meeting potential team players; meeting potential lawyers.

Quintiles: review of investments and divestments; geographic performance review visits; challenged the centralization of the business in the USA; reviewed the ways in which the business reported financial results; formed special committee which oversaw the privatization of the company in 2003; advised the founder, who was chairman and CEO, on many occasions on many issues.

U-POL: strategic review which emphasized geographic expansion; helped the company adjust from being a family business to being a private equity investment; oversaw the successful exit; appraised the CEO; guided the private equity house, especially concerning the executive team; advised on how to improve their logistics efficiency.

Vantec: led the strategic review to focus on sectors other than automotive; helped the business adjust from being a Nissan subsidiary to being a European private equity investment; served as the link between the private equity house and the executive board; advised senior management on issues such as account management, contracts and developments in global logistics; participated in business development; reviewed performance at locations; introduced potential purchasers of the business; introduced Exel as a business partner; independent assessment of the exit to Mizuho.

And all of this is in addition to the standard duties of the independent directors, such as attending board meetings and committee meetings.

The role of the chairman

In the UK, the role of chairman of the board has become much higher in profile and expectations of what the chairman can do, and must do, have increased. Stakeholders now expect chairmen to be engaged, energetic, and involved, and to do much more than simply chair board meetings and manage the corporate governance process. This is in sharp contrast to the USA, where the roles of chairman and CEO are often combined.

Chris Collins, the extremely effective chairman of the board of Forth Ports, describes the role as being that of a facilitator, someone who gets things moving. "It is important that the chairman and the CEO should get on," he says, "and the chairman should contribute to that relationship." CEOs have a job to do, he says, and the chairman should not hinder them in the performance of their duties, but at the same time the chairman is ultimately responsible to the shareholders for the company. The two need a working relationship with no clash of egos. "There is no room for two King Kongs," says Chris. "Today the CEO is usually the outward face of the company. This reality can require the exercise of tact by the chairman."

There is no one-size-fits-all prescription for an effective chairman. The right level of engagement will vary from company to company, often quite considerably, and within the same company it will vary over time depending on the company's stage in the business cycle, the competitive environment, and the experience and performance of the CEO. What is clear is that chairmen—even more than ordinary independents—need, in tennis parlance, an all-court game. The case studies earlier in this book show just how much influence and importance a good chairman can have.

A report from INSEAD in 2014 identified three key qualities in a good chairman: personal humility; listening, while at the same time both challenging and supporting the board; and the "guts" to do what is right.[55] Other reports identify features such as strategic vision, a clear sense of direction, gravitas, a good network of contacts, and the ability to bring people together. Another key attribute is the ability to understand the culture of companies, and to adapt to new cultures and ways of working. The chairman cannot impose himself or herself on the board and the company; he or she must be flexible and be able to work with others as a team.

Table 4.19 shows the role and qualities of a chairman we looked for at Forth Ports, and is a useful example of what the role involves. Again, the actual role will vary from company to company and time to time. This description should not be taken as a template.

Possibly the most critical role for any chairman, though, is ensuring effective succession planning. Chairmen, in the UK at least, cannot simply step in and take over when the CEO departs. They must ensure that the transition to a new CEO happens as smoothly as possible and that the right person is chosen, whether that person comes from inside or outside the company. Guiding the choice of CEO is one of the most important things a chairman does; and if the chairman gets it wrong, as happened at National Freight Corporation, the consequences can be horrendous.

Ask most chairmen and they will tell you that the hardest thing they have ever had to do was fire the CEO. Getting rid of underperforming board members

TABLE 4.19   Role and qualities of the chairman at Forth Ports

- Organisation of the composition, business and efficiency of the board
- Leadership of the board in strategy determination and measuring the achievement of business objectives independent directors
- Ensuring the board has accurate and clear visibility of results achieved and likely future trends
- Ensuring the board committees are properly established, composed and operated
- Ensuring with the CEO that effective relations are maintained with all major stakeholders including shareholders, customers and employees
- Enhancing the company's public standing and overall image
- Developing a strong working relationship with the CEO
- Facilitating the effective contribution of Independent directors and ensuring constructive relations between executive and independent directors
- Arranging the regular evaluation of the performance of the board, its committees and key directors

Qualities required

- Statesman/strong reputation, particularly in financial circles
- Conservative
- Long-term view of the business
- Perceptive reader of people/strong in empathy
- Excellent facilitator in shaping debates
- Long-term experience in dealing with institutions and regulatory authorities
- Financial acumen
- Strategic thinker
- International business experience
- Team leadership skills
- Company chairmanship experience

also ranks high on the list, along with factors such as dealing with market downturns, turning around failing businesses, dealing with bad press and managing large-scale crises. Raymond Way at Datrontech and Francis Peck at Michael Gerson are examples of chairmen in very difficult situations, when the job becomes much harder than it already is.

The other difficult thing that chairmen sometimes have to do is wind up companies that have failed. Francis Peck was in that position as chairman of Michael Gerson. Employed on the basis of four days a month, by the end he was working four days a week trying to find a buyer for the company before it ran out of money. "In the last weeks before the sale of the business, we were in almost weekly contact with the liquidator to ensure the business was trading legally," he recalls. Francis reminds us, too, that in these situations there are obligations to many stakeholders, not just the shareholders. One of his own priorities was to find a solution that would save the jobs of the workers and Michael Gerson and protect them from the mistakes that had been made by management.

As a final note, chairmen, like all independent directors, have to adjust to different kinds of ownership, especially when a company changes hands. Family businesses require a truly independent chairman who will stand up to the vested interests that these firms often contain and be prepared to sort out conflicts between family members. With private equity owned businesses, one has to adjust one's mindset and style in order to deal with owners who have often never actually run a business and may not even know very much about the sector or the company's operations. In public companies, one has to deal with activist shareholders and comply with a much tougher governance regime than is the case in the private sector.

Contributions of chairmen

The job of the chairman is capable of almost infinite expansion, but these are some of the key achievements of the chairmen in our eleven companies:

Biocompatibles
- provided strategic experience of clinical trials, helped set new strategy, made introduction to Quintiles, oversaw sale of the company

CH Jones
- led the strategic review, supervised the sale to private equity

Datrontech
- brought in turnaround specialist as CEO; took decision to wind up the company

Forth Ports
- brought the board together as a team to discuss strategy and other key issues

Keller
- led the MBO; pushed for and guided the global strategic review

Michael Gerson
- sought to change the strategy, liaised with investor, oversaw the sale

NFT
- built a strong management team, led thinking about new strategy, supported the CEO, oversaw the sale of the company

NovaQuest
- met with investors, liaised with Quintiles, developed strategy for a family of funds

Quintiles
- led strategic thinking, oversaw expansion and growth, took company private in 2003

U-POL
- liaison with private equity owners, supported the CEO, oversaw the sale of the company

Vantec
- developed strategy for new stand-alone company, oversaw sale to Mizhuo

The role of the senior independent director

In the UK, the Higgs Report of 2003 recommended, somewhat controversially, that boards appoint a senior independent director, originally as an additional channel of communication for shareholders should they be dissatisfied with the behavior of the chairman. At the time there were concerns that the senior independent director would undermine the authority of the chairman, and there were doubts about how truly independent senior independent directors would be (recall our earlier discussion in this book about "independence"). A decade on, the senior independent director's role has proved its worth and the appointment of a senior independent director is now enshrined in the Corporate Governance Code.

Far from undermining the chairman, a good senior independent director is a pillar of support. "Senior independent directors serve as a sounding board for chairmen," says the Institute of Directors (IOD), "and act as an intermediary for the other directors."[56] They are responsible for appraising the chairman, and for mediating and resolving disputes between chairmen and chief executives. As intended, they also serve as an alternative channel for communication with shareholders, and thus investor relations are a large part of the job. The IOD sums up the duties and responsibilities of the senior independent director as follows:

- Working closely with the chairman, acting as sounding board and support
- Acting as an intermediary for the other directors as and when necessary
- Being available to shareholders and other independents to address any concerns they feel have not been adequately dealt with through the usual channels of communication
- Meeting at least annually with the independents to review the chairman's performance and carrying out succession planning for the chairman's role
- Attending sufficient meetings with shareholders to obtain a balanced understanding of their issues and concerns[57]

The Changing Role of the Independent Director

As noted, the role of the independent director has changed greatly over the past two decades, becoming steadily more important. That role is still changing, and will continue to change into the foreseeable future. Here are some of the key trends to watch for.

Firstly, the number of independent directorships around the world will increase, as more companies are floated and more small- and medium-sized private companies begin to realize the value these independents bring to the board. This increase will come—must come—from an increasingly diverse pool of talent. We shall see more people from different backgrounds, more ethnic minorities, and, it is to be hoped sooner rather than later, more women. Ages will also fall; the current average age of a FTSE-350 independent director is 60, but that average will come down over time as more younger independent directors are appointed.

Globalization is an increasing force and companies are becoming steadily more international in terms of both markets and operations. Dual and triple listings will become more common as companies pursue capital in markets that offer different investor bases. Independent directors with international experience and who are aware of cultural sensitivities will be much in demand; those without such experience may struggle to stay relevant.

This expansion will come at a cost. Companies seeking IPOs in Western stock markets will come increasingly from countries with less developed codes of governance and rules of law. There will be more corporate scandals, and independents who get caught up in these will find themselves in court. Independent directors need to become much more vigilant, practicing due diligence, and only accepting those offers which do not carry significant reputational risk.

The issue of personal liability will increase in importance more generally, as traditional shareholders become more activist and demand better accounting. This, coupled with increasing public scrutiny, will put independent directors in the spotlight. At the same time, institutional investors in particular will come to rely ever more heavily on independent directors, and members of audit committees, in particular, can expect to have increasing interaction with shareholders.

Finally, since the collapse of Lehman Brothers in 2008, the relationship between CEOs and independent directors has changed fundamentally, on both sides of the Atlantic. CEOs are becoming more aware of their own vulnerability, and more willing to make use of the expertise and advice provided by independents. The issue of balance will become increasingly important as independent directors struggle to be both coach and referee at the same time.

The Independent Director

Sir Roger Carr, chairman of the Confederation of British Industry, describes the role of independent director as one that "relies on influence rather than power, with collegiate engagement, not dominant direction. It needs independence of mind as a deterrent to group think and the strength of character to support when appropriate, but challenge when necessary."[58] Sir Roger, like so many who have commented on the role, stresses the notion of independence of thought and action, and it really is almost impossible to stress this point too much. I shall round this section off by offering a selection of views from my own colleagues, past and present, about the value that a truly independent director brings to a board, and a company.

Charles Hammond, CEO Forth Ports

"The broad general experience of the non-executives meant that they would raise general points that we [the executive team] might not have thought about. It made us go away and think, have we got that covered? Are they right about that? Have we really addressed that properly?"

Justin Atkinson, CEO, Keller

"Independent directors will always spot a few things that you have missed, or that could be improved upon. Increased pressure from the non-executives over the years has been very good for the executives. It has certainly been very good for me."

Ron Wootten, managing partner, NovaQuest

"Independent directors are an extra set of eyes to make sure we are not being near-sighted. It is very important to have people with diverse backgrounds. If you populate your board with people of like experience, you don't get the diversity of thinking and challenging of initiatives, and this can lead to bad decisions."

Steve Edge, partner, Slaughter & May

"As a non-executive, you know that you're there to be a sounding board for the chief executive. You're there to support them, but you're also there to look for signs and use your experience to spot potential problems between shareholders and executives. If these do happen, you help to provide an intermediate ground for discussion. You're the custodian of shareholders' interests, but you're also management's friends and management's support. And if something goes wrong on your watch, you have to be prepared to explain."

Jeremy Curnock Cook, non-executive director, Biocompatibles

"There is no nice little route map you are given when you are developing a business. You really need to have people there who understand the business environment, and can bring an outsider's perspective when working on a high-risk program of technology development."

William Underhill, partner, Slaughter & May

"Good boards take dissent very seriously. Directors who are not happy should speak out, and a good chairman will find ways of discussing problems, sometimes outside of the meeting, or will look again at the decision."

Francis Peck, chairman, Michael Gerson

"Non-executive directors have got to have a breadth of vision, and not just look at what that business is doing at that time. They need think about how things can be financed. They need to make sure that standards are being set for the management of the business, agreed with the chairman, and then lower levels of management are also performing to the necessary standards. They hold management to account."

Dennis Gillings, chairman and CEO, Quintiles

"We live in a complex world, and we need more balance in working out issues. We may think we know the answers to questions, but we need to know what other people's answers might be. Will their answers reinforce what we already think? Or will they be the opposite of what we think? Are there factors to which we have not paid attention? Only once we have gone through this questioning and answering can we make decisions that are robust."

Patrick Wilson, Hawkpoint Partners

"The biggest job of the non-executive is to question, to make the executive team think outside the box. The most effective independent directors are those who ask, why are we doing this? What kind of business are we, and what kind of business do we want to be? What do we want to look like in five years, or ten years? Why do we want to look like that? What do we have to do to get there? The non-executive should question and probe and make them [the executives] think about things they don't normally think about."

Peter Waine, Hanson Green

"A good independent director needs constantly to have a degree of curiosity and a degree of courage. They are outsiders looking in, and they can see things that people who work with the business on a day-to-day basis will not necessarily see."

5

Conclusion

Throughout this book, two important themes have run continuously: firstly, the role of the independent director is more important than ever before; and secondly, the role of the independent director has never been harder, or more challenging. Independent, non-executive directors are no longer bystanders in the corporate world. They are on the frontline. If you want to be an independent director, or already are one, then this is the reality you must face.

The importance of the role was highlighted sharply by the banking crisis of 2008 and the subsequent economic downturn. A few large and powerful financial institutions ran into difficulties, and the rest of the economy suffered as a result. Bad strategy and bad governance at Royal Bank of Scotland, Lehman Brothers and others had a knock-on effect for the rest of us. Ordinary people put their hands in their pockets and found they had much less money than before. Many, not just in the banking sector, lost their jobs as the credit crunch took hold and companies went under. Those people in turn pointed the finger at the banking sector and blamed the bankers for their own losses.

Could it all have been avoided had the banks not made a series of errors in the years before 2008? I ask again the question that I asked several times during this book: where were the independent directors of those banks? What were they doing while all this went on? Why were they not raising concerns about strategy, risk, and governance? Had they done so, it is my belief that the crash might have been avoided, or at least, its consequences greatly reduced.

It is, perhaps, easy to be wise after the event. Hopefully, in future, independent directors *will* take responsibility and work to prevent such disasters from occurring. That is their duty as enshrined in regulation, and if they fail to carry it out, they can expect to suffer the consequences. Already we have seen independent directors appearing in court and, in the USA, going to prison.

Nor is the growing importance of the non-executive director confined to the financial sector. Scandals have hit companies in many sectors. For example, pharmaceuticals, a sector I know well, has been rocked by allegations of bribery and corruption in recent years. There is now a strong media focus on big pharma, and any allegation of malfeasance is likely to receive wide publicity, harming the companies involved and their shareholders. Non-executive directors need to be willing and able to step up and exercise greater governance and scrutiny to prevent these problems from happening.

Indeed as I am completing this book *The Times* is reporting that Britain's largest supermarket group Tesco is being investigated by the Serious Fraud Office. It follows the revelations from a whistleblower that the retailer had overstated its half year profit forecasts by more than a quarter of a billion pounds. Eight executives are suspended, the Chairman has resigned and Tesco has had more than £2billion wiped off its stock market value.

Apart from the rising interest in corporate governance and the demands for greater scrutiny and transparency, other forces are at work. Shareholders, still licking their wounds after 2008, are becoming more demanding. Some shareholders, notably hedge funds, are strongly activist and demand accountability from boards. Independent directors, as we saw earlier in the book, have an important role to play in bridge-building. At the same time, globalization is leading to more complex markets, and stretching companies as they try to bridge the cultural and political gaps between countries and continents. Independent directors with international experience are becoming very sought after, for they can help boards to understand these new markets and cultures and work out how to manage across borders.

Another important trend is the growing numbers of independent directors outside of the corporate world. Charities, hospitals, trust funds, schools, universities, non-governmental organizations, and all sorts of non-business, non-profit organizations are now seeing the value of this role. Names change: sometimes these directors are called governors, or trustees, but the role is essentially the same. The independence of thought and word that good corporate boards value so much is equally of value to the boards of non-profit institutions. Yet, the challenges for non-executive directors can be very different. Despite the similarity of role, the environment in which independent directors or trustees of charities or universities find themselves can be very different from that of business. Cultures, attitudes, ways of doing things are not what directors might expect, and they often have to work hard to adjust to their new environment. Not all succeed in doing so.

Lessons Learned

The case studies in Chapter 3 provided twelve examples of what independent directors do, and some of the key lessons learned. The themes in Chapter 4 went on to look at various aspects of the role of the independent director and comment on them. Here, I will sum up some of the key lessons learned.

First, in a well-run company the board works together as a team. Independent directors are part of that team, and must pull their weight. There can be no "us" and "them," no split between executives and non-executives. That does not mean that boards should be completely unanimous and think as one; far from it. Good discussion and debate are essential. We saw at Forth Ports how a good board works together and thrashes out contentious issues, rather than putting them to one side, and at NFT how the company thrived in large part thanks to an effective board that supported the CEO. At the same time, at Datrontech and Michael Gerson we saw what happened when boards don't work well together. If relationships go sour, then it is up to the independent directors — and especially the chairman — to find out what went wrong and fix it.

The ownership of a company has a very strong bearing on the role of the independent director, for two primary reasons. Firstly, independent directors are the bridge between the owners and the board; part of their task is to represent the views of owners and make their wishes known. Some owners, such as family owners and more pro-active private equity firms, are closely involved with the firm and want to keep their finger on the pulse. Others take a back seat, and only express their views if something goes wrong (for example, if profit or income targets are not met).

Also, whether a company is privately or publicly owned has a strong impact on the company's goals and targets. With publicly owned companies, the emphasis is on hitting short-term targets, and shareholder value is a prime concern. We saw in the Quintiles case how this affected the running of the company. In privately owned companies, the targets are longer term. Most private equity houses aren't greatly concerned about short-term issues so long as the trends are very positive, as the U-POL and NFT cases showed clearly. Their focus is on the exit, and building up the value of the company so that it can be sold at a very good multiple of earnings. Independent directors can find it very challenging to make the switch between these two mindsets, and I recommend that any would-be independent director should try to gain experience of both public ownership and private equity ownership as soon as possible.

That means that strategies for public and private companies are often very different (and in the non-profit sector, they are different again). There has in the past been a feeling in some quarters that independent directors should not get involved in strategy, which is the province of the executives. That view is fast disappearing. Today it is widely recognized that independent directors *must* get involved in strategy, which is one of the most important tasks that any board faces. As part of the board, independent directors are responsible for the company's strategy; it is as simple as that. Through training and experience, independent directors need to become familiar with a wide range of strategic issues and be comfortable with discussing them. Forth Ports, Quintiles Keller, Vantec, NFT, U-POL, NovaQuest, Biocompatibles, and CH Jones, among others, showed how much independent directors can contribute.

As a subset of strategy, globalization is also an issue that confronts boards. Again, independent directors have a role to play. As noted above, independent directors with international experience are worth their weight in gold to a company. The Quintiles and Keller cases showed this particularly strongly.

As I said earlier in the book, all business is risky. But there is risk, and then there is *risk*. Smart boards know what kinds of risks to take and what kinds to avoid. Biocompatibles, for example, knew how to manage risk as it developed its experimental technologies and made the transition from R&D-focused business to profitable company. At Datrontech, lack of understanding of risk by the executives plunged the company into a downward spiral of debt. Boards need the experience and wisdom of independent directors. They can help companies to identify risks and work out mitigation strategies. Many boards now have risk committees, with an independent director as chair. It follows, of course, that independent directors need to be able to understand risk and be capable of managing it effectively. Again, experience and maturity are important.

No matter how talented and diverse the board is, every board at some point needs to call on external advisors: lawyers, consultants, merchant bankers, accountants and auditors, headhunters, and many others. Managing these advisors is not always easy. The good ones are worth their weight in gold. The bad ones are ... bad, sometimes very bad. Independent directors can play a role in the management of advisors in several ways. Firstly, they can use their experience to help select advisors who will give value for money. Secondly, they can check on the credentials and background of potential advisors to see whether their reputation lives up to reality. Thirdly, they can help manage the relationship between advisors and the rest of the company. As we saw earlier, the relationship between external auditors and members of the audit committee is particularly important. In the case studies, the Keller case showed how useful consultants can be, while at NovaQuest, the setting up of the new fund would have been impossible without the assistance of specialist lawyers.

From the above, it can be seen that the relationship between executives and independent directors is of crucial importance, and no relationship is more important than that of the chief executive and the chairman (although this relationship is perhaps less important in the USA, where the chairman is often an executive, and sometimes the two roles are combined). Earlier we discussed at some length the nature of that relationship, but here I want to remind you of two key points. Firstly, one of the most important tasks of independent directors is to assist in the selection of senior executives, including the CEO but increasingly other posts as well. Getting these decisions wrong and hiring the wrong person can cripple a company or even kill it. NFT and Vantec provided good examples of the importance of getting the right people into top posts.

And secondly, there is the often-made point that independent directors are not executives. There is a limit to their duties and responsibilities, a line that they must not cross. If independent directors get involved in day-to-day management, then they quickly cease to be independent. They need an element of detachment; they need to stand back and look at the larger picture, while the executives grapple with more immediate responsibilities. That is what independent directors do; that is why they exist.

If this book does only one thing, then I hope it shows the vital importance of the independent director's role. Through their contributions to governance, scrutiny and oversight, strategy and risk management, and through their effective partnerships with executives, independent directors are not just important board members; they are key members of the team that guides the company. I would go so far as to say they are indispensable. They bring their own experience and backgrounds, and create a diversity of thought and ideas in the boardroom. They challenge and test received wisdom, and offer new thinking. Sometimes, they shake the executive out of their complacency; sometimes, they cause a stir and, as one of my colleagues says, every independent director should be prepared at times to be the most unpopular person in the room. Above and beyond all else, they make people think; and through thinking comes better understanding and better decisions.

Future Challenges

I said earlier that the role of the independent director has changed greatly in the past few years. It is inevitable that the role will continue to change, and that the challenges and responsibilities will grow greater. Here are what I see as the main issues in the years ahead.

Firstly, boards are no longer solely concerned with maximizing shareholder value. Other pressures, from shareholders, regulators, and the public, are growing and will continue to grow. Among these are the demand for better governance and more transparency, and the rising pressure for companies to demonstrate their commitment to sustainability. Independent directors and chairmen will need to develop their own skills in these areas in order to work with the executives and play their parts as members of the board team.

Secondly, corporate governance is becoming more comprehensive and international in its coverage. Companies operating internationally will need to comply with different codes in different jurisdictions, not just the one where the company is domiciled. Independent directors need to be aware of their responsibilities, and potential liabilities, in each jurisdiction.

The push for independent directors to be fully involved in the development of business strategy, including the review of strategic options, will continue. Cursory oversight of strategy will not be sufficient.

Increasingly, globalization is affecting every business, large or small. There will no longer be a place for directors with experience of domestic markets only. Independent directors and chairmen will have to gain international experience if they are to play a full part as board members.

Independent directors and chairmen will also come under steadily increasing scrutiny from regulators, investors, employees, and the media, and the danger of civil or criminal prosecution for failures will increase. Risk management will therefore become ever more important. Independent directors will need to be totally involved in the development of a proactive, company-wide approach to risk. A full understanding of the discipline of risk management, including best practice for risk avoidance, will be essential.

Greater fluidity in the ownership of public companies, coupled with the increasingly activist approach of some shareholders, means that the emphasis on short-term performance will increase. This poses a challenge for investor relations, and will put more pressure on independent directors. Their roles as independent board members and representatives of shareholder interests could become conflicted.

Increasingly, Private equity houses will turn to the "buy and build" model and become more involved in the businesses in which they invest, helping to identify opportunities for growth and then ensuring those opportunities are taken. Independent directors in PE-owned companies will need to adapt to this more hands-on style, and experience of private equity ownership will become even more valuable.

Succession planning at board and senior management level will become a high-priority issue, and independent directors will be expected to play a role in managing the succession of senior posts across the business.

As business becomes more complex, the role of professional advisors will become more important. More businesses will use these advisors, in greater numbers and in a variety of capacities. Independent directors will continue to be involved in the management of these advisors to ensure that they give fair advice and best value for money.

Executive mobility is an increasing trend, and the time that CEOs and other senior executives spend in their posts is shortening. As churn among executives increases, it will be the responsibility of independent directors and chairman to become guardians of the long-term interest and value of companies. They will become repositories of the company's culture and wisdom. This too could lead to conflict, as directors may need to push back against new executives who attempt to act against the company's best long-term interests.

All of these activities will increase the time pressures on independent directors. They will be required to give more time to their duties, and to use that time more effectively, in order to get things done.

Finally, the combined pressures and challenges of the role mean that the quality of independent directors and chairmen must improve. Selection standards will rise, and more and better training for the role will eventually be provided. One very important aspect of this is for boards to become much more diverse for example with a greater Proportion of women board members. Regulators are already intervening in the selection of independent directors in financial services, for example, and it is likely that this intervention will increase.

A Final Note

The world of business has changed greatly since I first entered it over forty years ago. The rise of globalization means that nearly every business now has to confront international competition and work in international markets. Regulation has increased many times over, and businesses of every sort are governed by far more regulations than before, making the task of the director that much more difficult. Technology has ramped up the complexities that we face; technology has been a great enabler and we can do things in business now that we used only to dream about, but the rapid pace of change and evolution makes it very hard to keep up with technological developments. The business world, like the world itself, has become a much more complex place. Yet through it all there has been continuity too. The need for trust, the importance of personal relationships, the power of good communications, the need for leadership—these continue to be as important as they have always been. Nor are they likely to go away.

Personally, I have found being an independent director to be a very satisfying part of my career, and life. The work has been very demanding, and there have been disappointments along the way. But the challenges have been fascinating, and the work has been intellectually stimulating. I have enjoyed the international dimension, and it has been a real pleasure to work with different companies and management teams in very different businesses and sectors. The diversity of the work has been one of its main pleasures.

Most of all, though, there has been the chance to make a difference, to help build up companies that provide more and better services to customers, to improve the value of companies for shareholders, to guide boards and executive teams to realize at least some of their dreams. I believe strongly that independent directors can be a force for good. Despite all the pressures, challenges, and risks, this is a job that is very much worth doing. I hope that others will feel inspired to become independent directors; and for those who do, I end this book with a few remarks on building a portfolio.

6

chapter

Building a Portfolio

Having described the role of the independent director in detail, and from multiple perspectives, it is time to consider how one gets started as an independent director and how one builds up a portfolio. First, of course, one must be qualified to do the job. Primarily, that means executive experience. One needs to have been there, to have walked the walk, and to understand how businesses are run, before one can even think of becoming an independent or non-executive director.

What kind of experience is the right experience? It is important to have sector experience, as this is what many stakeholders are looking for. I noted earlier how private equity houses are increasingly making sector experience a top priority (this is because most PE houses lack sector experience of their own, and are looking for a surrogate on the board who can fill this gap). However, high-level experience in a particular branch of management, such as marketing or operations, can also be helpful. In my own case, my executive experience was in general management and a number of the companies I have worked with have had a strong emphasis on logistics, even if they were not in the logistics sector as such. My early experience with Quintiles also gave me experience of pharmaceuticals, which led to my later appointment at Biocompatibles.

However, a diversity of experience is also important. As a sector or functional specialist it is easy to get bogged down, to see the world from just that one perspective. But independent directors are there to provide a broader range of experience, a wider world-view. That becomes very difficult if the director has only a limited range of experience to draw upon. My own experience certainly suggests that a diverse portfolio, built up over time, gives a greater range of prior experience. This range of experience not only improves effectiveness as a director, but also opens the doors to a broader range of positions and a more diverse portfolio. A virtuous circle then develops, with diverse experience leading to still greater diversity and breadth.

Here, in summary, is the range of my own portfolio across several dimensions:

Ownership: public, private equity, private

Size: large, medium, small

Geography: USA, Europe, Asia

Sectors: logistics, construction, pharmaceuticals, manufacturing, medical devices, information technology, chilled foods, ports, property, financial services

Getting Started

Management search agencies, or headhunters, are one of the best places to find out about potential independent director roles. Some of these, such as Hanson Green, specialize in independent and non-executive roles and will help you find out what roles are available that might suit you. However, it is important not to just blindly accept the first role that is offered.

Stuart Vincent, managing director of Rothschild Corporate Finance Advisory practice, offers a cautionary note at this stage. "People need to think very hard about the risks and rewards of being a non-executive director," he says. "The role has very significant responsibilities and affects your reputation over the whole of your working life. When things go wrong, people remember them forever." He advises prospective independent directors to do due diligence on companies before joining. Find out what their reputation is, meet with auditors and advisors and even other board members and gather as much information as possible before making a decision. Make sure that the company has a future, and that you are not walking into a minefield.

In Chapter 4, I quoted the list of questions from Spencer Stuart that all prospective independent directors should ask themselves. It is worth repeating that list here:

- What do I have to offer?
- How will I find the right board?
- How much due diligence should I do? (Spencer Stuart adds: "be rigorous")

- Do I have the time?
- Can I contribute?
- Will I learn?
- Will it be fun?
- What is the time commitment?
- Is my current employer fully supportive?
- Should I expect a board induction?

The last point is particularly significant. No independent directors should be expected to turn up at his or her first board meeting and hit the ground running. Some kind of induction and working-in period is essential so that the new director can get to know the company.

Once on a board, it is important to ease into the position gently. Do not feel you have to impress your colleagues at every turn, and do not feel you have to speak on every item on the agenda. It is more important in the first instance to listen, very carefully, and learn as much as you can about the company and the board and how it operates. Then, concentrate on building relationships with your board colleagues; once you have done so, when you do speak, they will be more likely to listen. Ensure that you prepare carefully for meetings; under-preparedness or ignorance of key issues will not always endear you to your busy colleagues. I also advise that new directors concentrate on a particular issue, which is in line with their own experience or background and make that their own province. This gives them a platform from which to offer meaningful advice.

Here is a short list of dos and don'ts for independent directors.

Do:

- Understand the business and its sector.
- Study the company completely, especially its history.
- Read independent reports on the business.
- Focus on strategic development and growing the team.
- Visit locations, especially overseas locations, and see what is happening on the ground.
- Listen to all staff at every level.
- Commit time to work with board colleagues.

Don't:

- Panic when there is a problem (for example, a profits warning must be issued).
- React in an emotional way.

• Avoid problems or issues, but confront them directly.
• Lecture other board members, especially about corporate governance.
• Get involved in too much detail at board meetings. If a complex issue arises, sort it out in committees or working groups, or through private conversations.

And here are the rules that I have found to be useful in my own work as an independent director:

1. Tailor your advice to the specific needs of the company. General ideas might be interesting to discuss, but they don't solve problems. Look at what the company really needs, right now and in the future, and don't get too hung up on theory.
2. Take time to educate and persuade. Not everyone will see the world the way you do; that is fine. Get involved in discussions, be prepared to give and take. If you believe in your position, and you are right, then in time others will agree with you. Don't try to force the issue, and especially don't try to hector or override your colleagues. They won't thank you for doing so.
3. Be consistent. Vacillating from one view to another means people don't know what you are really thinking.
4. Speak your mind. Be truthful, though of course remembering to be courteous as you do. If the board proposes an action with which you do not agree, say so, and why. Don't hide your views because you don't want to disagree with your colleagues and friends. Your responsibility is not to them; it is to the company and its investors.
5. Take your colleagues with you. Work to achieve a consensus of views, a course of action to which everyone can sign up. "Majority rules" is not good enough. Use persuasion and reasoned argument to get everyone on-side.
6. Build a reputation that you can be proud of. That means, most of all, being sure that you do the right thing and that your own course of action has always been the honorable one. Not every company succeeds; I myself have been involved in failures and disappointments. But even in these worst cases, it is important to come out with your own head up, knowing that you did the right thing for everyone involved.

The End Game

That reputation, of course, extends beyond individual companies; as Stuart Vincent says, it follows you for life. If you have a good reputation, you will find that more companies want you on their boards and your portfolio will increase. Here are a few simple rules that will help you build that portfolio and maintain that reputation.

Firstly, choose carefully which offers to accept. Especially for younger directors, there might be a temptation to jump at any offer, which is presented. It is, after all, flattering to be asked. But not every offer is equal. Work out a plan for your own portfolio and choose the offers that will help you develop your new career as an independent director.

Secondly, build a balanced portfolio. I discussed above the benefits of variety and diversity in terms of size, sector, geography, and ownership. Make sure there is an element of diversity in your plan, and choose offers that will help you gain experience and develop more fully.

Thirdly, avoid too many problem companies. What constitutes a "problem company"? The term can range from everything from complete basket cases on the verge of bankruptcy to fundamentally sound companies facing serious issues. The former are to be avoided. The latter can be useful in terms of developing skills and experience, and of course if you are part of a board that does turn a company around, there is a great deal of satisfaction to be had. But problem companies are a strain on one's time and intellectual resources, and can take away energies that are needed elsewhere. Recall how Frances Peck, chairman of Michael Gerson, ended up working four days a week for just that one company. Too many problem companies in a portfolio can lead to overwork and burnout.

Fourthly, avoid conflicts of interest. This is another reason for seeking diversity; the further apart your companies are in terms of sector and ownership, the less likely you are to find conflicts of interest.

Fifthly, enjoy contributing to the companies with which you are involved. If you find one day that you have stopped enjoying it, then it is probably time to move on.

Sixthly, learn about different sectors. Even if your portfolio ends up concentrated in one or two sectors, broaden your mind by learning about other sectors in any way you can. It is surprising how much good practice can be learned by benchmarking, even informally, against companies in other sectors.

Seventhly, the financial rewards for independent directors are not inconsiderable. This is as it should be, given the increasing importance and challenge

The good	The bad	The ugly
Independence	Poor communicator	Irresponsible
Integrity	Goes native	Believes shareholders are irrelevant
Listening skills	Low attention level	Personal interest prevails
Cultural flexibility	Unprepared for board meetings	Low attendance at board meetings
Professional	Does not visit operations	Corrupt, or is prepared to tolerate corruption
Entrepreneurial	Does not contribute to value creation	Never challenges the executives
	Wrong balance regarding corporate governance	Poor business judgment
	Tries to do the executive job	

FIG 6.1 / The good, the bad, and the ugly

of the role. Ensure that you negotiate a compensation package that is commensurate with your experience, skill and likely contribution to the company.

Let me end this book by summing up some of the characteristics of successful and unsuccessful independent directors, what I call the good, the bad, and the ugly directors (see Figure 6.1). As I said in the introduction to this book, the choice is yours!

Notes

1   Introduction

1. Stefan Stern, "Bidets, Baubles – and Boards," *Financial Times*, April 24, 2014.
2. Peter Whitehead, "Non-executive Director: A Task for which No One Is Qualified," *Financial Times*, April 10, 2013.
3. Ibid.
4. Alastair Walmsley, 'Foreword', Corporate Governance for Main Market and AIM Companies, 2012, http://www.londonstockexchange.com/companies-and-advisors/aim/publications/documents/corpgov.pdf
5. Ibid.

2   Executive Experience

1. There are a number of good books on NFC and the employee ownership scheme, including Sir Peter Thompson, *Sharing the Success: the Story of NFC*, London: Collins, 1990; Sandy McLachlan, *The National Freight Buy-out*, Basingstoke: Macmillan, 1983; and Geoffrey Lewis, *Corporate Strategy in Action: The Strategy Process in British Road Services*, London: Routledge & Kegan Paul, 1988.
2. Thompson, *Sharing the Success*, p. 162.
3. NFC subsequently disappeared from view. What happened is outside of the scope of this story, but anyone interested will find plenty of material online. Exel, however, continues to thrive.
4. Sandy McLachlan, *National Freight Buy-out*, p. 182.

3   Case Studies

1. 'Analysis: Datrontech bullish with Mulford at helm', *V3*, August 12, 1997.
2. *Financial Times*, March 23, 2011.
3. Ibid.

4 Themes

1. Ram Charan, *Boards at Work: How Boards Create Competitive Advantage*, San Francisco: Jossey-Bass, 1998; Neville Bain, *The Effective Board: Building Individual and Board Success*, London: Institute of Directors, 2009; Morten Huse, *Boards, Governance and Value Creation: The Human Side of Corporate Governance*, Cambridge: Cambridge University Press, 2007; Jay W. Lorsch, *The Future of Boards: Meeting the Governance Challenges of the Twenty-First Century*, Boston: Harvard Business Review Press, p. 201.

2. Richard Koch, *The Financial Times Guide to Strategy: How to Create, Pursue and Deliver a Winning Strategy*, London: FT Books, 2006, p. 223.

3. "Non-Executive Roles 'Of Little or No Value to the Business'," *Financial Times*, April 10, 2013.

4. Samuel A. Malone, *Greed, Fraud and Corruption: A Guide to Organisational Ethics*, London: Management Books, 2000, p. 234.

5. http://www.mckinsey.com/insights/strategy/High-performing_boards_whats_on_their_agenda?

6. Iain Martin, *Making It Happen: Fred Goodwin, RBS and the Men Who Blew Up the British Economy*, London: Simon & Schuster, 2013, pp. 2, 9.

7. Geoff Beattie and Beverly Behan, "How to Run a Board," *Ivey Business Journal*, October 2013. I will discuss the role of the chairman more fully later in this chapter.

8. Huse, pp. 310 ff.

9. John R. Engen, "What Directors Think," *Corporate Board Member*, https://www.boardmember.com/MagazineArticle_Details.aspx?id=9134

10. Eversheds Board Report, 2013, p. 10.

11. 'Using Social Media', Korn/Ferry Institute Briefing, 2011, http://www.kornferry institute.com/briefings-magazine/spring-2011/using-social-media

12. Charan, *Boards at Work*, p. 35.

13. Beattie and Behan, "How to Run a Board," *Ivey Business Journal*, 2013.

14. For variations in valuation, see "From Bogus to Brilliant," *Board Prospects*, 2014, http://boardprospects.hivefire.com/articles/719614/board-evaluation-from-bogus-to-brilliant/.

15. Lorsch, *The Future of Boards*, Boston: Harvard Business Review Press, 2012, p. 118.

16. Ibid, p. 119.

17. Adolph A. Berle and Gardiner C. Means, *The Modern Corporation and Private Property*, New York: Macmillan, 1932.

18. http://www.worldbank.org/ifa/rosc_cgoverview.html

19. Morten Huse, *Boards, Governance and Value Creation: The Human Side of Corporate Governance*, Cambridge: Cambridge University Press, 2007.

20. Jay W. Lorsch and Andy Zelleke, "Should the CEO be the Chairman?," *Sloan Management Review*, Winter, 2005, http://sloanreview.mit.edu/article/should-the-ceo-be-the-chairman/

21. Jaap W. Winter, "Shareholder Engagement and Stewardship: The Realities and Illusions of Institutional Share Ownership," SSRN Research Network, 2011, http://papers.ssrn.com/sol3/papers.cfm?abstract_id=1867564

22. Institute of Directors, *Handbook of International Corporate Governance*, London: Kogan Page, p. 52.

23. Ibid, p. 30.

24. *Handbook of International Corporate Governance*, p. 37.

25. "Shareholders Alone Should Not Decide on AstraZeneca," *Financial Times*, May 9, 2014.

26. "Shareholder Activism: Battle for the Boardroom," *Financial Times*, April 23, 2014.

27. "Hedge Funds Should Not Be The Only Activitist Investors," *Financial Times*, February 26, 2014.

28. John Wood and Thames Fulton, "Independent Directors for a Family Business," Heidrick & Struggles Governance letter, n.d.

29. http://www.efinancialnews.com/story/2013-02-04/private-equity-manoeuvres-for-elbow-room

30. http://www.ameinfo.com/blog/finance-and-economy/private-equity-optimism-replaces-years-frustration/

31. References to Andrews, Mintzberg, 1–2 others.

32. Richard Koch, *The Financial Times Guide to Strategy*, London: FT Books, 2006.

33. Johnson, P. (2013), "A Theory of Business Strategy," http://www.exeter.ox.ac.uk/node/255

34. The terms "internationalization" and "globalization" are often used interchangeably. Technically, an international business is one that operates in and/or trades across more than one country, but not necessarily doing so on a worldwide basis, while a global business is one with complete global reach and presence. In practice, this can be a distinction without a difference.

35. "Bad News for Western Jobs as Ideas Are Also Made in China," *Financial Times*, May 1, 2014.

36. Speech to the IMCA, Seattle, April 2013.

37. Kenichi Ohmae, *The Borderless World: Power and Strategy in the Interlinked Economy*, New York: HarperBusiness, 1990; Ohmae, *The Next Global Stage: Challenges and Opportunities in Our Borderless World*, Engelwood Cliffs: Wharton School Publishing; Janet Morrison, *The Global Business Environment*, Basingstoke: Palgrave Macmillan, 2011; Sumantra Ghoshal and Christopher Bartlett, *Managing Across Borders: The Transnational Solution*, Boston: Harvard Business School Press, 2002; Ravi Venkatesan, *Conquering the Chaos: Win in India, Win Everywhere*, Boston: Harvard Business Review Press, 2013.

38. Geert Hofstede, *Culture's Consequences: International Differences in Work-Related Values*, Beverley Hills: Sage, 1980; Project GLOBE, www.globe.org.uk

39. C.K. Prahalad, *The Fortune at the Bottom of the Pyramid*, Engelwood Cliffs: Wharton School Publishing, 2004; Vijay Mahajan, *Africa Rising: How 900 Million*

African Consumers Offer More Than You Think, Engelwood Cliffs: Wharton School Publishing, 2008; Mahajan, *The Arab World Unbound: Tapping Into the Power of 350 Million Consumers*, New York: John Wiley, 2012.

40. Aidan Manktelow, *Guide to Emerging Markets: The Business Outlook, Opportunities and Obstacles*, London: Economist Books, 2014.
41. Paul Hopkin, *Fundamentals of Risk Management*, London: Kogan Page, p. 100.
42. http://www.allenovery.com/news/en-gb/articles/Pages/Directors-under-scrutiny.aspx
43. Thomas S. Coleman, *A Practical Guide to Risk Management*, London: Research Foundation of the CFA Institute, 2011; Michel Crouhy, Dan Galai and Robert Mark, *The Essentials of Risk Management*, 2nd edn, New York: McGraw-Hill, 2014.
44. Institute of International Finance, "IIF Report on Market Best Practice, Principles of Conduct and Best Practice," p. 10.
45. George Gilder, *The Spirit of Enterprise*, New York: Simon & Schuster, 1984, p. 246.
46. Jamie Oliver and Tony Goodwin, *How They Blew It: The CEOs and Entrepreneurs Behind Some of the World's Most Catastrophic Business Failures*, London: Kogan Page, 2013.
47. "A Task for Which No One is Qualified," *Financial Times*, April 10, 2013.
48. Ibid.
49. http://www.nedaglobal.com/downloads/NED_Awards_Book_2012.pdf
50. Jeffrey N. Gordon, "The Rise of Independent Directors in the United States, 1950-2005: Of Shareholder Value and Stock Market Prices," Columbia Law and Economics Working Paper 301.
51. "The Good Servant," *The Director*, January 2012.
52. "Celebrating NEDs Who Keep Their Heads," *The Director*, February 2008.
53. "Bidets, Baubles – and Boards," *Financial Times*, April 24, 2014.
54. "The Good Servant," *The Director*, January 2012.
55. "What Makes a Good Chairman?," INSEAD report, http://knowledge.insead.edu/corporate-governance/what-makes-a-good-chairman
56. http://www.iod.com/guidance/briefings/cgbis-role-of-the-senior-independent-director-sid
57. Ibid.
58. http://www.nedaglobal.com/downloads/NED_Awards_Book_2012.pdf

Index

Printed and bound in Great Britain by
CPI Group (UK) Ltd, Croydon, CR0 4YY